DeepSeek R1

A Hands-on Guide to Building Collaborative Multi-agent Systems for Solving Complex Tasks.

©
Written By
Morgan Devline

Copyright

DeepSeek R1: A Hands-on Guide to Building Collaborative Multi-agent Systems for Solving Complex Tasks

Table of Contents

Preface

About This Book

Welcome to **DeepSeek R1: A Hands-on Guide to Building Collaborative Multi-agent Systems for Solving Complex Tasks**. This book is designed to help you understand and apply DeepSeek R1—an advanced platform for creating and managing intelligent, collaborative agents. Through detailed explanations, step-by-step tutorials, and real-world examples, this guide aims to empower you to build robust multi-agent systems that can tackle complex tasks effectively.

In this book, you will explore the core principles behind multi-agent systems (MAS), discover the unique features of DeepSeek R1, and learn best practices for designing agents that work together to solve challenging problems. We have taken great care to provide:

- **Clear Explanations**: Each concept is broken down into understandable parts, ensuring you gain a solid grasp of the topic before moving on.
- **Practical Examples**: Every important concept is illustrated using code snippets, diagrams, or tables, whenever relevant. These examples are carefully selected to mirror real-world scenarios, helping you see how theory translates into practice.
- **Hands-on Projects**: At the end of most chapters, you will find projects or exercises that reinforce the lessons learned. By working through these tasks, you will gain practical experience in building and optimizing multi-agent systems with DeepSeek R1.

Whether you're looking to explore new AI paradigms, streamline workflows in your organization, or simply deepen your knowledge of multi-agent systems, this book provides a structured path to mastery. We hope you find the material both engaging and rewarding as you progress toward becoming a proficient DeepSeek R1 user.

Who Should Read This Book

We have written this guide to cater to a broad audience, including:

1. **Developers and Engineers**: If you have a background in software development—especially in AI, machine learning, or distributed

systems—this book will help you integrate multi-agent capabilities into your projects.

2. **Researchers and Academics**: If you are studying or teaching multi-agent systems, AI, or related fields, the in-depth explanations and real-world examples will serve as valuable references and teaching materials.

3. **Technical Managers and Team Leads**: If you oversee engineering teams, you can use this book to understand the potential and limitations of multi-agent systems in practical settings. This knowledge will aid in project planning and team guidance.

4. **Enthusiasts and Self-Learners**: If you are curious about AI and want to dive into collaborative agent-based approaches, you will find step-by-step instructions and exercises to get hands-on experience, even without a formal technical background.

Because we keep the language clear and use numerous examples, readers at various levels of expertise can follow along. We also provide pointers to more advanced topics for those who want to delve deeper into the theory or cutting-edge research.

How to Use This Book

To maximize learning and retention, we recommend the following approach:

1. **Read Sequentially**
The book is organized to guide you from fundamental concepts to advanced implementations. If you are new to DeepSeek R1 or multi-agent systems, begin at the first chapter and progress step by step. This method ensures you build a solid foundation before tackling more complex material.

2. **Experiment with Code Examples**
Where applicable, you'll find code examples and demonstrations. We encourage you to type out or copy these snippets into your development environment and experiment with them. Don't be afraid to break things—you often learn best by troubleshooting and tweaking examples to see how they behave.

3. **Explore Hands-On Projects**
Most chapters contain end-of-chapter projects or exercises that reinforce the topics covered. Working through these exercises is an excellent way to solidify your knowledge. You will learn how to set up agents, implement communication protocols, handle conflicts, and optimize overall system performance.

4. **Refer to Tables, Diagrams, and Appendices**
   When a concept is better explained visually, we provide tables or diagrams to illustrate key points. Each table is clearly labeled and contains accurate, well-organized data. You will also find reference materials in the appendices, including a glossary of terms, an API reference for DeepSeek R1, and links to additional resources.
5. **Use the Book as a Reference**
   Once you are comfortable with the basics, feel free to jump to chapters that address specific topics or challenges you are facing. Each chapter stands on its own while still connecting to the broader context, making the book a useful reference for quick look-ups and advanced topics.
6. **Engage with the Community**
   Throughout the book, we highlight ways to connect with other DeepSeek R1 users, including online forums and community-driven platforms. By engaging with others, you can share insights, ask questions, and stay updated on the latest developments.

Acknowledgments

A project of this magnitude would not be possible without the support, expertise, and collaboration of many individuals. We would like to extend our sincerest gratitude to:

- **Technical Reviewers**: Their meticulous feedback ensured the examples and explanations in each chapter are accurate, consistent, and up to date.
- **Industry Experts**: Several professionals graciously offered their time to share insights and case studies, helping us showcase real-world applications of DeepSeek R1 in diverse fields.
- **Beta Readers**: Early adopters and readers who tested the projects, worked through the code examples, and provided constructive feedback to refine the book's structure and content.
- **Design and Editorial Team**: Their expertise in polishing the manuscript, improving layout, and enhancing readability helped create a cohesive and professional final product.
- **Open-source and AI Community**: The ever-evolving research and open-source contributions in artificial intelligence, distributed systems, and multi-agent technologies inspired many of the topics and examples presented here.

Finally, we would like to thank **you**, the reader, for choosing to embark on this journey with us. Your curiosity and passion for learning drive us to explore new frontiers in AI and share our findings in a clear, accessible manner. We hope this book helps you develop the knowledge and confidence to build innovative, collaborative multi-agent systems with DeepSeek R1.

Book Features

Below is an in-depth overview of the key features you will find in this book, **DeepSeek R1: A Hands-on Guide to Building Collaborative Multi-agent Systems for Solving Complex Tasks**. These elements are designed to give you a **comprehensive, practical, and engaging** learning experience. Throughout the book, you will encounter **tables**, **code examples**, and **diagrams** that have been crafted to be **complete, accurate,** and clearly explained, ensuring you can follow along and replicate the results on your own.

1. Hands-On Projects and Exercises

To help you move beyond theory and into real-world application, many chapters include **hands-on projects** and **exercises**. These practical tasks serve several purposes:

1. **Reinforcement of Learning**
   - By applying newly acquired knowledge to build or modify agents, you deepen your understanding of key concepts.
   - The process of writing and debugging code helps clarify theoretical points in a tangible way.
2. **Step-by-Step Guidance**
   - Each project is broken down into clear steps.
   - Code snippets are provided and explained in detail, making it easier to follow along and implement the features in your own environment.
3. **Incremental Complexity**
   - Initial exercises focus on foundational tasks, ensuring beginners can gain confidence.

o Later projects introduce more advanced topics, guiding you toward professional-level proficiency with DeepSeek R1.

4. **Realistic Scenarios**
   o Exercises simulate challenges you might face in industry contexts, such as dynamic task allocation, conflict resolution, or scaling an agent-based system.
   o This real-world emphasis ensures that the skills you develop can be directly transferred to your professional or research projects.

2. Visual Aids and Diagrams

While textual explanations are essential, **visual aids** often provide a clearer understanding of complex structures and workflows. Throughout the book, you will encounter:

1. **Flowcharts and Process Diagrams**
   o These illustrate how agents interact with one another and with the environment.
   o When learning about communication protocols or coordination strategies, a visual map can help you see how messages and data move through the system.
2. **System Architecture Illustrations**
   o Complex architectures, such as multi-agent platforms with layered structures, are explained through labeled diagrams.
   o You can quickly grasp how various modules or components connect within DeepSeek R1.
3. **Tables for Comparative Overviews**
   o When multiple methods, algorithms, or configurations are discussed, tables are used to summarize and compare their features, pros, and cons.
   o Each table is meticulously formatted to ensure readability and clarity.
4. **Annotated Screenshots**
   o Key parts of the DeepSeek R1 interface, configuration files, or tool settings may be showcased with annotations, making it easier to recognize elements when working in your own setup.

3. Real-World Case Studies

To bridge the gap between theory and practical applications, this book provides **case studies** that demonstrate how DeepSeek R1 is used to solve **real-world problems**:

1. **Industry-Specific Examples**
   - You will see how multi-agent systems can enhance operations in sectors like manufacturing, healthcare, logistics, and more.
   - These examples illustrate the versatility of DeepSeek R1 across different domains.
2. **Detailed Analysis**
   - Each case study offers an in-depth look at the project's objectives, the challenges faced, and the solutions implemented.
   - Technical details, such as agent roles, communication mechanisms, and performance metrics, are dissected so you can understand the reasoning behind each decision.
3. **Lessons Learned**
   - Beyond just showcasing successes, case studies highlight pitfalls and recommended best practices.
   - This candid reflection helps you anticipate and avoid common mistakes in your own projects.
4. **Scalable Solutions**
   - Many of these cases focus on growing systems, illustrating how to manage increasing agent counts and data volumes.
   - Strategies for load balancing, fault tolerance, and robustness are highlighted.

---

4. Expert Insights and Interviews

To offer diverse viewpoints and real-life experiences, we include **insights** from professionals and **interviews** with experts who have hands-on experience in multi-agent systems, AI development, or DeepSeek R1 specifically:

1. **Practical Advice**
   - Experts share tips that are not always apparent from official documentation, giving you insider knowledge on how to

optimize agent behavior and streamline development workflows.

2. **Industry Success Stories**
   - Case studies become more compelling when accompanied by firsthand accounts from engineers or project managers who overcame unique hurdles.
   - Real data and performance outcomes demonstrate what you can achieve with DeepSeek R1 in production environments.

3. **Emerging Trends**
   - Interviews often touch on the future of multi-agent systems, ethical considerations, and how AI is shaping different industries.
   - This forward-looking perspective can help you stay ahead of rapid technological changes.

4. **Actionable Recommendations**
   - You will learn about problem-solving approaches, recommended tools, and best practices that can speed up your development cycle.
   - These insights are often informed by real-world successes and failures, saving you from trial-and-error in your projects.

---

5. Supplementary Materials

In addition to the core content, you will find various **supplementary materials** to support your learning:

1. **Appendices**
   - Technical references, such as API documentation, a glossary of terms, or advanced configuration guides, are located in the appendices.
   - These sections can be referred to repeatedly for clarifications or advanced use cases.

2. **Online Resources**
   - Links to external resources, such as online tutorials, webinars, or official DeepSeek R1 forums, are provided to help you delve deeper into specialized topics.
   - Community forums and discussion platforms are great places to seek help, share knowledge, and stay updated on the latest developments.

3. **Sample Code Repositories**

- Where applicable, code examples discussed in the book are made available in publicly accessible repositories (such as GitHub).
- This allows you to download, run, and customize solutions quickly, accelerating your learning process.
4. **Best Practice Checklists**
   - You may find condensed checklists summarizing the do's and don'ts of multi-agent system development, agent coordination, or security measures.
   - These checklists make it easier to apply your newly gained knowledge in real projects without forgetting critical steps.

6. Interactive Elements

Learning is most effective when **active engagement** is encouraged. Accordingly, the book contains **interactive components** that prompt you to participate:

1. **Quizzes and Self-Assessments**
   - Brief quizzes appear at the end of certain chapters, helping you gauge your grasp of the material.
   - These question sets also serve as a quick revision tool, ensuring you haven't missed important concepts.
2. **Discussion Questions**
   - Open-ended questions are provided to spark deeper thinking and encourage you to articulate your own understanding of the material.
   - These prompts are useful for classroom or group learning settings, facilitating discussion and collaboration.
3. **Project Suggestions**
   - Beyond step-by-step exercises, you'll find suggestions for extending a project, integrating advanced features, or applying the concepts to a fresh scenario.
   - This autonomy fosters creativity and challenges you to shape the system to your unique needs.
4. **Community Engagement**
   - Readers are encouraged to share their results, challenges, and custom projects on relevant online platforms.
   - Engaging with peers can broaden your perspective and lead to valuable networking opportunities.

7. Up-to-Date Content

The field of **multi-agent systems** and **AI** evolves rapidly, and staying current is vital:

1. **Latest DeepSeek R1 Features**
   - This book covers the most recent version of DeepSeek R1 as of its publication date.
   - Whenever new updates or releases occur, references and code examples are designed to be easily adaptable.
2. **Recent Research and Industry Trends**
   - Wherever relevant, recent academic research or industry case studies are cited to provide you with the most contemporary insights.
   - This ensures that the solutions you learn are not only theoretically sound but also reflective of current best practices.
3. **Future-Proofing Your Skills**
   - In addition to showing you how to solve immediate problems, the book highlights emerging technologies and areas of innovation.
   - By understanding ongoing trends, you can make your agent-based systems more adaptable to future needs and expansions.
4. **Community and Continuous Updates**
   - Readers are guided on how to stay informed through official DeepSeek R1 documentation, community channels, and online portals.
   - As new challenges emerge, you can rely on the active community and future book editions or errata for assistance.

Final Note

By combining **hands-on projects**, **visual aids**, **real-world case studies**, **expert perspectives**, **supplementary materials**, **interactive elements**, and **up-to-date content**, this book aims to deliver a well-rounded and engaging learning experience. Every **table**, **diagram**, and **code example** is carefully verified for **accuracy** and presented with **thorough explanations** so you can implement and adapt what you learn with confidence.

I hope these features make your journey through **DeepSeek R1** and multi-agent systems both enlightening and enjoyable. Dive in, experiment, and let your curiosity guide you to unlock the full potential of collaborative AI systems.

Chapter 1: Introduction to Multi-agent Systems (MAS)

Multi-agent systems (MAS) represent a vibrant field in artificial intelligence, focusing on how multiple intelligent entities (agents) can work together to solve complex tasks. This chapter provides an overview of what multi-agent systems are, explains their historical evolution and relevance in modern AI, explores different types of agents, and examines the core components that define a MAS. All examples, tables, and explanations presented here are designed to be **clear**, **complete**, and **easy to follow**, making it straightforward for you to grasp the foundational concepts.

---

1. What is a Multi-agent System?

Definition and Key Concepts

A **multi-agent system (MAS)** is a collection of autonomous entities, known as **agents**, which interact within an environment to achieve individual or shared goals. Each agent operates with a certain degree of **independence**, but the overall system's performance often depends on **cooperation**, **coordination**, or **competition** among these agents.

- **Agent**: An autonomous program or entity capable of making decisions and taking actions to achieve specific objectives.
- **Environment**: The world (physical or virtual) in which agents operate. It can provide information to agents through sensors and receive actions or outputs from agents.
- **Interaction**: Communication or signals exchanged among agents or between agents and their environment. Interaction can be direct (e.g., message passing) or indirect (e.g., sensing changes in the environment).

Key Characteristics of a MAS:

1. **Multiple Agents**
   - At least two agents are required; however, practical systems often involve dozens or hundreds of agents.

2. **Autonomous Behavior**
   o Each agent makes independent decisions based on its goals, knowledge, or programming.
3. **Local Views**
   o Agents typically have limited or partial knowledge about the entire environment, focusing on local information or assigned tasks.
4. **Decentralized Control**
   o There is no single leader agent that controls all others; instead, decision-making is distributed.
5. **Communication and Coordination**
   o Agents communicate to coordinate actions, share information, or negotiate solutions.

Below is a simple **table** summarizing the fundamental differences between a **single-agent system** and a **multi-agent system**:

Feature	Single-Agent System	Multi-agent System
Number of Decision-Makers	One main controller or program	Multiple autonomous agents
Autonomy	Centralized decisions	Distributed decisions
Interaction	Limited or none with other entities	Agents communicate and coordinate via direct or indirect means
Complexity	May be simpler to design but can struggle with large-scale tasks	Can handle complex, large-scale tasks by dividing responsibilities among multiple agents
Fault Tolerance	Single point of failure	Failure of one agent may not collapse the entire system

Historical Evolution of MAS

- **Early Roots (1970s–1980s)**
  Researchers began exploring distributed AI, recognizing that a single, monolithic system might struggle with tasks requiring diverse expertise or parallel computation.
- **Growth in the 1990s**
  The field matured with frameworks supporting cooperative problem-

solving. Concepts such as **contract nets**, **negotiation protocols**, and **blackboard systems** gained popularity.

- **Mainstream Adoption (2000s–Present)**
  Advances in **networked systems**, **cloud computing**, and **machine learning** accelerated the practical use of MAS in robotics, e-commerce, logistics, and simulation of social behaviors.
- **Modern Trends**
  Current research focuses on scalability, real-time decision-making, agent learning (e.g., reinforcement learning), and ethical considerations in autonomous agent interactions.

Importance and Relevance in Modern AI

Multi-agent systems are increasingly relevant across industries:

1. **Robotics and Automation**
   - Teams of robots (e.g., in a factory) coordinate tasks, improving efficiency and reducing operational risks.
2. **Smart Grids**
   - Decentralized energy systems rely on agents to manage power distribution and consumption in real time.
3. **Healthcare**
   - Collaborative agents can assist medical professionals in diagnosis, patient monitoring, and resource allocation.
4. **Transportation**
   - Autonomous vehicles communicate with each other and with infrastructure systems to optimize traffic flow and enhance safety.
5. **Gaming and Simulations**
   - MAS approaches power complex simulations involving multiple virtual agents, such as non-player characters (NPCs) in video games or intelligent opponents in strategic simulators.

---

2. Types of Agents in MAS

Although agents share general characteristics, they differ in how they perceive the environment and make decisions. Below are five commonly referenced agent types:

2.1. Autonomous Agents

- **Definition**: Agents that operate without continuous human intervention, guided by their internal goals and decision processes.
- **Key Feature**: They can sense their environment, process information, and execute actions to achieve objectives.
- **Example**: A cleaning robot that autonomously navigates a house, adjusting its path based on furniture placement and dirt detection.

2.2. Collaborative Agents

- **Definition**: Agents that work together, sharing information and resources to accomplish a shared or compatible goal.
- **Key Feature**: Cooperation through communication protocols or mechanisms (e.g., messaging, blackboard systems).
- **Example**: A group of drones working in tandem to map a disaster-hit area, where each drone covers a portion of the area and shares its findings.

2.3. Reactive Agents

- **Definition**: Agents that respond **immediately** to changes in the environment with no (or limited) internal model of the world.
- **Key Feature**: Behavior is often defined by condition-action rules ("if condition, then action").
- **Example**: A thermostat that switches heating on or off based on the current temperature compared to a threshold.

2.4. Proactive Agents

- **Definition**: Agents that do not merely react; they **plan** ahead and take the initiative to fulfill long-term goals.
- **Key Feature**: They can deliberate, forming strategies or sequences of actions in advance.
- **Example**: An intelligent personal assistant that schedules tasks ahead of time, anticipating user needs.

2.5. Learning Agents

- **Definition**: Agents that improve their behavior or decision-making over time by learning from experience or data.

- **Key Feature**: Employing machine learning or reinforcement learning algorithms to adapt to changing environments or refine strategies.
- **Example**: A recommendation system that tailors suggestions based on user interactions and preferences.

Below is a brief **table** summarizing the defining attributes of each agent type:

Agent Type	Defining Attribute	Typical Example
Autonomous	Operates independently, minimal human oversight	Cleaning robot adjusting its path
Collaborative	Coordinates with others, shared goals	Drones mapping a disaster area
Reactive	Immediate response to environmental changes	Simple thermostat (condition-action rules)
Proactive	Goal-driven, takes initiative, plans ahead	Smart personal assistant
Learning	Improves over time via experience or data	Recommendation system (machine learning)

3. Core Components of MAS

A multi-agent system typically consists of several fundamental components that collectively define how agents operate and interact within their environment.

3.1. Agents

- **Definition**: The individual entities that perceive, decide, and act.
- **Responsibilities**: Each agent may have specialized capabilities or tasks. In a logistics MAS, for instance, one agent may handle route planning while another manages fleet maintenance.
- **Attributes**: Includes internal state (memory or knowledge), goals, and strategies for action.

3.2. Environment

- **Definition**: The domain or context in which agents operate. This could be physical (a factory floor) or virtual (a simulated marketplace).
- **Attributes**: May contain resources (energy, data), obstacles, or competing entities.
- **Role**: Provides stimuli to agents and receives their actions, shaping the feedback loop that influences decision-making.

3.3. Communication Mechanisms

- **Definition**: The methods or protocols by which agents exchange information and coordinate.
- **Examples**: Message passing, event broadcasting, shared memory or blackboard systems, or even direct physical signals (e.g., robotic swarm coordination via sensors).
- **Significance**: Effective communication ensures agents can share goals, negotiate roles, and avoid conflicts.

Basic Example of an Agent-to-Agent Message (Pseudocode):

```python
# A simple message structure in Python-like pseudocode

class AgentMessage:
    def __init__(self, sender_id, receiver_id, content):
        self.sender_id = sender_id
        self.receiver_id = receiver_id
        self.content = content

# Example of creating and sending a message
message = AgentMessage(sender_id="Agent1",
                       receiver_id="Agent2",
                       content={"task": "collect_data",
"priority": "high"})

# Assume Agent2's inbox is a list
Agent2.inbox.append(message)
```

- **Explanation**:
    o `sender_id`: Identifies who sent the message.
    o `receiver_id`: Identifies the intended recipient.
    o `content`: May hold instructions, requests, or any relevant data.

o   Agents handle messages by reading their inbox, parsing content, and determining the appropriate response or action.

3.4. Coordination and Cooperation Strategies

- **Definition**: Rules and methods agents use to work effectively together, sharing tasks or objectives.
- **Techniques**:
    1. **Negotiation**: Agents discuss and reach agreements on task allocation or resource sharing.
    2. **Contract Net Protocol**: A classic approach where one agent (the manager) publishes a task, and other agents (bidders) submit proposals.
    3. **Plan Merging**: In proactive systems, agents may merge individual plans to reduce conflicts and improve efficiency.

High-Level Coordination Example (Pseudocode):

```python
# Simple manager-agent coordination scenario

manager_agent.broadcast_task("Data Collection",
required_agents=2)

# Agents that can handle data collection respond:
for agent in agent_list:
    if agent.can_handle("Data Collection"):
        manager_agent.receive_bid(agent.id,
bid_details=agent.create_bid())

# Manager selects best bids:
selected_agents =
manager_agent.select_agents_based_on_criteria(criteria="lowes
t_time")
manager_agent.assign_task("Data Collection", selected_agents)
```

- **Explanation**:
    o   `broadcast_task`: The manager agent announces a needed task.
    o   `receive_bid`: The manager collects offers from suitable agents.
    o   `select_agents_based_on_criteria`: The manager chooses the best agents according to set criteria (e.g., time, cost, or efficiency).

o This approach allows multiple agents to coordinate without a single agent dictating every step in an overly centralized manner.

4. Applications of MAS

Multi-agent systems (MAS) have proven their versatility across various industries, providing robust solutions to complex problems. Below are some of the most common applications:

4.1. Robotics

- **Collaboration and Task Division**: In modern manufacturing facilities, multiple robots (agents) can coordinate tasks like assembly, welding, or packaging. Each robot may specialize in a specific function, improving efficiency and reducing errors.
- **Swarm Robotics**: In scenarios like search and rescue missions, a group of lightweight robots can disperse over an area, each agent gathering data independently and sharing findings to cover more ground quickly.

4.2. Autonomous Vehicles

- **Traffic Coordination**: Self-driving cars (agents) communicate with one another and with traffic infrastructure to optimize routes, reduce congestion, and enhance safety.
- **Fleet Management**: Ride-sharing and delivery services often use MAS principles to schedule and dispatch vehicles dynamically, maximizing resource usage and cutting down wait times.

4.3. Healthcare Systems

- **Patient Monitoring**: Smart sensors and software agents track patient vitals, environmental conditions, and medication schedules, alerting medical staff to anomalies in real time.
- **Resource Allocation**: Hospitals use MAS to manage bed availability, operating rooms, and staff rosters, ensuring patients receive timely care while optimizing facility utilization.

- **Diagnostics and Decision Support**: Agent-based diagnostic systems can aggregate patient data from various sources, apply different algorithms or expert rules, and then recommend treatment strategies.

4.4. Finance and Trading

- **Algorithmic Trading Agents**: Financial markets rely on agents that execute trades based on predictive algorithms. These agents can react within microseconds to market fluctuations, buying or selling assets automatically.
- **Risk Management**: Multi-agent setups help assess market risk by modeling different scenarios, incorporating diverse data feeds, and enacting real-time adjustments to portfolios.

4.5. Smart Grids and IoT

- **Distributed Energy Management**: Agents balance energy supply and demand, scheduling when to draw from or feed into the grid. This becomes especially important with renewable energy sources, such as solar or wind power, which can fluctuate.
- **IoT Device Coordination**: In a smart home or factory, various sensors, appliances, and machines (all acting as agents) work together to optimize energy usage, streamline maintenance, or enhance user comfort and safety.

5. Challenges in MAS Development

While MAS offers powerful solutions, there are inherent challenges that developers and researchers must address:

5.1. Scalability

- **Problem**: As the number of agents grows, communication overhead and resource management can become overwhelming.

- **Example**: A system managing hundreds of autonomous delivery robots must ensure that each robot's coordination messages do not saturate the network or slow down decision-making.
- **Possible Approaches**:
  - Hierarchical architectures where smaller groups of agents communicate with a "super-agent" or manager.
  - Efficient data structures and protocols that reduce message duplication.

5.2. Coordination and Synchronization

- **Problem**: Agents must often coordinate actions to avoid conflicts and achieve overall goals. If not done properly, agents may duplicate efforts or interfere with each other.
- **Example**: Two factory robots might both try to pick up the same item at once, causing collisions or system errors.
- **Possible Approaches**:
  - **Scheduling Algorithms**: Assign tasks and time slots so that only one agent operates in a given area at a time.
  - **Synchronization Mechanisms**: Use of locks, tokens, or event-based signals to control access to shared resources.

5.3. Conflict Resolution

- **Problem**: Agents with different objectives or limited resources may come into conflict over strategies or resource usage.
- **Example**: In a trading system, multiple agent-based algorithms might compete for the same profitable trade, driving up costs.
- **Possible Approaches**:
  - **Negotiation Protocols**: Agents discuss terms and try to arrive at a mutually acceptable solution.
  - **Auction-Based Methods**: Agents bid for resources, and the highest bidder wins (often used in contract net protocols).

5.4. Security and Privacy

- **Problem**: Decentralized environments introduce vulnerabilities, such as unauthorized agent access or message tampering. Furthermore, data privacy is a concern when agents share sensitive information.
- **Example**: In healthcare, patient data must be protected while agents exchange vital information across hospital networks.

- **Possible Approaches**:
  - ○ **Encryption**: Secure data exchange between agents.
  - ○ **Authentication and Authorization**: Ensure only trusted agents can join or interact within the system.
  - ○ **Privacy-Preserving Techniques**: Techniques like differential privacy or secure multiparty computation can allow data sharing without exposing sensitive details.

5.5. Ethical Considerations

- **Problem**: Autonomous agents can make decisions with significant real-world impact, raising concerns about accountability, fairness, and unintended consequences.
- **Example**: A self-driving car deciding between multiple collision scenarios may face ethical dilemmas if human lives are at stake.
- **Possible Approaches**:
  - ○ **Regulatory Guidelines**: Agents must comply with laws and industry standards.
  - ○ **Responsible AI Frameworks**: Implementing transparency, explainability, and ethical decision-making heuristics in agent architectures.

6. End-of-Chapter Projects

Project 1: Designing a Simple Reactive Agent

Objective: Create a basic agent that **reacts** to changes in its environment using a simple condition-action rule. This project will familiarize you with the core concept of **reactive agents** and show you how agents can sense and respond to immediate environmental stimuli.

Project Overview

1. **Environment Setup**:
   - ○ You will simulate an environment containing **temperature** data.
   - ○ The agent will read the current temperature and decide whether to turn a cooling fan on or off.
2. **Reactive Behavior**:

- o Define a simple rule:
  - If temperature > 25°C, **fan** = ON
  - Else, **fan** = OFF
3. **Implementation Steps**:

   0. Create an `Environment` class to store and update temperature.
   1. Implement a `ReactiveAgent` class with a `sense()` method to read the temperature and an `act()` method to determine the fan state based on the condition.

Example Code (Python-like Pseudocode)

```python
python

class Environment:
    def __init__(self, initial_temperature):
        self.temperature = initial_temperature

    def update_temperature(self, new_temp):
        self.temperature = new_temp

class ReactiveAgent:
    def __init__(self, name):
        self.name = name
        self.fan_state = "OFF"

    def sense(self, environment):
        return environment.temperature

    def act(self, temperature):
        if temperature > 25:
            self.fan_state = "ON"
        else:
            self.fan_state = "OFF"

    def report_state(self):
        print(f"[{self.name}] Current Fan State:
{self.fan_state}")

# ---- Simulation Code ----
# Step 1: Create an environment and a reactive agent
room_env = Environment(initial_temperature=22)
simple_agent = ReactiveAgent(name="Agent1")

# Step 2: Agent senses environment and acts accordingly
current_temp = simple_agent.sense(room_env)
simple_agent.act(current_temp)
simple_agent.report_state()   # Expected Fan State: OFF
```

```
# Step 3: Change the environment and see how the agent reacts
room_env.update_temperature(28)
current_temp = simple_agent.sense(room_env)
simple_agent.act(current_temp)
simple_agent.report_state()   # Expected Fan State: ON
```

Explanation of the Code

- **Environment Class**: Holds the current temperature. The `update_temperature()` method allows the temperature to be changed, simulating real-world fluctuations.
- **ReactiveAgent Class**: Contains two primary methods:
  - **sense()**: Reads the temperature from the `Environment`.
  - **act()**: Applies the condition-action rule to set `fan_state`.
- **Simulation Code**: Demonstrates how the environment changes and how the agent reacts to the updated temperature.

Extensions

- **Additional Conditions**: Expand the rule to handle multiple thresholds (e.g., below 15°C = heater ON, above 25°C = fan ON).
- **Multiple Agents**: Implement more than one reactive agent, each responding to its own sensor readings in the same environment or separate environments.

---

7. Quizzes and Self-Assessments

Quiz 1: Fundamentals of MAS

Test your understanding of the **basic concepts** introduced in this chapter by answering the following questions. Feel free to refer back to the text or code examples as needed.

1. **Definition of an Agent**
   - **Question**: What is an agent in the context of a multi-agent system, and what are its core responsibilities?
2. **Application Domains**
   - **Question**: Name two industries where MAS is utilized, and briefly describe the role agents play in each.

3. **Agent Types**
   - **Question**: Distinguish between a reactive agent and a proactive agent. Provide a simple real-world example for each.
4. **Coordination vs. Cooperation**
   - **Question**: How do you differentiate coordination from cooperation in MAS, and why are they both important?
5. **MAS Challenges**
   - **Question**: Identify one key challenge in MAS development (e.g., scalability, conflict resolution) and mention a common approach or technique to address it.
6. **Short Coding Prompt**
   - **Question**: Outline the basic structure (in pseudocode) of a message-passing protocol where one agent can send a task request to another agent.

Answer Key (Suggested):

1. **Core Responsibilities**: An agent autonomously perceives its environment and acts toward a goal.
2. **MAS in Industries**:
   - **Robotics**: Multiple robots coordinate tasks on a production line.
   - **Finance**: Trading agents make autonomous decisions to buy or sell stocks.
3. **Reactive vs. Proactive**:
   - **Reactive** agents respond immediately to environmental changes (e.g., thermostat).
   - **Proactive** agents plan ahead and may initiate actions (e.g., scheduling tasks).
4. **Coordination vs. Cooperation**:
   - **Coordination** ensures agents do not conflict with each other's actions (scheduling, avoiding collisions).
   - **Cooperation** implies working together toward a common goal, sometimes requiring shared strategies or resource pooling.
5. **MAS Challenge Example**:
   - **Scalability** can be addressed using hierarchical architectures, reducing communication overhead by breaking large systems into manageable clusters.
6. **Message-Passing Protocol** (Pseudocode Example):

```python
message = {"sender": "AgentA", "receiver": "AgentB",
"task_request": "CollectSensorData"}
AgentB.inbox.append(message)
```

By reviewing these **applications**, **challenges**, **projects**, and **quiz** questions, you should now have a **clear understanding** of how multi-agent systems operate, where they are commonly deployed, and what obstacles you may face when developing MAS solutions. In the next chapters, you will delve deeper into **agent design**, **communication protocols**, and advanced **reasoning** strategies that will expand your capabilities for building effective and innovative multi-agent systems.

Chapter 2: Overview of DeepSeek R1

DeepSeek R1 is a powerful platform for building and deploying multi-agent systems, designed to address complex problems through **coordinated** and **intelligent** agent behaviors. In this chapter, we will explore the evolution of DeepSeek R1, its architecture, core features, and how it compares with other MAS tools. We will also look at real-world use cases and success stories, followed by a practical project to help you gain hands-on experience with DeepSeek R1's architecture. All explanations, tables, and code examples are written in a **clear, simple style**, ensuring that you can follow along easily.

---

1. Introduction to DeepSeek R1

What is DeepSeek R1?

DeepSeek R1 is an advanced **multi-agent system (MAS) framework** that combines **reasoning**, **collaboration**, and **task management** capabilities under one unified platform. It is designed to streamline the development of agent-based applications by providing robust tools and libraries that handle complex interactions among agents, data processing, and decision-making.

Key Attributes:

1. **Scalability**: Capable of managing large numbers of agents in distributed environments.
2. **Adaptability**: Offers dynamic resource allocation, enabling agents to adapt to real-time data and changing environments.
3. **User-Friendly APIs**: Provides interfaces that simplify agent definition, communication, and coordination.

Whether you are developing a fleet of autonomous drones or managing distributed warehouse robots, DeepSeek R1 aims to reduce the overhead of handling multi-agent tasks, allowing you to focus on **solution logic** instead of low-level infrastructure.

Evolution from DeepSeek to DeepSeek R1

DeepSeek was originally developed as a **search and query tool** for large-scale data systems, leveraging intelligent agents to parse, index, and retrieve information. Over time, developers realized that the underlying architecture could be expanded to support broader **multi-agent functionalities**. With the addition of **advanced reasoning** modules, **real-time coordination**, and **enhanced APIs**, DeepSeek evolved into **DeepSeek R1**—a next-generation platform that goes beyond information retrieval, facilitating collaborative problem-solving and distributed decision-making.

Milestones:

- **DeepSeek 0.5**: Focused on data indexing and search-driven agents.
- **DeepSeek 0.9**: Introduced basic agent coordination features and a plugin system for third-party integrations.
- **DeepSeek R1**: Comprehensive suite for MAS, including advanced reasoning, modular architecture, and expanded multi-agent coordination tools.

2. DeepSeek R1 Architecture

System Components

DeepSeek R1's architecture is **modular**, allowing you to mix and match components based on your specific needs. Here are the main building blocks:

1. **Agent Manager**
   - Coordinates the creation, lifecycle, and termination of agents.
   - Keeps track of agent capabilities, states, and roles.
2. **Communication Layer**
   - Provides **messaging** protocols (e.g., publish-subscribe, direct message passing) and handles network communication.
   - Ensures reliable and secure data exchange among agents, even in distributed setups.
3. **Task Scheduler**
   - Allocates tasks to agents based on resource availability, priorities, or specialized skills.

o Supports dynamic reallocation if an agent fails or if new agents become available.

4. **Reasoning Engine**
   o Powers **advanced decision-making**, such as rule-based reasoning, probabilistic models, or machine learning integrations.
   o Helps agents evaluate multiple strategies and choose optimal actions.

5. **Data Storage and Knowledge Base**
   o Central or distributed databases where agents can share information, store learned patterns, or retrieve domain knowledge.
   o May include specialized AI models for classification, prediction, or anomaly detection.

Below is a **simplified diagram** of DeepSeek R1's architecture:

```lua
           +------------------------------+
           |      Reasoning Engine        |
           |  (rule-based, ML models, etc.)
           +------------------------------+
                          ^
                          |
           +------------------------------+
           |      Task Scheduler          |
           |  (task distribution,         |
           |    prioritization)           |
           +------------------------------+
                          ^
                          |
   +----------------+----------------+-----------+
   |          Communication Layer                |
   | (message routing, direct or pub-sub protocols)|
   +----------------+----------------+-----------+
                          |
                          v
           +------------------------------+
           |         Agent Manager        |
           |  (agent lifecycle,           |
           |    registration)             |
           +------------------------------+
                          |
                          v
           +-------------------------------------------+
           |      Data Storage & Knowledge Base        |
```

```
|  (databases, knowledge graphs, AI models)|
+-----------------------------------------+
```

Integration with Existing Systems

DeepSeek R1 is **highly extensible**, supporting various integration patterns:

- **API and SDK**: Offers a set of libraries (e.g., in Python, Java, or C++) that integrate directly into your application code.
- **Microservices**: Runs as modular services in containerized environments (e.g., Docker, Kubernetes), enabling distributed deployments.
- **Plugin Architecture**: Allows third-party tools to hook into **communication**, **task scheduling**, or **data processing**, making it easier to adopt specialized components (e.g., a custom machine learning model).

3. Core Features and Capabilities

Advanced Reasoning

One of the highlights of DeepSeek R1 is its **Reasoning Engine**, which supports different methods to evaluate complex situations and make informed decisions:

1. **Rule-Based Reasoning**
   o Ideal for systems governed by well-defined rules or regulations (e.g., industrial automation).
2. **Probabilistic Models**
   o Agents can handle uncertainty using Bayesian networks, Markov Decision Processes, or fuzzy logic.
3. **Machine Learning Integration**
   o Incorporates ML frameworks (TensorFlow, PyTorch, scikit-learn) to enable **reinforcement learning**, **predictive analytics**, and **pattern recognition** within agents.

Multi-agent Coordination

Effective **coordination** lies at the heart of multi-agent systems, and DeepSeek R1 excels in this domain by providing:

- **Communication Protocols**: Messaging services that support broadcast, directed messaging, or subscription-based models.
- **Coordination APIs**: Simplifies group decision-making by abstracting complexities like consensus algorithms, negotiation, or conflict resolution.
- **Scalable Topologies**: You can opt for centralized, decentralized, or hybrid coordination structures to match your system's needs.

Task Distribution and Management

Task management is crucial in any distributed system. DeepSeek R1's **Task Scheduler** automatically:

1. **Analyzes Agent Capabilities**: Assigns tasks to agents with matching skill sets.
2. **Handles Prioritization**: Ensures critical tasks are handled before low-priority tasks.
3. **Reallocates Resources**: Dynamically reassigns tasks if an agent is overloaded or becomes unavailable.

Decision-making Processes

DeepSeek R1 facilitates **real-time decision-making** for agents through:

- **Event-Driven Triggers**: Agents react to events (e.g., sensor alerts, data updates) with minimal latency.
- **Contextual Evaluation**: Decisions can incorporate **historical data**, **current environment states**, and **predicted future trends**.
- **Customization**: Developers can define custom logic for each agent's decision flow, from simple condition-action rules to elaborate planning algorithms.

4. Comparative Analysis

DeepSeek R1 vs. Other MAS Tools

Below is a comparative **table** highlighting how DeepSeek R1 stacks up against some general MAS frameworks:

Feature	DeepSeek R1	Generic MAS Tool A	Generic MAS Tool B
Architecture	Modular & task-focused	Often monolithic	Varies, partial plugins
Reasoning Engine	Integrated rule-based & ML	Minimal or external	Basic rule engine
Scalability	Built-in distributed support	Moderate	High, but needs manual integration
Task Scheduling	Native dynamic scheduler	Typically manual	Some scheduling features
Community/Support	Active forums, official docs	Limited	Decent user forums
Ease of Integration	API, SDK, microservices	Mostly library-based	Partial microservices
Learning Curve	Moderate (comprehensive docs)	Variable	Intermediate

Interpretation:

- **DeepSeek R1** focuses on **comprehensive features** like **advanced reasoning** and **task scheduling** out of the box.
- **Generic MAS Tools** may require additional libraries or manual coding to achieve similar levels of functionality and integration.

Unique Selling Points of DeepSeek R1

1. **All-in-One Framework**: Provides a **unified solution** for reasoning, task management, and communication.
2. **High-Level Abstractions**: Simplifies agent development with **prebuilt APIs** for coordination, reducing the need for boilerplate code.

3. **Advanced Decision Engines**: Combines classical AI methods (rule-based) with modern ML, making it suitable for a wide range of applications—from simple automation to data-driven tasks.
4. **Robust Community**: Active user forums, official documentation, and regular updates ensure timely support and feature enhancements.

---

5. Use Cases and Success Stories

Industry Implementations

- **Automated Warehouses**: Major e-commerce companies use DeepSeek R1 to coordinate thousands of warehouse robots, ensuring items are picked, packed, and shipped efficiently.
- **Healthcare Networks**: Hospitals and clinics integrate sensor data and patient records, with agents managing real-time alerts to optimize triage and resource usage.
- **Smart City Management**: Municipal systems for traffic lights, public transportation, and energy grids run on agent-based coordination, reducing congestion and improving sustainability metrics.

Case Studies Highlighting DeepSeek R1's Impact

1. **Global Logistics Firm**
   - **Challenge**: Managing a global fleet of delivery vehicles and drones under rapidly changing weather and traffic conditions.
   - **Solution**: DeepSeek R1's **Task Scheduler** and **Communication Layer** enabled real-time re-routing of vehicles, reducing delivery delays by 25%.
   - **Key Benefit**: The company scaled from 300 to 2,000 delivery agents across continents without revamping the entire system architecture.
2. **Healthcare Data Aggregation**
   - **Challenge**: Consolidating data from multiple hospital departments and third-party labs in real time.
   - **Solution**: Agents using DeepSeek R1's **Reasoning Engine** identified critical cases, flagged conflicting data, and initiated direct communication with on-call medical staff.

- Key Benefit: Improved patient outcomes and reduced administrative overhead by automating data validation and triage.
3. **Smart Grid Stabilization**
   - **Challenge**: Balancing energy distribution during peak usage periods.
   - **Solution**: DeepSeek R1's **multilayer architecture** allowed the creation of neighborhood-level agents to manage local power flows, while regional agents coordinated overarching demands.
   - **Key Benefit**: Energy savings of up to 15% in certain test regions, along with more stable electricity supply.

---

6. End-of-Chapter Projects

Project 2: Exploring DeepSeek R1's Architecture

Objective: Familiarize yourself with the **core components** of DeepSeek R1 by deploying a **minimal prototype** that includes agent creation, basic communication, and simple task management.

Project Overview

1. **Setup**:
   - Install or clone the DeepSeek R1 SDK/Library.
   - Configure a local or cloud-based environment to run your agents.
2. **Architecture Implementation**:
   - **Agent Creation**: Implement at least **two** agents capable of sending messages back and forth.
   - **Task Scheduler**: Define a **basic** task that can be broadcast to both agents. The scheduler will pick the best agent to handle it.

- o **Reasoning**: Add a **simple rule-based** logic for one agent. For example, if the message is of type `"DATA_REQUEST"`, the agent will respond with `"DATA_PROVIDED"`.

Example Code (Pseudocode)

```python
python

# Assuming we have a DeepSeek R1 library with key classes

from deepseek_r1 import AgentManager, TaskScheduler,
AgentBase

# 1. Define a simple agent with minimal reasoning
class SimpleAgent(AgentBase):
    def on_message(self, message):
        if message.content_type == "DATA_REQUEST":
            # Simple rule: If asked for data, respond with
data
            response = {
                "sender": self.agent_id,
                "receiver": message.sender,
                "content_type": "DATA_PROVIDED",
                "payload": "SampleData123"
            }
            self.send_message(response)
        else:
            print(f"[{self.agent_id}] Received an unknown
message type.")

# 2. Initialize Manager, Scheduler, and Agents
agent_manager = AgentManager()
scheduler = TaskScheduler()

agent1 = SimpleAgent(agent_id="Agent1")
agent2 = SimpleAgent(agent_id="Agent2")

agent_manager.register_agent(agent1)
agent_manager.register_agent(agent2)

# 3. Basic Task Setup
task = {
    "task_id": "RequestData",
    "requirements": {"data_query": "Required"}
}

# The scheduler picks the best agent for the job (basic
selection for now)
selected_agent = scheduler.select_best_agent([agent1,
agent2], task)
```

```
print(f"Selected agent: {selected_agent.agent_id}")

# 4. Simulate Task Execution
# Agent sends a message to itself or another agent
message = {
    "sender": "Scheduler",
    "receiver": selected_agent.agent_id,
    "content_type": "DATA_REQUEST",
    "payload": "Please provide data"
}
selected_agent.send_message(message)

# 5. Run the system (assuming there's an event loop or main
execution thread)
agent_manager.run()  # This would keep agents active,
listening for messages
```

Explanation of Key Sections

- **SimpleAgent**: Inherits from a hypothetical `AgentBase` class in the DeepSeek R1 library. Implements **rule-based** logic in the `on_message` method.
- **AgentManager**: Handles registration and lifecycle. `register_agent()` ensures each agent is tracked properly.
- **TaskScheduler**: Chooses an agent for the given task. Here, we used a simple selection method; in advanced cases, it could analyze agent capabilities or priorities.
- **Message Flow**: The `DATA_REQUEST` message triggers a response of type `DATA_PROVIDED`, demonstrating basic **communication** and **decision-making** logic.

Extensions

- **Complex Conditions**: Expand the agent's reasoning to handle multiple message types or utilize ML models.
- **Multiple Task Types**: Create tasks with different constraints to see how the scheduler handles them.
- **Distributed Environment**: Launch agents on separate machines or containers, testing network reliability and scalability.

7. Quizzes and Self-Assessments

Quiz 2: DeepSeek R1 Overview

Test your understanding of **DeepSeek R1** by answering the following questions. Refer to code examples or text above as needed.

1. **Architecture**
   o **Question**: List three major components of DeepSeek R1's architecture and briefly describe their functions.
2. **Core Features**
   o **Question**: What type of reasoning methods does the DeepSeek R1 Reasoning Engine support? Give a brief explanation of each.
3. **Integration**
   o **Question**: Name two ways DeepSeek R1 can integrate with existing systems or third-party tools.
4. **Comparative Analysis**
   o **Question**: Identify one unique selling point of DeepSeek R1 compared to generic MAS tools.
5. **Use Cases**
   o **Question**: Describe one real-world scenario where DeepSeek R1 is used, and highlight the main benefit it provides.
6. **Short Coding Prompt**
   o **Question**: Outline the steps to set up a minimal DeepSeek R1 application with two agents and a simple message exchange.

Answer Key (Suggested):

1. **Components**:
   o **Agent Manager** handles agent lifecycle; **Task Scheduler** distributes tasks; **Reasoning Engine** manages advanced decision-making.
2. **Reasoning Methods**:
   o **Rule-Based** for deterministic logic, **Probabilistic** for handling uncertainty, **Machine Learning** for data-driven adaptability.
3. **Integration**:
   o **API/SDK** for direct integration with application code, **Plugin Architecture** for extending or customizing key modules (e.g., communication, data processing).

4. **Unique Selling Point**:
   - o DeepSeek R1 includes **task scheduling and advanced reasoning** out of the box, reducing the need for separate frameworks or manual coding.
5. **Use Case Example**:
   - o **Automated Warehouses**: Robots coordinate picking and packing, resulting in faster order fulfillment and lower operational errors.
6. **Minimal Application Steps**:
   - o **Setup** the AgentManager, create two agents, register them, **send a test message**, run the system's main loop.

This chapter has provided a **comprehensive overview** of **DeepSeek R1**, from its origins and architecture to its key features and real-world applications. You've learned how it stacks up against other MAS tools, what unique value it brings to multi-agent development, and how you can set up a basic system using its APIs and scheduling features.

Chapter 3: Getting Started with DeepSeek R1

Welcome to **Chapter 3**, where we focus on setting up your environment and getting your very first **DeepSeek R1** project running. By the end of this chapter, you will know the **hardware and software requirements**, how to **install** DeepSeek R1 on different platforms, and how to **configure** a development environment that suits your needs. We will also guide you through **creating your first project**, exploring the **user interface**, and **navigating** the documentation and community resources. All examples in this chapter are provided in a **clear, professional style**, ensuring you can easily follow along and replicate them on your own system.

1. System Requirements

Before installing **DeepSeek R1**, it is crucial to verify that your system meets the necessary **hardware** and **software** requirements.

1.1. Hardware Specifications

Requirement	Minimum Specification	Recommended Specification
Processor (CPU)	Dual-core CPU (2.0 GHz or higher)	Quad-core CPU (3.0 GHz or higher)
Memory (RAM)	8 GB	16 GB or more
Storage	20 GB free disk space	50 GB+ (especially for large projects)
Graphics (GPU)	Not strictly required unless using ML integrations	Dedicated GPU for advanced ML tasks

1. **CPU**: A minimum dual-core CPU ensures that you can run multiple agents simultaneously without significant performance degradation. A faster, multi-core CPU enhances parallel processing.

2. **RAM**: While 8 GB can handle small to medium MAS projects, 16 GB or more is advisable for complex simulations or heavy data processing.
3. **Storage**: Keep at least 20 GB of free space, as DeepSeek R1's libraries, logs, and additional data can grow over time.
4. **GPU (Optional)**: If you plan on integrating machine learning components or handling large-scale simulations, a dedicated GPU can significantly accelerate processing.

1.2. Software Dependencies

Dependency	Minimum Version	Recommended Version
Operating System	Windows 10 / macOS 10.15 / Linux (Ubuntu 20.04)	Latest OS patch level
Python	3.7+	3.9+
Java (Optional)	8	11+ (if using Java-based APIs)
Docker (Optional)	19.03+	Latest Stable Release

1. **Operating System**: DeepSeek R1 officially supports Windows, macOS, and popular Linux distributions like Ubuntu or CentOS.
2. **Python**: A large portion of DeepSeek R1's tools and examples are written in Python, so ensure you have Python 3.7 or higher installed.
3. **Java**: Some advanced features or plugins may require Java. If you're only using Python-based APIs, Java may not be necessary.
4. **Docker**: If you want to run DeepSeek R1 in containerized environments (recommended for production), Docker is an optional but powerful tool.

2. Installation Guide

This section provides a **step-by-step** installation process for **Windows, macOS**, and **Linux**, along with common troubleshooting tips.

2.1. Step-by-Step Installation on Various Platforms

2.1.1. Windows

1. **Download the Installer**
   - o Visit the official DeepSeek R1 website or repository.
   - o Download the latest **DeepSeek R1 Windows Installer (.exe)**.
2. **Run the Installer**
   - o Double-click the `.exe` file.
   - o Follow the on-screen prompts:
     - ▪ Accept the license agreement.
     - ▪ Choose an installation directory (default is `C:\Program Files\DeepSeekR1`).
     - ▪ Complete the installation.
3. **Configure Environment Variables**
   - o Open **Control Panel → System → Advanced System Settings → Environment Variables**.
   - o Under **System variables**, select `Path` → **Edit** → Add the path to the DeepSeek R1 `bin` folder (e.g., `C:\Program Files\DeepSeekR1\bin`).
   - o Click **OK** to save.
4. **Verify Installation**
   - o Open **Command Prompt** and type:

   ```bash

   deepseek --version
   ```

   - o If the version number appears, the installation is successful.

2.1.2. macOS

1. **Download the Package**
   - o Obtain the **DeepSeek R1 DMG package** from the official website.
2. **Install**
   - o Double-click the `.dmg` file to open the installer.
   - o Drag the **DeepSeek R1** icon into your **Applications** folder.
3. **Terminal Setup** (Optional)

o   If you need to run DeepSeek R1 commands from the
    Terminal, link the `deepseek` executable to a known directory
    (e.g., `/usr/local/bin`):

```bash
bash

sudo ln -s /Applications/DeepSeekR1/bin/deepseek
/usr/local/bin/deepseek
```

4. **Verify Installation**
   o   Open **Terminal** and type:

```bash
bash

deepseek --version
```

   o   A version check confirms the tool is successfully installed.

2.1.3. Linux (Ubuntu Example)

1. **Install Dependencies**
   o   Update and install necessary packages:

```bash
bash

sudo apt-get update
sudo apt-get install python3 python3-pip openjdk-
11-jdk
```

2. **Download & Extract**
   o   Download the **DeepSeek R1 Linux tarball** (`.tar.gz`) or use
       a package manager if available.
   o   Navigate to the download directory and extract:

```bash
bash

tar -xvzf deepseek_r1_linux.tar.gz
```

3. **Add to PATH**
   o   Suppose the extracted folder is `~/deepseek_r1`. Edit
       `~/.bashrc` or `~/.zshrc`:

```bash
bash
```

```
echo 'export PATH="$PATH:$HOME/deepseek_r1/bin"'
>> ~/.bashrc
source ~/.bashrc
```

4. **Verify Installation**
   - o Open a new Terminal session:

```
bash

deepseek --version
```

   - o If you see DeepSeek R1's version details, the installation is complete.

2.2. Troubleshooting Common Installation Issues

1. **Command Not Found**
   - o **Cause**: The environment variable `PATH` might not be correctly set.
   - o **Solution**: Recheck your system's PATH settings, ensure the `bin` directory for DeepSeek R1 is included.
2. **Permission Denied**
   - o **Cause**: Insufficient permissions to access or run executable files.
   - o **Solution**: On Linux/macOS, run `chmod +x deepseek` or use `sudo` if necessary.
3. **Missing Dependencies**
   - o **Cause**: Required software like Python, Java, or Docker is not installed or outdated.
   - o **Solution**: Check your versions and install or update the missing dependencies.
4. **Version Conflicts**
   - o **Cause**: Running multiple versions of Python or Java might lead to conflicts.
   - o **Solution**: Use a dedicated virtual environment for Python and ensure your `JAVA_HOME` points to the correct Java version.

3. Setting Up the Development Environment

To create and manage DeepSeek R1 projects effectively, set up a **development environment** that aligns with your workflow and application requirements.

3.1. IDE Recommendations

1. **Visual Studio Code (VS Code)**
   - **Plugins**: Extensions like Python, Java, Docker, and code formatting tools.
   - **Integrated Terminal** for running DeepSeek R1 commands.
2. **PyCharm**
   - Ideal for Python-heavy projects with built-in debugging, virtual environment management, and code inspection.
3. **Eclipse or IntelliJ IDEA (If Using Java)**
   - Streamlined integration with Java-based projects, offering robust refactoring and debugging features.

3.2. Configuring DeepSeek R1 for Development

Example: Configuring VS Code with DeepSeek R1 (Pseudocode)

1. **Install VS Code**
   - Download and install from the official website (https://code.visualstudio.com).
2. **Add Extensions**
   - **Python**: Provides syntax highlighting, IntelliSense, and debugging.
   - **DeepSeek R1 Tools** (if available): Adds additional code snippets and direct integration with the DeepSeek R1 engine.
3. **Create a Project Folder**

   ```bash
   mkdir ~/deepseek_projects/hello_deepseek
   cd ~/deepseek_projects/hello_deepseek
   ```

4. **Initialize a Python Virtual Environment**

   ```bash
   ```

```
python3 -m venv venv
source venv/bin/activate
```

5. **Install DeepSeek R1 Python SDK (if using pip)**

```bash
bash
```

```
pip install deepseek-r1-sdk
```

6. **Launch VS Code**

```bash
bash
```

```
code .
```

7. **Configure Launch Settings**
   - In VS Code, go to **Run and Debug → Create a launch.json file**, setting it to recognize Python and your newly created environment.

4. First Steps with DeepSeek R1

Once your environment is ready, you can create your **first DeepSeek R1 project** and explore the **basic configuration** options and **user interface (UI)**.

4.1. Creating Your First Project

1. **Directory Setup**
   - Create a dedicated folder for your project (e.g., `my_first_deepseek_project`).
   - Initialize version control if desired (`git init`).
2. **Basic Python Script Example**

```python
python

# hello_deepseek.py
from deepseek_r1_sdk import AgentManager, AgentBase

class HelloAgent(AgentBase):
    def on_start(self):
        print(f"{self.agent_id} starting up...")
```

```
    def on_message(self, message):
        print(f"Received message: {message}")

if __name__ == "__main__":
    manager = AgentManager()
    agent = HelloAgent(agent_id="Agent_1")
    manager.register_agent(agent)
    manager.run()
```

- o **Explanation**:
  - ▪ `HelloAgent` is a simple class extending `AgentBase`, implementing basic **on_start** and **on_message** methods.
  - ▪ `Manager` handles agent lifecycle.
  - ▪ `manager.run()` starts the system, allowing the agent to receive messages (if any).
3. **Run Your Script**

```bash
python hello_deepseek.py
```

- o You should see console output confirming the agent's startup.

4.2. Understanding the User Interface

While DeepSeek R1 can be used entirely via **command-line** or **API** calls, it also provides an **optional UI** or **web-based dashboard** for monitoring:

1. **Agent Monitoring**
   - o View a list of active agents, their states (e.g., running, paused), and resource usage.
2. **Task & Job Overview**
   - o Shows assigned tasks, priorities, and overall progress.
3. **System Logs**
   - o Consolidates logs from various agents, highlighting errors or warnings in a centralized location.

4.3. Basic Configuration and Customization

1. **Configuration Files**

- o Typically located in a file like `deepseek_config.yaml` or `deepseek.json`.
- o Contains settings for **network ports**, **data storage**, and **agent defaults**.

2. **Logging Level**
   - o Adjust levels (`DEBUG`, `INFO`, `WARN`, `ERROR`) to manage verbosity.
   - o Useful for troubleshooting or performance profiling.

3. **Plugin Management**
   - o Enable or disable plugins (e.g., machine learning modules, specialized schedulers) in configuration files.

5. Navigating DeepSeek R1 Documentation

To unlock DeepSeek R1's full potential, you need to become familiar with the available **documentation and community** channels.

5.1. Key Resources

- **Official Docs**: Often hosted on the DeepSeek R1 website, providing detailed references for APIs, agent classes, and deployment guides.
- **Developer Guides**: Step-by-step tutorials, best practices, and example projects.
- **Knowledge Base/FAQ**: Addresses common questions, offering quick tips for new users.

5.2. Community and Support Channels

- **User Forum**: A place to ask technical questions, share projects, and get feedback from other developers.
- **Slack/Discord Channels**: Real-time chat for instant help, announcements, or discussions on new features.
- **Issue Tracker (e.g., GitHub)**: Report bugs, request features, or check the status of known issues.
- **Professional Support**: For enterprise-level projects, DeepSeek R1 may offer premium support packages, providing dedicated troubleshooting and consulting.

6. End-of-Chapter Projects

Project 3: Setting Up Your Development Environment

Objective: Validate your **DeepSeek R1** setup and create a simple agent-driven script to ensure your environment works as intended.

Project Outline

1. **Install/Verify Dependencies**
   - Check Python, Java (if required), and Docker (optional) versions.
2. **Create a Project Folder**
   - Name it `my_env_setup_project`.
3. **Initialize a Virtual Environment**
   - `python3 -m venv env` → `source env/bin/activate`
4. **Install DeepSeek R1 SDK**
   - `pip install deepseek-r1-sdk`
5. **Implement a Simple Agent**
   - Copy or modify the **HelloAgent** example from Section 4.1.
6. **Run and Observe Output**
   - Confirm that your agent starts and logs basic messages.

Sample Code

```python
# my_env_setup_project/agent_setup.py
from deepseek_r1_sdk import AgentManager, AgentBase

class EnvTestAgent(AgentBase):
    def on_start(self):
        print(f"{self.agent_id} has started successfully in
our new environment.")

if __name__ == "__main__":
    manager = AgentManager()
    agent = EnvTestAgent(agent_id="Env_Agent_1")
    manager.register_agent(agent)
    manager.run()
```

Expected Result

- The console should print a startup message from your agent, indicating that **DeepSeek R1** is correctly installed and configured.

---

7. Quizzes and Self-Assessments

Quiz 3: Getting Started with DeepSeek R1

Test your knowledge from this chapter by answering the following questions. Use the sections above for reference if needed.

1. **System Requirements**
   - **Question**: What is the minimum recommended RAM for running DeepSeek R1, especially for complex projects?
   - **Hint**: Refer to the hardware specifications table.
2. **Installation**
   - **Question**: Name two common installation issues you might face on Linux and how to resolve them.
3. **Development Environment**
   - **Question**: Why is it recommended to use a Python virtual environment when setting up DeepSeek R1 on a machine?
4. **First Steps**
   - **Question**: What command would you type to verify that DeepSeek R1 is installed successfully on a Windows system?
5. **Basic Customization**
   - **Question**: How can you change the logging level for DeepSeek R1 agents to reduce console output?
6. **Documentation and Community**
   - **Question**: Mention one benefit of using the official DeepSeek R1 forum or Slack/Discord channel.
7. **Short Coding Prompt**
   - **Question**: Write a minimal Python script that creates one agent, assigns it a unique ID, and prints "Hello from [AgentID]".

Answer Key (Suggested):

1. **Minimum Recommended RAM**: 16 GB for complex or large-scale agent tasks.
2. **Installation Issues**:

- o **Command Not Found**: Fix by adding the DeepSeek R1 `bin` folder to your PATH.
  - o **Permission Denied**: Run `chmod +x deepseek` or use `sudo` to adjust file permissions.
3. **Python Virtual Environment**: Avoids dependency conflicts and keeps your project's libraries isolated.
4. **Verify Installation on Windows**: `deepseek --version` in **Command Prompt**.
5. **Logging Level**: Adjust the `deepseek_config.yaml` or environment variable to set `LOG_LEVEL` to `WARN` or `ERROR`.
6. **Community Benefit**: Quick feedback from other developers, timely answers to technical issues, and a place to share experiences or solutions.
7. **Coding Prompt**:

```python
python

from deepseek_r1_sdk import AgentManager, AgentBase

class MyTestAgent(AgentBase):
    def on_start(self):
        print(f"Hello from {self.agent_id}")

if __name__ == "__main__":
    manager = AgentManager()
    agent = MyTestAgent(agent_id="UniqueAgent_123")
    manager.register_agent(agent)
    manager.run()
```

In this chapter, you learned how to **install** and **configure** DeepSeek R1 across different operating systems, set up a **development environment** in popular IDEs, and create a **basic project**. You also explored key **troubleshooting** steps and discovered how to navigate the official documentation and community channels for support. By completing the **End-of-Chapter Project** and testing your knowledge with the **Quiz**, you are now well-prepared to delve into more advanced features of DeepSeek R1 in the following chapters.

Chapter 4: Designing Agents in DeepSeek R1

Designing agents is a critical step in building effective **multi-agent systems (MAS)** using **DeepSeek R1**. This chapter provides an in-depth look at the **architecture** of agents, strategies for **defining roles**, various **communication protocols**, and how to implement **agent behaviors**. We also cover **best practices** to ensure scalability, autonomy, and robustness. By the end of this chapter, you will be equipped with practical knowledge to design agents that can function reliably in complex environments. All tables, code examples, and explanations are presented in a **clear, professional style**, ensuring they are **complete** and **easy to follow**.

---

1. Agent Architecture

1.1. Structural Design of Agents

Agents in DeepSeek R1 often follow a **layered architecture**, which helps organize functionalities and separate concerns. A **typical** layered structure might look like this:

```diff
+----------------------------------+
| High-Level Reasoning Layer       | (Planning, Goal
Management)
+----------------------------------+
| Decision-Making / Strategy Layer | (Utility-based, Rule-
based, or ML-driven logic)
+----------------------------------+
| Perception & Communication Layer | (Handles incoming
messages, environment data)
+----------------------------------+
| Action Layer                     | (Executes actions, sends
messages)
+----------------------------------+
```

- **High-Level Reasoning Layer**: Oversees the agent's long-term goals and plans (e.g., "Coordinate with other agents to complete a manufacturing process").

- **Decision-Making / Strategy Layer**: Implements algorithms (rule-based, machine learning, or heuristic) that determine the best action given the current context.
- **Perception & Communication Layer**: Gathers data from the environment or other agents, interpreting messages.
- **Action Layer**: Carries out physical or logical actions, such as moving in a real-world environment or sending response messages.

Benefits of a Layered Approach:

- **Separation of Concerns**: Each layer handles distinct tasks, making the system easier to maintain.
- **Modularity**: Enhances reusability because a change in one layer (e.g., updating perception algorithms) doesn't necessarily disrupt the others.
- **Scalability**: Easy to add or remove layers without redesigning the entire agent.

1.2. Modular vs. Monolithic Agents

Modular Agents

- **Definition**: Agents whose functionalities are divided into smaller modules or components, each addressing a specific function (communication, reasoning, memory, etc.).
- **Advantages**:
    - **Ease of Maintenance**: Swapping or upgrading modules without affecting the entire system.
    - **Team Collaboration**: Different team members can work on individual modules independently.
    - **Incremental Development**: Start with a basic module and add more advanced modules over time.

Monolithic Agents

- **Definition**: Agents that implement all functionalities in a single, tightly integrated system.
- **Advantages**:
    - **Simplified Setup**: May be quicker to implement initially for small projects.
    - **Performance**: Fewer layers of abstraction, which can reduce overhead in certain scenarios.

- **Drawbacks**:
  - o **Difficult to Scale**: Growth in complexity can make maintenance or modifications cumbersome.
  - o **Less Flexible**: Harder to repurpose or extend agent functionalities without rewriting core code.

Choosing Between Modular and Monolithic

- For **small, focused** tasks with limited complexity, monolithic agents can suffice.
- For **larger systems** or projects expected to evolve over time, adopting a **modular** structure is generally best.

---

2. Defining Agent Roles and Responsibilities

2.1. Role Assignment Strategies

When multiple agents operate together, it is often helpful to assign **distinct roles**. Some common strategies include:

1. **Role-by-Expertise**: Each agent specializes in a specific function (e.g., data collection, analysis, or resource allocation).
2. **Role-by-Task**: Roles align with tasks (e.g., "Transport Agent," "Quality-Control Agent," "Inventory Agent" in a factory).
3. **Dynamic Role Assignment**: Agents switch roles on the fly, based on their current load, performance metrics, or emergent system needs.

Example Table of Potential Roles in a Warehouse System:

Agent Role	Primary Responsibilities	Skills/Capabilities Needed
Inventory Agent	Track stock levels, reorder thresholds	Database queries, forecasting

Agent Role	Primary Responsibilities	Skills/Capabilities Needed
Packaging Agent	Package items, coordinate box sizes and materials	Packaging protocols, resource management
Delivery Agent	Plan routes, dispatch vehicles	Route optimization, scheduling algorithms
Maintenance Agent	Monitor robot health, schedule repairs	Diagnostic tools, communication with robots

2.2. Specialization and Generalization in Agents

Specialized Agents

- **Focused Capabilities**: Trained or programmed for a **specific** set of tasks.
- **Performance Optimization**: Better at handling domain-specific problems, as they can use specialized algorithms or data structures.
- **Limited Flexibility**: Not as adaptable if new tasks or requirements emerge outside their area of expertise.

Generalist Agents

- **Broad Skill Set**: Capable of handling **multiple** tasks, though perhaps less optimally than a specialized agent.
- **Increased Resilience**: If one agent fails, another can step in, mitigating single points of failure.
- **Training Overhead**: May require more complex decision-making or learning algorithms to handle varied tasks efficiently.

Balancing Specialization and Generalization

- In large-scale systems, you might combine specialized agents for critical tasks with generalist agents that fill gaps or handle overflow.

3. Agent Communication Protocols

3.1. Message Formats and Standards

In DeepSeek R1, agents communicate through **messages**. Standardization in message formats ensures smooth exchange of information:

1. **JSON**: A lightweight, human-readable format commonly used in web technologies.
2. **XML**: Structured data with a focus on hierarchies, useful when messages need strict validation or metadata.
3. **Binary Formats** (e.g., Protocol Buffers): More efficient in terms of bandwidth, beneficial for large or frequent message exchanges.

Example of a JSON Message:

```json
json

{
  "sender": "Agent_Inventory",
  "receiver": "Agent_Packaging",
  "message_type": "STOCK_UPDATE",
  "payload": {
    "item_id": 123,
    "current_quantity": 40
  }
}
```

- **Explanation**: This message informs the **Packaging Agent** about the current stock level of a particular item.

3.2. Synchronous vs. Asynchronous Communication

1. **Synchronous Communication**
   o **Definition**: The sender waits for a response before proceeding.
   o **Use Cases**: Situations where **immediate confirmation** is necessary (e.g., critical resource allocation).
   o **Drawbacks**: Can lead to **bottlenecks** if the system is large or if agents frequently wait for replies.
2. **Asynchronous Communication**
   o **Definition**: The sender sends a message and continues its process without waiting. The receiver handles the message in its own time.
   o **Use Cases**: Scenarios where agents can operate **independently** or in parallel, such as event-driven data processing.

- o **Drawbacks**: Ensuring consistency can be more challenging. Agents need to handle message queues and potential communication delays.

Choosing a Communication Model

- **Synchronous** is best for **small, critical tasks** requiring confirmations, while **asynchronous** suits **large, distributed systems** to maximize parallelism.

4. Implementing Agent Behaviors

4.1. Reactive Behaviors

- **Definition**: Agents respond **immediately** to environmental changes, typically using **condition-action** rules.
- **Example**: A thermostat agent that turns the heater on if the temperature drops below 20°C, otherwise off.
- **Advantages**:
  - o Low computational overhead.
  - o Highly predictable.
- **Limitations**:
  - o Lacks foresight or planning.
  - o Not ideal for tasks requiring strategic decision-making.

4.2. Proactive Behaviors

- **Definition**: Agents take the **initiative**, planning ahead and setting goals.
- **Example**: A scheduling agent that books maintenance appointments before a device hits a critical wear level.
- **Key Aspects**:
  - o **Goal-driven**: Agents define objectives and work towards them.
  - o **Planning**: Agents may simulate or evaluate multiple future states before taking action.
- **Benefits**:
  - o Better at handling long-term or complex tasks.
  - o Can adapt when the environment changes unpredictably.

4.3. Adaptive and Learning Behaviors

- **Definition**: Agents improve **over time** using data, feedback, or trial-and-error methods.
- **Approaches**:
  - **Reinforcement Learning**: Agents learn by maximizing a reward signal.
  - **Supervised / Unsupervised**: Agents may use external training data or identify patterns without explicit labels.
- **Example**: A trading agent that refines its strategy by learning from historical market data and current trends.
- **Challenges**:
  - Requires more **computational resources**.
  - **Risk of Overfitting** or poor decisions if training data is incomplete or biased.

5. Best Practices in Agent Design

5.1. Ensuring Scalability

1. **Distributed Architecture**: Avoid single points of control. Use decentralized coordination where possible.
2. **Load Balancing**: Monitor agent workloads. Migrate tasks from overloaded agents to less busy ones automatically.
3. **Caching and Local State**: Minimize repeated network calls by storing frequently accessed data locally.

5.2. Maintaining Agent Autonomy

1. **Minimal Dependencies**: Each agent should operate with minimal reliance on external services or other agents, reducing inter-dependencies.
2. **Self-contained Modules**: If one module fails, other modules within the agent should continue functioning.
3. **Local Decision Rights**: Agents should handle local decisions (e.g., immediate sensor data) without always waiting for global directives.

5.3. Designing for Robustness and Fault Tolerance

1. **Redundant Agents**: Deploy multiple agents that can perform the same function, preventing system collapse if one fails.
2. **Graceful Degradation**: If an agent loses partial functionality, it should still handle a reduced scope of tasks rather than stop completely.
3. **Automated Recovery**: Allow agents to **restart** or **reinitialize** themselves if they encounter errors, and ensure communication protocols can handle transient failures.

---

6. End-of-Chapter Projects

Project 4: Designing and Implementing Agent Roles

Objective: Learn how to assign **roles** to agents and **implement** distinct behaviors (reactive, proactive, or adaptive) using DeepSeek R1's libraries.

Project Outline

1. **System Concept**:
   o You will create a simplified **warehouse scenario** with **two agents**:
      1. **StockAgent** (Reactive)
      2. **OrderAgent** (Proactive)
2. **Agent Behavior Requirements**:
   o **StockAgent**:

      ▪ **Reactive** to inventory requests.
      ▪ If it receives a message `"CHECK_STOCK"`, it replies with the current stock level.

   o **OrderAgent**:

      ▪ **Proactive** in restocking items once a threshold is reached.

- Periodically checks stock levels; if below 10 units, sends a "RESTOCK" message.

3. **Implementation Steps**:

```python
# warehouse_agents.py
from deepseek_r1_sdk import AgentManager, AgentBase, TaskScheduler

class StockAgent(AgentBase):
    def __init__(self, agent_id, initial_stock=20):
        super().__init__(agent_id)
        self.stock_level = initial_stock

    def on_message(self, message):
        if message.get("content_type") == "CHECK_STOCK":
            response = {
                "sender": self.agent_id,
                "receiver": message["sender"],
                "content_type": "STOCK_LEVEL",
                "payload": {"stock": self.stock_level}
            }
            self.send_message(response)
        elif message.get("content_type") == "RESTOCK":
            # Increase stock by a fixed amount
            self.stock_level += 10
            print(f"[{self.agent_id}] Restocked! New level: {self.stock_level}")

class OrderAgent(AgentBase):
    def on_start(self):
        # Proactive check - schedule a recurring task
        self.scheduler_id = TaskScheduler.schedule_repeating(self.check_stock, interval=5)

    def check_stock(self):
        # Request current stock from StockAgent
        msg = {
            "sender": self.agent_id,
            "receiver": "StockAgent",
            "content_type": "CHECK_STOCK"
        }
        self.send_message(msg)

    def on_message(self, message):
        if message.get("content_type") == "STOCK_LEVEL":
            current_stock = message["payload"]["stock"]
```

```python
        if current_stock < 10:
            restock_msg = {
                "sender": self.agent_id,
                "receiver": "StockAgent",
                "content_type": "RESTOCK"
            }
            self.send_message(restock_msg)
```

4. **Run and Observe**:

```python
python

# main.py
from deepseek_r1_sdk import AgentManager
from warehouse_agents import StockAgent, OrderAgent

if __name__ == "__main__":
    manager = AgentManager()

    stock_agent = StockAgent(agent_id="StockAgent",
initial_stock=8)
    order_agent = OrderAgent(agent_id="OrderAgent")

    manager.register_agent(stock_agent)
    manager.register_agent(order_agent)

    manager.run()
```

   o **Explanation**:
     ▪ **StockAgent** is reactive; it replies to `"CHECK_STOCK"`
        queries and updates stock levels upon receiving
        `"RESTOCK"`.
     ▪ **OrderAgent** is proactive; it periodically checks the
        stock level, triggering a restock if needed.
5. **Expected Output**:
   o **OrderAgent** requests stock updates every 5 seconds.
   o If **StockAgent** reports a level below 10, a `"RESTOCK"`
      message is sent, increasing the stock.

Extensions

- **Adaptive Behavior**: Enhance **OrderAgent** to learn from purchasing
  trends, adjusting restock quantities dynamically.
- **Additional Agents**: Introduce a **DeliveryAgent** or **PackagingAgent**
  to see how messages propagate through the system.

7. Quizzes and Self-Assessments

Quiz 4: Agent Design Principles

Test your understanding of **agent design** in DeepSeek R1 by answering the following questions. You can refer to the project or code snippets above for guidance.

1. **Agent Architecture**
   - **Question**: What is one advantage of using a layered agent architecture in DeepSeek R1?
2. **Modular vs. Monolithic Agents**
   - **Question**: Provide one advantage and one disadvantage of building agents in a monolithic style.
3. **Roles and Responsibilities**
   - **Question**: In what scenario might dynamic role assignment be preferable over static roles?
4. **Communication Protocols**
   - **Question**: Differentiate between synchronous and asynchronous communication, and give one example of when each would be most appropriate.
5. **Behavior Types**
   - **Question**: How does a **proactive** agent differ from a **reactive** agent in terms of decision-making approach?
6. **Best Practices**
   - **Question**: Describe one method for maintaining agent autonomy in a large multi-agent system.
7. **Short Coding Prompt**
   - **Question**: Write a pseudocode snippet that shows how an agent would decide whether to take a **reactive** or a **proactive** approach based on a configuration file setting.

Answer Key (Suggested):

1. **Layered Architecture Advantage**: Separates concerns, making it easier to maintain and update individual layers without affecting the entire agent.
2. **Monolithic Agent**:
   - **Advantage**: Easier to set up for small, simple tasks.

      o **Disadvantage**: Difficult to scale or modify once the system grows in complexity.

3. **Dynamic Role Assignment**: Useful in environments where workloads or resource availability change rapidly (e.g., a variable manufacturing line).
4. **Synchronous vs. Asynchronous**:
      o **Synchronous**: Sender waits for a response (e.g., confirming resource allocation).
      o **Asynchronous**: Sender continues without waiting, ideal for large distributed systems to avoid bottlenecks.
5. **Proactive vs. Reactive**: Proactive agents plan ahead and set goals, while reactive agents simply respond to environmental stimuli.
6. **Maintaining Autonomy**: Keep internal logic and data localized so agents can make decisions independently, with minimal reliance on centralized directives.
7. **Coding Prompt** (Pseudocode):

```python
config = load_config("agent_config.yaml")
approach = config.get("behavior_approach", "reactive")
# default to "reactive"

if approach == "proactive":
    agent_behavior = ProactiveBehaviorModule()
else:
    agent_behavior = ReactiveBehaviorModule()

agent = MyAgent(behavior_module=agent_behavior)
agent.start()
```

In this chapter, you have learned about **agent architecture**, how to **define roles**, the importance of **communication protocols**, and the difference between **reactive, proactive,** and **adaptive behaviors**. We also discussed **best practices** for designing agents that are **scalable**, **autonomous**, and **robust**. By experimenting with the **end-of-chapter project**, you will gain practical insight into creating well-structured and capable agents within **DeepSeek R1**.

Armed with these skills, you are now prepared to **expand** your agent designs further, integrating them into larger systems and leveraging advanced **reasoning** and **coordination** features introduced in upcoming chapters.

Chapter 5: Communication and Coordination Among Agents

Communication and coordination lie at the **heart** of any successful multi-agent system (MAS). In **DeepSeek R1**, these aspects are heavily emphasized, ensuring that agents can share information efficiently, coordinate tasks, and make collaborative decisions. This chapter explores various **communication models**, mechanisms for **coordination**, **synchronization** techniques, collaborative **decision-making** approaches, and strategies for **handling communication failures**. By following the examples and best practices outlined here, you will be equipped to design robust multi-agent interactions that scale seamlessly. All tables, diagrams, and code examples provided are **clear, accurate, and easy to follow**.

---

1. Inter-Agent Communication

1.1. Communication Models

In multi-agent systems, agents must exchange information to fulfill tasks effectively. Two broad models of communication in MAS are:

1. **Direct (Peer-to-Peer) Communication**
   - o **Definition**: Each agent communicates directly with targeted agents via point-to-point messages.
   - o **Use Cases**: Ideal for smaller systems or scenarios where agents have specific roles and known recipients (e.g., an inventory agent always informing a packaging agent).
   - o **Pros/Cons**:
     - **Pro**: Low overhead, straightforward implementation.
     - **Con**: Doesn't scale as easily when the number of agents grows large.
2. **Indirect (Shared Space or Publish/Subscribe) Communication**
   - o **Definition**: Agents publish messages to a channel or shared data structure (e.g., blackboard, message queue) that other agents can subscribe to or read from.

- o **Use Cases**: Large or dynamic systems where the set of interested agents can change over time (e.g., sensor data for multiple monitoring agents).
- o **Pros/Cons**:
  - ▪ **Pro**: Decouples senders from receivers, improving scalability.
  - ▪ **Con**: Slightly more complex to set up and maintain.

Example Table: Communication Model Comparison

Feature	Direct (Peer-to-Peer)	Indirect (Publish/Subscribe)
Scalability	Limited by the number of connections	High, as publishers do not need knowledge of subscribers
Complexity	Lower initial complexity	Higher complexity but more flexible
Best for	Small, static networks	Large, dynamic systems
Fault Tolerance	Depends on handling agent failures	Can be higher if brokers or blackboards are replicated

1.2. Messaging Systems in DeepSeek R1

DeepSeek R1 provides a **Messaging Layer** that supports both **direct** and **publish/subscribe** patterns. Here's how it typically works:

- **Agent Manager Registration**
  - o Agents register with the **AgentManager**, which maintains a global directory mapping agent IDs to network addresses or message queues.
- **Message Object**
  - o A standard message object contains fields like `sender`, `receiver`, `content_type`, and `payload`.
  - o By default, JSON is used for ease of serialization and debugging.
- **Publish/Subscribe**

- o Agents can **subscribe** to topics (e.g., "InventoryUpdates"), and any **published** messages on that topic are routed to them automatically.

Basic Pseudocode Example:

python

```
# direct_message.py
from deepseek_r1_sdk import AgentManager, AgentBase

class SenderAgent(AgentBase):
    def send_direct_message(self, receiver_id, payload):
        message = {
            "sender": self.agent_id,
            "receiver": receiver_id,
            "content_type": "DIRECT_MSG",
            "payload": payload
        }
        self.send_message(message)

class ReceiverAgent(AgentBase):
    def on_message(self, message):
        if message.get("content_type") == "DIRECT_MSG":
            print(f"[{self.agent_id}] Received direct message from {message['sender']}: {message['payload']}")

if __name__ == "__main__":
    manager = AgentManager()

    sender = SenderAgent(agent_id="Sender1")
    receiver = ReceiverAgent(agent_id="Receiver1")

    manager.register_agent(sender)
    manager.register_agent(receiver)

    manager.run()

    # At runtime, sender can call:
    sender.send_direct_message("Receiver1", {"info": "Hello from Sender1"})
```

- **Explanation**: This simplified snippet demonstrates a **direct (peer-to-peer)** communication scenario in DeepSeek R1.

2. Coordination Mechanisms

2.1. Centralized vs. Decentralized Coordination

1. **Centralized Coordination**
   - o **Definition**: A single "master" or "manager" agent coordinates all tasks and resource allocations.
   - o **Advantages**:
     - ▪ Clear line of control.
     - ▪ Simplified logic since one agent manages global decisions.
   - o **Disadvantages**:
     - ▪ Single point of failure.
     - ▪ Can become a bottleneck in large systems.
2. **Decentralized Coordination**
   - o **Definition**: Multiple agents share responsibilities, each making decisions based on local information or partial system views.
   - o **Advantages**:
     - ▪ Improves scalability; no single point of failure.
     - ▪ Agents can adapt to local changes quickly.
   - o **Disadvantages**:
     - ▪ More complex to implement.
     - ▪ Risk of conflicts or overlapping efforts if not carefully designed.

2.2. Coordination Languages and Protocols

In **DeepSeek R1**, you can implement coordination using established protocols:

- **Contract Net Protocol (CNP)**
  - o A manager agent announces tasks ("calls for proposals"), and other agents bid for them. The manager awards the contract to the best bid.
- **Blackboard Systems**
  - o Agents post partial solutions or requests on a shared blackboard. Other agents read or update the blackboard, gradually converging on a solution.
- **Negotiation Protocols**
  - o Agents follow rules to negotiate resource allocation, scheduling, or conflict resolution (e.g., auctions, bartering).

Example: Contract Net in Pseudocode:

```python
# contract_net.py
class ManagerAgent(AgentBase):
    def announce_task(self, task_details):
        # Broadcast a "Call for Proposals" message
        cfp_message = {
            "sender": self.agent_id,
            "receiver": "ALL",  # or a specific group
            "content_type": "CALL_FOR_PROPOSALS",
            "payload": task_details
        }
        self.send_message(cfp_message)

    def on_message(self, message):
        if message.get("content_type") == "PROPOSAL":
            # Evaluate the proposal and respond with
ACCEPT_PROPOSAL or REJECT_PROPOSAL
            best_bid = self.evaluate_proposal(message)
            if best_bid:
                # Send acceptance
                accept_msg = {
                    "sender": self.agent_id,
                    "receiver": message["sender"],
                    "content_type": "ACCEPT_PROPOSAL",
                    "payload": {"task_id":
task_details["task_id"]}
                }
                self.send_message(accept_msg)
            else:
                # Reject
                reject_msg = {
                    "sender": self.agent_id,
                    "receiver": message["sender"],
                    "content_type": "REJECT_PROPOSAL",
                    "payload": {}
                }
                self.send_message(reject_msg)

class WorkerAgent(AgentBase):
    def on_message(self, message):
        if message.get("content_type") ==
"CALL_FOR_PROPOSALS":
            # Check if can handle the task, then send a
proposal
            proposal_msg = {
                "sender": self.agent_id,
                "receiver": message["sender"],
                "content_type": "PROPOSAL",
                "payload": {"cost": 10, "time_needed": 5}
            }
```

```
        self.send_message(proposal_msg)
    elif message.get("content_type") ==
"ACCEPT_PROPOSAL":
        # Execute the task
        self.perform_task(message["payload"]["task_id"])
```

3. Synchronization Techniques

3.1. Time-based Synchronization

- **Definition**: Agents perform actions or exchange data at fixed intervals or synchronized "ticks."
- **Examples**:
  - o **Step-based Simulations**: Each agent updates its state every second or every iteration.
  - o **Periodic Polling**: Agents check for new messages or sensor updates at set intervals.

Advantages:

- Predictable timing, simpler scheduling.
- Useful for simulations or scenarios where **global time** is crucial.

Disadvantages:

- May lead to **idle waiting** if agents have to align with a global clock.
- Introduces overhead in large systems with frequent communication intervals.

3.2. Event-based Synchronization

- **Definition**: Agents react to events (e.g., a message arrival, sensor reading change) in real time without relying on a fixed clock.
- **Examples**:
  - o **Asynchronous Messaging**: The agent triggers specific behaviors upon receiving a new message.
  - o **Interrupt-driven**: External triggers cause agent behaviors to fire immediately.

Advantages:

- Efficient resource usage, as agents act only when needed.
- More natural for real-world scenarios where events are unpredictable.

Disadvantages:

- Harder to debug if multiple asynchronous events happen concurrently.
- Requires robust concurrency handling to avoid race conditions.

4. Collaborative Decision Making

4.1. Consensus Algorithms

When multiple agents must agree on a shared outcome (e.g., distributed ledger consensus, or a unified course of action), consensus algorithms are crucial.

- **Examples**:
    - **Paxos**: A fault-tolerant algorithm ensuring a majority consensus.
    - **Raft**: Simplifies understanding and implementation while maintaining fault tolerance.
- **Use Cases**:
    - Distributed computing (replication, consistency).
    - Multi-agent negotiations where unanimous decisions are critical.

4.2. Distributed Decision-Making Models

1. **Voting Systems**
    - Each agent votes on a proposal; the majority outcome wins.
    - Straightforward but may not reflect agent expertise differences.
2. **Market-Based Approaches**
    - Agents "buy" or "sell" resources or tasks, and supply-demand dynamics lead to equilibrium solutions.
    - Effective in resource allocation and load balancing.
3. **Game-Theoretic Models**

- o Agents act as rational players aiming to maximize their own utility.
- o Complex but can capture real-world negotiation or conflict scenarios (e.g., auctions).

DeepSeek R1 Implementation Tip:

- Combine **Task Scheduler** with a **Market-Based** plugin to enable dynamic bidding for tasks. This ensures tasks are handled by agents most capable or least busy at any given time.

---

5. Handling Communication Failures

5.1. Error Detection and Recovery

Multi-agent systems must anticipate disruptions, such as network outages or agent crashes.

1. **Heartbeat Mechanisms**
   - o Agents periodically send "I'm alive" messages to a coordinator or peer.
   - o If no heartbeat is received within a set timeframe, the system infers the agent may be offline.
2. **Automatic Retries**
   - o Failed message deliveries can be retried a configurable number of times.
   - o After repeated failures, fallback strategies (e.g., reassigning tasks) may be triggered.

5.2. Ensuring Reliable Communication

1. **Message Acknowledgments**
   - o Sender requires a confirmation message (ACK). If not received, it re-sends or logs an error.
2. **Redundant Communication Paths**

- o In critical systems, messages can be sent through multiple channels or brokers to avoid single points of failure.
3. **Checkpointing**
    - o Agents periodically save their state. If a crash occurs, they can restart from the last checkpoint with minimal data loss.

6. End-of-Chapter Projects

Project 5: Implementing Inter-Agent Communication

Objective: Develop a simple scenario where agents use **both** direct communication and a **publish/subscribe** mechanism to coordinate a shared task.

Project Outline

1. **Scenario**:
    - o **SensorAgent**: Publishes sensor readings (e.g., temperature, humidity) to a topic called "SensorData."
    - o **ControllerAgent**: Subscribes to "SensorData." When the temperature exceeds a threshold, it sends a direct message to **ActuatorAgent** to turn on a cooling system.
    - o **ActuatorAgent**: Receives direct messages from **ControllerAgent**, then logs or acts on commands (e.g., turning a fan on).
2. **Implementation Steps**:

```python
# sensor_controller_actuator.py
from deepseek_r1_sdk import AgentManager, AgentBase

class SensorAgent(AgentBase):
    def on_start(self):
        self.publish_sensor_data()

    def publish_sensor_data(self):
        import random
        temp = random.randint(18, 35)
        message = {
            "sender": self.agent_id,
            "receiver": "TOPIC:SensorData",
```

```python
                "content_type": "SENSOR_READING",
                "payload": {"temperature": temp}
            }
        self.send_message(message)
        # Schedule next reading
        self.timer(5, self.publish_sensor_data)  # publish
every 5 seconds

class ControllerAgent(AgentBase):
    def on_message(self, message):
        if message.get("content_type") == "SENSOR_READING":
            temp = message["payload"]["temperature"]
            if temp > 30:
                # Direct message to ActuatorAgent
                control_msg = {
                    "sender": self.agent_id,
                    "receiver": "ActuatorAgent",
                    "content_type": "COOLING_ON",
                    "payload": {}
                }
                self.send_message(control_msg)
                print(f"[{self.agent_id}] Temperature {temp}
- Cooling system triggered.")

class ActuatorAgent(AgentBase):
    def on_message(self, message):
        if message.get("content_type") == "COOLING_ON":
            print(f"[{self.agent_id}] Received cooling
command. Turning fan ON.")

if __name__ == "__main__":
    manager = AgentManager()

    sensor = SensorAgent(agent_id="SensorAgent")
    controller = ControllerAgent(agent_id="ControllerAgent")
    actuator = ActuatorAgent(agent_id="ActuatorAgent")

    # Register agents
    manager.register_agent(sensor)
    manager.register_agent(controller)
    manager.register_agent(actuator)

    # Subscribe ControllerAgent to the SensorData topic
    manager.subscribe_to_topic("ControllerAgent",
"SensorData")

    manager.run()
```

Explanation of Key Sections

- **SensorAgent**:
  - **Publish Sensor Data**: Generates a random temperature and publishes it to a topic every five seconds.
- **ControllerAgent**:
  - **Subscribe**: Listens for **SENSOR_READING** messages from the "SensorData" topic.
  - **Decision**: If the temperature is above 30, sends a direct message to **ActuatorAgent**.
- **ActuatorAgent**:
  - **React**: Receives **COOLING_ON** messages and logs an action.

Expected Result

- Every five seconds, the sensor publishes a random temperature.
- If the reading is over 30, the controller triggers the actuator, turning on a "cooling system."
- You will see log messages in the console illustrating the flow of messages.

7. Quizzes and Self-Assessments

Quiz 5: Communication and Coordination

Test your understanding of **multi-agent communication and coordination** in DeepSeek R1 by answering the following questions. Feel free to revisit code examples and discussions from earlier sections as needed.

1. **Communication Models**
   - **Question**: Explain one advantage of using a publish/subscribe approach over a peer-to-peer model.
2. **Coordination**
   - **Question**: Differentiate between a **centralized** and a **decentralized** coordination approach. Give one real-world example for each.
3. **Synchronization Techniques**
   - **Question**: Compare **time-based** and **event-based** synchronization, including one advantage of each.
4. **Collaborative Decision Making**

- o **Question**: What is the main purpose of a **consensus algorithm**, and in what situation would it be critical for multiple agents to reach consensus?
5. **Communication Failures**
   - o **Question**: Name two methods to detect or handle agent communication failures in DeepSeek R1 systems.
6. **Short Coding Prompt**
   - o **Question**: Write a pseudocode snippet where an agent checks every 10 seconds if it has received a heartbeat from another agent, and if not, logs an error or triggers a re-registration procedure.

Answer Key (Suggested):

1. **Publish/Subscribe Advantage**: Decouples senders from receivers, allowing flexible subscription to topics without needing explicit peer relationships.
2. **Centralized vs. Decentralized**:
   - o **Centralized**: One manager agent allocates tasks (e.g., a single dispatch center for taxis).
   - o **Decentralized**: Each agent decides based on local data (e.g., swarm of drones distributing area coverage).
3. **Time-based vs. Event-based Synchronization**:
   - o **Time-based**: Regular intervals, predictable but may waste resources if few events occur.
   - o **Event-based**: React only when an event happens, saving resources but needing more careful concurrency handling.
4. **Consensus Algorithm**: Ensures all agents agree on a shared value or outcome. Critical in scenarios requiring consistent data replication (e.g., distributed ledgers) or unified decisions (e.g., resource allocation in a fault-tolerant system).
5. **Communication Failures**:
   - o **Heartbeat Mechanisms**, **Automatic Retries**, **Message Acknowledgments**, or **Fallback Strategies** like reassigning tasks.
6. **Coding Prompt** (Pseudocode):

```python
class HeartbeatMonitorAgent(AgentBase):
    def on_start(self):
        self.last_heartbeat_time = get_current_time()
        # Schedule check every 10 seconds
```

```
        self.timer(10, self.check_heartbeat)

    def receive_heartbeat(self):
        self.last_heartbeat_time = get_current_time()

    def check_heartbeat(self):
        if get_current_time() -
self.last_heartbeat_time > 10:
            print("[HeartbeatMonitorAgent] No heartbeat
received for over 10s. Triggering re-registration.")
            # Initiate re-registration or error
handling
```

In this chapter, you gained a **comprehensive overview** of how **agents** in **DeepSeek R1** communicate and coordinate their actions. We discussed **communication models** (direct vs. publish/subscribe), **coordination mechanisms** (centralized vs. decentralized), **synchronization techniques** (time-based vs. event-based), and collaborative **decision-making** frameworks (consensus algorithms, distributed models). We also addressed **communication failures** and how to ensure reliability in fault-prone environments.

By completing the **end-of-chapter project** and reflecting on the **quiz**, you are now equipped with the fundamental concepts and techniques to design collaborative multi-agent interactions in **DeepSeek R1**. In subsequent chapters, we will explore more advanced reasoning and decision-making strategies that build on these foundational communication and coordination principles.

Chapter 6: Advanced Reasoning and Decision-Making with DeepSeek R1

Agents in a multi-agent system (MAS) often need to make **intelligent** decisions based on **rules, probabilities**, or **utility** measures. **DeepSeek R1** provides a robust **Reasoning Engine** that aids agents in these tasks by integrating various AI reasoning methods. This chapter introduces different types of reasoning, explores the architecture of DeepSeek R1's Reasoning Engine, and demonstrates how to build **complex decision-making** models— including **rule-based**, **probabilistic**, and **utility-based** frameworks. We also discuss how to handle **uncertainty** using probabilistic models and fuzzy logic. All tables, code examples, and explanations are presented in a **clear, professional manner**, ensuring they are **complete** and easy to follow.

---

1. Introduction to AI Reasoning

1.1. Types of Reasoning: Deductive, Inductive, Abductive

Reasoning refers to the process of drawing conclusions from existing information or observations. There are three primary reasoning approaches in AI:

1. **Deductive Reasoning**
   - **Definition**: Deriving specific conclusions from general premises or rules that are assumed to be true.
   - **Example**: If "All cars have wheels" and "X is a car," then "X has wheels."
   - **Use Cases**: Formal logic-based systems, rule engines, and scenarios where domain knowledge is well-defined and certain.
2. **Inductive Reasoning**
   - **Definition**: Inferring general rules or patterns from specific examples or observations.
   - **Example**: Observing that 100 swans in a region are white might lead you to infer that "All swans are white" (though it could be disproven by finding a single non-white swan).

- o **Use Cases**: Machine learning tasks such as classification, regression, or pattern discovery, where data drives rule creation.
3. **Abductive Reasoning**
    - o **Definition**: Making the best possible explanation for an observation when multiple explanations are possible.
    - o **Example**: If your agent observes footprints near a vending machine and the machine is empty, it might hypothesize "Someone recently bought items" as a plausible explanation.
    - o **Use Cases**: Diagnosing system faults, medical diagnosis, or any scenario where partial data leads to one (or several) likely hypotheses.

1.2. Reasoning vs. Learning in AI

Although reasoning and learning overlap in AI systems, they address different aspects of **intelligence**:

- **Reasoning**: Uses **explicit logic** or **knowledge structures** to derive conclusions. It typically requires a well-defined set of rules or knowledge to operate.
- **Learning**: Involves **adaptation** and **improvement** over time, using data or feedback loops (e.g., machine learning). The system's behavior changes with new inputs or outcomes.

Table: Key Differences Between Reasoning and Learning

Aspect	Reasoning	Learning
Approach	Works with predefined rules or inferred logic	Adapts models from data over time
Knowledge Base	Relies on explicit domain knowledge	Builds knowledge from examples or reward signals
Typical Methods	Rule-based systems, logic inference, knowledge graphs	Supervised, unsupervised, or reinforcement learning
Advantages	Highly interpretable decisions	Flexible, can handle large amounts of data and find hidden patterns

Aspect	Reasoning	Learning
Disadvantages	Limited if domain knowledge is incomplete or incorrect	Less transparent "black box" models, risk of overfitting

2. DeepSeek R1's Reasoning Engine

2.1. Architecture and Capabilities

The **Reasoning Engine** in DeepSeek R1 is designed to integrate **multiple** reasoning paradigms—rule-based logic, probabilistic inference, and utility-based decision-making—under a **unified framework**. Key components include:

1. **Knowledge Base (KB)**
   o Stores **rules**, **facts**, and **domain models**. Agents can query or update the KB during runtime.
2. **Inference Module**
   o Processes rules or logic statements to derive conclusions. Supports deductive, inductive, and abductive methods.
3. **Probabilistic Engine**
   o Handles uncertain or incomplete information using Bayesian networks, Markov decision processes, or custom probability models.
4. **Integration Layer**
   o Connects the Reasoning Engine with external data sources, machine learning models, or specialized domain services.

Below is a **simplified diagram** of how the Reasoning Engine fits into DeepSeek R1:

sql

```
+------------------------------------+
|          Reasoning Engine          |
| +---------+ +------------------+ |
| | Inference| | Probabilistic    | |
| | Module  | |    Module        | |
| +---------+ +------------------+ |
|      ^               ^           |
|      |               |           |
```

```
|  Knowledge Base <->+                |
+----------+---------+---------------+
           |
+----------v---------+
|    Integration     |
|   (External APIs,  |
|    ML Models, etc.) |
+--------------------+
```

2.2. Integrating External Knowledge Bases

1. **Local Databases**: Your agents may reference SQL or NoSQL databases containing domain facts (e.g., parts inventory, medical records).
2. **Online Knowledge Repositories**: Pull data from services like **Wikidata**, **DBpedia**, or specialized ontologies in healthcare, finance, or manufacturing.
3. **Ontology and Semantic Web**: Use **OWL** or **RDF** to represent complex relationships. DeepSeek R1 can parse these structures to enhance inference with domain-specific logic.

Example of Reasoning Engine Initialization in Pseudocode:

```python
python

from deepseek_r1_sdk import AgentBase, ReasoningEngine

class KnowledgeAgent(AgentBase):
    def on_start(self):
        self.reasoning_engine = ReasoningEngine()
        # Load domain-specific rules
        self.reasoning_engine.load_rules("domain_rules.json")
        # Connect to external knowledge base

self.reasoning_engine.connect_knowledge_base("http://example-ontology.org/api")

    def reason_about_fact(self, fact):
        conclusion = self.reasoning_engine.infer(fact)
        print(f"Inferred conclusion: {conclusion}")
```

- **Explanation**: The agent loads domain rules and connects to an external knowledge base, enabling advanced inference tasks.

3. Decision-Making Frameworks

3.1. Rule-Based Systems

A **rule-based system** uses **if-then** or **production** rules to make decisions:

- **Structure**:
    - **Condition (IF)**: A logical test on the agent's data or environment.
    - **Action (THEN)**: What the agent should do if the condition is true.
- **Advantages**:
    - **Transparent**: Easy to understand and modify.
    - **Good for stable domains** where rules do not change frequently.
- **Limitations**:
    - Hard to maintain in rapidly evolving domains.
    - Rules can conflict if not well-managed.

Example Rule:

```scss
IF temperature > 30°C AND humidity < 50% THEN cool_down()
```

Use in DeepSeek R1:

```python
rule = {
    "conditions": [
        {"field": "temperature", "operator": ">", "value": 30},
        {"field": "humidity", "operator": "<", "value": 50}
    ],
    "action": "cool_down"
}
reasoning_engine.add_rule(rule)
```

3.2. Probabilistic Reasoning

Probabilistic reasoning helps agents **deal with uncertainty**:

1. **Bayesian Networks**
    - Graphical models linking variables with conditional probabilities.
    - **Example**: Diagnosing a machine fault based on sensor readings.
2. **Markov Decision Processes (MDPs)**
    - Captures sequential decisions where outcomes are partly random.
    - **Example**: An autonomous vehicle deciding whether to accelerate or brake based on traffic predictions.

Advantages:

- More **realistic** in uncertain or noisy domains.
- Can combine multiple uncertain sources of data (e.g., sensor readings, partial observations).

Example (Pseudocode for Bayesian Inference):

```python
# Simple Bayesian Inference
# P(Disease | Symptom) = [P(Symptom | Disease) * P(Disease)]
/ P(Symptom)

disease_prob = 0.01  # prior
symptom_given_disease = 0.8
symptom_prob = 0.05  # from population data

posterior = (symptom_given_disease * disease_prob) /
symptom_prob
print(f"Posterior Probability: {posterior}")
```

3.3. Utility-Based Decision Making

Agents use **utility functions** to **quantify preferences** among different outcomes:

- **Definition**: A function $U(x)$ that assigns a numerical "score" to a state x, indicating desirability.
- **Example**: In logistics, an agent might have a utility function balancing **delivery cost** vs. **delivery time**.
- **Approach**:
    1. Generate possible actions or states.

2. Compute each action's utility.
3. Choose the **action** with the **highest utility**.

Pros/Cons:

- **Pro**: Clear, mathematically grounded approach.
- **Con**: Requires carefully designed utility functions to represent real-world trade-offs.

High-Level Example:

python

```python
def utility_function(cost, time, reliability):
    # Weighted combination of factors
    return -cost + (-time * 0.5) + (reliability * 2)

def choose_best_action(actions):
    best_action = None
    best_utility = float('-inf')
    for action in actions:
        util = utility_function(action.cost, action.time,
action.reliability)
        if util > best_utility:
            best_utility = util
            best_action = action
    return best_action
```

4. Implementing Complex Decision Trees

4.1. Designing Decision Trees in DeepSeek R1

Decision trees help structure sequential decisions or conditions in a **hierarchical** manner. In DeepSeek R1, you can store tree nodes as **JSON** or as **objects** and incorporate them into the **Reasoning Engine**.

Basic Example (Pseudocode):

python

```python
decision_tree = {
    "node_id": "start",
    "condition": "temperature > 30",
    "yes_branch": {
```

```
        "node_id": "turn_on_ac",
        "action": "AC_ON"
    },
    "no_branch": {
        "node_id": "check_humidity",
        "condition": "humidity < 40",
        "yes_branch": {"action": "SPRINKLER_ON"},
        "no_branch": {"action": "DO_NOTHING"}
    }
}
```

Explanation:

- If **temperature** > 30, take the **yes_branch** (turn AC on).
- Otherwise, check **humidity** < 40. If yes, turn sprinkler on; if no, do nothing.

4.2. Optimizing Decision Paths

Large decision trees may suffer from **redundant checks** or **imbalanced branching**. Optimization techniques include:

1. **Pruning**: Remove branches that rarely occur or yield minimal gains.
2. **Caching/Subtree Reuse**: Store results for repeated sub-decisions.
3. **Heuristic Ordering**: Test the most critical or high-probability conditions first to reduce unnecessary evaluations.

5. Handling Uncertainty and Incomplete Information

5.1. Probabilistic Models

Agents can maintain **probabilistic models** of the environment when data is uncertain or incomplete:

- **Bayesian Updates**: As new evidence arrives, update prior probabilities to posterior probabilities.
- **Particle Filters**: Useful in robotics, tracking states like position or velocity amid noise.

Practical Example:

- An **inspection agent** might estimate the chance of **machine failure** based on partial sensor data. Each new reading updates the agent's probability distribution.

5.2. Fuzzy Logic in Decision Making

- **Definition**: Fuzzy logic deals with degrees of truth, rather than strict true/false evaluations.
- **Example**: "Temperature is high" might be 0.7 true, instead of a hard cutoff at 30°C.
- **Implementation**:
    1. **Fuzzification**: Convert numeric input to fuzzy sets (e.g., "Low," "Medium," "High").
    2. **Inference**: Apply fuzzy rules (IF Temperature is HIGH THEN SpeedFan = FAST).
    3. **Defuzzification**: Translate fuzzy output back into a crisp action.

Advantages:

- More **human-like** reasoning.
- Smooth handling of borderline cases or noisy data.

6. End-of-Chapter Projects

Project 6: Building a Decision-Making Framework

Objective: Create a **multi-step decision framework** that combines **rule-based** logic for initial filtering with a **probabilistic** step for uncertain outcomes.

Scenario

- A **DeliveryAgent** determines whether to **accept** or **reject** a same-day delivery request based on:
    1. **Rule-based** checks (e.g., do we have enough available vehicles?).
    2. **Probabilistic** estimate of traffic conditions to see if on-time delivery is likely.

Implementation Steps

1. **Rules for Vehicle Availability**:

```python
from deepseek_r1_sdk import AgentBase, ReasoningEngine

class DeliveryAgent(AgentBase):
    def on_start(self):
        self.reasoning_engine = ReasoningEngine()
        # Load some basic rules
        rule_vehicle_avail = {
            "conditions": [
                {"field": "available_vehicles",
"operator": ">", "value": 0}
            ],
            "action": "PROCEED_TO_PROBABILISTIC_CHECK"
        }

self.reasoning_engine.add_rule(rule_vehicle_avail)

    def evaluate_delivery_request(self, request):
        # Step 1: Rule-based check
        facts = {
            "available_vehicles":
request.get("available_vehicles", 0)
        }
        outcome =
self.reasoning_engine.evaluate_rules(facts)
        if "PROCEED_TO_PROBABILISTIC_CHECK" in outcome:
            # Step 2: Probabilistic approach
            success_prob =
self.estimate_traffic_probability(request)
            if success_prob > 0.75:
                print("Delivery Accepted")
            else:
                print("Delivery Rejected - High traffic
risk")
        else:
            print("Delivery Rejected - No available
vehicles")
```

```
def estimate_traffic_probability(self, request):
    # Simple Bayesian or any custom logic
    # e.g., prior for normal traffic
    prior = 0.8
    # If time of day is rush hour, reduce
probability
    if request.get("time_of_day") == "rush_hour":
        return prior * 0.5
    return prior
```

2. **Triggering the Decision**:

python

```
if __name__ == "__main__":
    agent = DeliveryAgent(agent_id="DeliveryAgent1")
    # Example request
    request_info = {
        "available_vehicles": 2,
        "time_of_day": "rush_hour"  # or "off_peak"
    }
    agent.evaluate_delivery_request(request_info)
```

Explanation:

- The agent uses a **rule-based** system to check **vehicle availability**.
- If the rule passes, it applies a **probabilistic** method to decide if traffic conditions allow on-time delivery.
- The final verdict is printed out as **Accepted** or **Rejected**.

Extensions

- **Utility Functions**: Factor in **delivery distance**, **cost**, or **priority** using a utility-based approach.
- **Learning Component**: Update the traffic probability based on **actual outcomes** of previous deliveries (reinforcement learning).

7. Quizzes and Self-Assessments

Quiz 6: Advanced Reasoning Techniques

Assess your understanding of **advanced reasoning and decision-making** in DeepSeek R1 by addressing the questions below. Refer to the examples and explanations in this chapter for guidance.

1. **Types of Reasoning**
   - **Question**: Distinguish between **deductive** and **inductive** reasoning. Provide an example where each is most suitable.
2. **DeepSeek R1's Reasoning Engine**
   - **Question**: List two key modules within the Reasoning Engine and briefly describe their roles.
3. **Decision-Making Frameworks**
   - **Question**: Name one advantage and one limitation of using **rule-based systems**.
4. **Complex Decision Trees**
   - **Question**: Why might you choose to prune or reorder branches in a decision tree?
5. **Uncertainty Management**
   - **Question**: Compare **probabilistic models** with **fuzzy logic** in terms of how they handle uncertain information.
6. **Short Coding Prompt**
   - **Question**: Write a pseudocode snippet where an agent uses a **utility function** to choose between two possible tasks: "ShortDelivery" (lower cost but high time) and "ExpressDelivery" (higher cost but less time).

Answer Key (Suggested):

1. **Deductive vs. Inductive**:
   - **Deductive**: Goes from general rules to specific cases (e.g., "All humans are mortal → Socrates is mortal"). Best suited where domain rules are certain.
   - **Inductive**: Goes from specific examples to broader generalizations (e.g., "Observing many white swans → Inferring all swans are white"). Good for data-driven discovery.
2. **Reasoning Engine Modules**:
   - **Inference Module**: Processes logical or rule-based statements.
   - **Probabilistic Module**: Handles uncertain information, using Bayesian or Markov models.
3. **Rule-Based Systems**:
   - **Advantage**: High interpretability, straightforward to modify.

- o **Limitation**: Can grow large and complex, making maintenance difficult if rules conflict or the domain changes.
4. **Decision Tree Optimization**:
   - o **Pruning**: Removes rarely used or insignificant branches to reduce complexity and improve performance.
   - o **Reordering**: Tests high-impact or high-likelihood branches first to shorten decision paths.
5. **Probabilistic vs. Fuzzy Logic**:
   - o **Probabilistic**: Uses probabilities to handle uncertain events or incomplete data, focusing on how likely an event is.
   - o **Fuzzy Logic**: Deals with degrees of truth (partial membership), focusing on how strongly a property applies.
6. **Utility Function (Pseudocode)**:

```python
python

shortDeliveryUtility = -cost_short + -time_short * 0.5
expressDeliveryUtility = -cost_express + -time_express
* 0.5

if expressDeliveryUtility > shortDeliveryUtility:
    choose("ExpressDelivery")
else:
    choose("ShortDelivery")
```

Conclusion

In this chapter, you explored **advanced reasoning** and **decision-making** in **DeepSeek R1**, learning how to:

- **Distinguish** between **deductive**, **inductive**, and **abductive** reasoning styles.
- **Use** DeepSeek R1's **Reasoning Engine** with rule-based, probabilistic, or utility-based decision frameworks.
- **Design** complex decision trees and handle uncertainty with **probabilistic models** or **fuzzy logic**.
- **Implement** a multi-step decision-making framework incorporating both **rule-based** checks and **probabilistic** estimations.

By experimenting with the **end-of-chapter project** and reflecting on the **quiz**, you can deepen your practical understanding of agent-driven decision-making processes. In upcoming chapters, we will continue to refine agent capabilities by integrating **learning** and exploring **scalable** multi-agent **coordination** with advanced AI tools.

Chapter 7: Task Allocation and Load Balancing

In multi-agent systems (MAS), **task allocation** and **load balancing** are key mechanisms that ensure agents work efficiently and effectively. **DeepSeek R1** offers robust features for distributing tasks among agents, monitoring performance, and adapting to changing workload conditions. This chapter explores the **basics** of task allocation, common **load balancing** strategies, **implementation details** in DeepSeek R1, and real-world use in a **smart factory** case study. We also provide a **project** to help you practice dynamic task allocation and a **quiz** for self-assessment. All **tables**, **code examples**, and **explanations** are provided in a clear, thorough manner.

---

1. Understanding Task Allocation

1.1. Task Types and Characteristics

In a MAS, **tasks** can vary widely depending on the domain. Before assigning a task to an agent, it helps to identify **task characteristics**:

1. **Complexity**
   - **Simple**: Requires a single agent (e.g., a sensor reading).
   - **Complex**: May need multiple agents collaborating (e.g., coordinating a manufacturing process).
2. **Resource Requirements**
   - **Minimal**: Low CPU or memory usage, no special tools needed.
   - **High**: Demands specialized hardware or large memory.
3. **Time Sensitivity**
   - **Real-Time**: Must complete within strict deadlines (e.g., responding to safety hazards).
   - **Flexible**: Can be queued or deferred.
4. **Dependencies**
   - **Independent**: No prerequisites or required sequencing.
   - **Dependent**: Must wait on other tasks to finish (e.g., assembly line steps).

Table: Example Task Types and Characteristics

Task	Complexity	Resource Requirements	Time Sensitivity	Dependencies
Inventory Check	Simple	Low (basic queries)	Flexible	None
Robotic Assembly	Complex	Specialized hardware	Real-Time	Previous assembly steps completed
Data Analysis	Medium	High CPU for ML tasks	Flexible	Data collection task finished
Emergency Alert	Simple	Low or moderate	Real-Time	Triggered by sensor event

1.2. Allocation Strategies

Allocation strategies define how tasks are assigned to agents:

1. **Centralized Allocation**
   - **Definition**: A single "manager" agent or module receives tasks and delegates them to workers.
   - **Advantages**:
     - Simplified control, easy to implement.
     - Straightforward performance monitoring.
   - **Disadvantages**:
     - Single point of failure.
     - Scalability concerns for large MAS.
2. **Distributed (or Decentralized) Allocation**
   - **Definition**: Each agent participates in deciding which agent should take on the next task, often via negotiation or bidding.
   - **Advantages**:
     - Eliminates single point of failure.
     - Scales better for large systems.
   - **Disadvantages**:
     - More complex to implement.
     - Potential for conflicts or inefficient allocations if not well managed.
3. **Hybrid Approaches**
   - **Definition**: Mix centralized and distributed strategies (e.g., localized clusters with a central coordinator).

- o **Use Cases**: Large-scale or geographically distributed systems requiring some level of hierarchical control.

---

2. Load Balancing Techniques

2.1. Static vs. Dynamic Load Balancing

1. **Static Load Balancing**
   - o **Definition**: Allocation decisions are made **before** tasks begin or at fixed intervals without continuous feedback.
   - o **Example**: Assigning each agent a set of predefined tasks at the start of a shift.
   - o **Advantages**:
     - Low overhead, simple.
   - o **Disadvantages**:
     - Fails to adapt to changes in agent availability or workload spikes.
2. **Dynamic Load Balancing**
   - o **Definition**: Allocation is adjusted in **real-time** based on agent performance, resource usage, or other factors.
   - o **Example**: A cloud-based system that automatically reassigns tasks to less busy agents when workloads spike.
   - o **Advantages**:
     - Optimizes resource utilization and responsiveness.
   - o **Disadvantages**:
     - Higher complexity in monitoring and decision-making.

2.2. Algorithms for Efficient Load Distribution

Various algorithms address load balancing, depending on system requirements:

1. **Round Robin**
   - o Cycles through available agents, assigning one task to each in turn.
   - o **Pro**: Simple, easy to implement.
   - o **Con**: Does not account for variations in agent capabilities or task complexity.

2. **Least Loaded**
    o   Always assigns a new task to the agent with the smallest current workload.
    o   **Pro**: Balances tasks more evenly.
    o   **Con**: Requires frequent updates on agent load status.
3. **Priority-Based**
    o   Agents or tasks have **priority** levels; higher priority tasks are assigned first or to the most capable agents.
    o   **Pro**: Accommodates critical tasks promptly.
    o   **Con**: Lower priority tasks might be delayed indefinitely (starvation) if not managed carefully.
4. **Market-Based (Auction)**
    o   Agents "bid" on tasks based on their capability or availability, and the manager picks the best "bid."
    o   **Pro**: Tends to yield optimal matches of tasks to agent strengths or availability.
    o   **Con**: Overhead in running auctions, can be complex to implement.

3. Implementing Task Allocation in DeepSeek R1

3.1. Configuring Task Managers

DeepSeek R1 simplifies task management through:

1. **TaskManager** or **Scheduler** Components
    o   Responsible for receiving **task requests**, determining which agent should handle them, and distributing work.
    o   Can integrate different allocation algorithms (e.g., round robin, market-based).
2. **Agent Registration**
    o   Agents register their **capabilities**, resource limits, and preferences.
    o   The **TaskManager** uses this metadata to allocate tasks intelligently.

Example of a Task Allocation Configuration (Pseudocode):

```python
# config.py
task_allocation_strategy = {
    "algorithm": "least_loaded",  # or "round_robin",
"auction"
    "update_frequency": 5         # in seconds for dynamic
checks
}
```

3.2. Assigning Tasks to Appropriate Agents

After **configuring** the TaskManager, tasks can be **submitted** and **assigned**:

High-Level Steps:

1. **Submit Task**: An agent (or external system) creates a task object specifying task details (type, priority, required resources).
2. **Evaluate Agent Pool**: The TaskManager checks agent states:
   o CPU usage, memory, specialized skills, etc.
3. **Allocate Task**: The TaskManager assigns the task to the **optimal** agent based on the chosen strategy.
4. **Execution**: The agent processes the task, updating status upon completion or failure.

Code Snippet:

```python
# task_manager_example.py
from deepseek_r1_sdk import TaskManager, AgentManager,
AgentBase

# 1. Define TaskManager with a chosen strategy
task_manager = TaskManager(strategy="least_loaded")

class WorkerAgent(AgentBase):
    def capabilities(self):
        return {"cpu_power": 2, "has_camera": False}

    def on_task_received(self, task):
        print(f"[{self.agent_id}] Received task:
{task['description']}")
        # Perform task here
        self.complete_task(task)

if __name__ == "__main__":
```

```
manager = AgentManager()
agent1 = WorkerAgent(agent_id="Agent1")
agent2 = WorkerAgent(agent_id="Agent2")
manager.register_agent(agent1)
manager.register_agent(agent2)

# 2. Submit a new task
new_task = {
    "task_id": "T001",
    "description": "Inspect conveyor belt",
    "required_capabilities": {"has_camera": False}
}
task_manager.submit_task(new_task)
manager.run()
```

- **Explanation**:
  - o The `TaskManager` uses **least_loaded** strategy.
  - o On `submit_task()`, it evaluates available agents (Agent1 and Agent2) and assigns the task to the least loaded.
  - o The chosen agent executes `on_task_received()` and processes the task.

4. Monitoring and Adjusting Task Distribution

4.1. Real-time Monitoring Tools

DeepSeek R1 provides mechanisms to track system load and agent performance:

1. **Agent Status**: Agents periodically report metrics like CPU, memory usage, or queue length.
2. **Task Dashboard**: A web UI or console tool that shows which agent is handling which tasks, current load, and performance.
3. **Logs and Metrics**: Automatic logging of task start/end times, errors, and resource usage.

4.2. Adaptive Load Balancing Mechanisms

Adaptive strategies dynamically respond to changing conditions:

1. **Load Thresholds**

- o If an agent's load exceeds a threshold (e.g., 80% CPU usage), tasks are reallocated to a less busy agent.
2. **Feedback Loops**
     - o The system continually monitors performance metrics and "learns" from them. Overloaded agents can signal the scheduler to reduce incoming tasks.
3. **Predictive Allocation**
     - o Based on historical data, the system anticipates surges (e.g., peak hours) and preemptively shifts tasks.

Example (Pseudocode for Adaptive Check):

python

```
# adaptive_load_balancing.py
def adaptive_rebalance():
    for agent in manager.get_registered_agents():
        load = agent.get_current_load()
        if load > 80:
            # Move tasks from this agent to others
            redistribute_tasks(agent)
```

- **Explanation**: This function periodically checks agent load, redistributing tasks if an agent is near capacity.

5. Case Study: Task Allocation in a Smart Factory

Scenario Overview

A **smart factory** uses **robotic agents** for assembly, **inspection agents** for quality control, and **logistics agents** for packaging and shipping. **DeepSeek R1** coordinates these tasks in real time, ensuring each agent is optimally loaded and tasks are completed on schedule.

Challenges:

- **Varied Task Complexity**: Assembly tasks might require certain robotic arms, while inspection tasks need sensors.
- **High Throughput**: Thousands of tasks per hour.

- **Dynamic Conditions**: Machines can go offline for maintenance, or sudden bulk orders can increase workload.

Implementation Highlights

1. **Registration**
   - **RoboticArmAgent** registers capabilities like "precision_gripper: True."
   - **InspectionAgent** registers "camera_resolution: HD."
2. **Task Manager Configuration**
   - The factory manager sets an **auction-based** allocation strategy for high-priority tasks.
   - Lower priority tasks can use **round robin** to ensure fairness.
3. **Real-Time Monitoring**
   - Agents continuously report sensor data, resource usage, and task completion times to a central dashboard.
4. **Adaptive Reallocation**
   - If a robotic arm agent experiences a mechanical fault, tasks are automatically reassigned to another arm with similar capabilities.

Results:

- **Increased Efficiency**: Tasks allocated to the most suitable agent, reducing errors and bottlenecks.
- **Resilience**: Automatic redistribution minimized downtime when an agent failed.
- **Scalability**: The system accommodated seasonal peaks by dynamically spinning up more agents or reconfiguring tasks.

---

6. End-of-Chapter Projects

Project 7: Implementing Dynamic Task Allocation

Objective: Practice **dynamic** task assignment in DeepSeek R1. You will create multiple agents with varying capabilities and implement a basic **adaptive** strategy to handle load spikes.

Outline

1. **Create Agents**
   - ○ **LightWorker**: Handles simple tasks quickly.
   - ○ **HeavyWorker**: Capable of complex tasks but processes them more slowly.
2. **Dynamic Load Monitoring**
   - ○ Each agent reports its **current load** (e.g., number of tasks in queue).
3. **Adaptive Strategy**
   - ○ The **TaskManager** rechecks load every 3 seconds. If any agent exceeds a certain threshold, tasks are moved to another agent.

Sample Code (Pseudocode)

```python
# dynamic_allocation.py
from deepseek_r1_sdk import TaskManager, AgentManager,
AgentBase, time

class LightWorker(AgentBase):
    def __init__(self, agent_id):
        super().__init__(agent_id)
        self.current_load = 0

    def on_task_received(self, task):
        self.current_load += 1
        print(f"[{self.agent_id}] Received task
{task['task_id']}, load={self.current_load}")
        time.sleep(2)  # simulate work
        self.current_load -= 1
        self.complete_task(task)

class HeavyWorker(AgentBase):
    def __init__(self, agent_id):
        super().__init__(agent_id)
        self.current_load = 0

    def on_task_received(self, task):
        self.current_load += 2  # heavier tasks
        print(f"[{self.agent_id}] Received heavy task
{task['task_id']}, load={self.current_load}")
        time.sleep(5)  # simulating heavy work
        self.current_load -= 2
        self.complete_task(task)

def adaptive_allocation(task_manager):
    for agent in agent_manager.get_registered_agents():
```

```
        if agent.current_load > 3:
            # Redistribute tasks to less busy agents
            # (Implementation: reassign queued tasks if
possible)
            print(f"Reallocating tasks from {agent.agent_id}
due to high load.")

if __name__ == "__main__":
    agent_manager = AgentManager()
    task_manager = TaskManager(strategy="custom")  # We'll
implement a custom approach

    light1 = LightWorker(agent_id="Light1")
    heavy1 = HeavyWorker(agent_id="Heavy1")

    agent_manager.register_agent(light1)
    agent_manager.register_agent(heavy1)

    # Submit a batch of tasks
    for i in range(10):
        task = {
            "task_id": f"T{i}",
            "description": "Mixed complexity task"
        }
        task_manager.submit_task(task)

    # Periodically run our adaptive logic
    while True:
        adaptive_allocation(task_manager)
        time.sleep(3)
```

- **Explanation**:
  - **LightWorker** increments its load by 1 for each new task, while **HeavyWorker** increments by 2.
  - The **adaptive_allocation** function checks if any agent has a load > 3, and if so, tries to redistribute tasks (implementation can vary).

Expected Outcome

- **Light1** may handle many quick tasks, while **Heavy1** manages fewer but more intensive tasks.
- The system attempts to keep loads balanced by identifying overloaded agents and reallocating tasks as needed.

7. Quizzes and Self-Assessments

Quiz 7: Task Allocation and Load Balancing

Test your knowledge of task allocation and load balancing in DeepSeek R1. Refer to the code examples and discussions for guidance.

1. **Task Types**
   - **Question**: Give an example of a time-sensitive task versus a flexible task, and explain why their time sensitivity matters for allocation.
2. **Allocation Strategies**
   - **Question**: What is one advantage and one disadvantage of a **centralized** task allocation strategy?
3. **Load Balancing**
   - **Question**: Differentiate between **static** and **dynamic** load balancing, and provide a scenario where dynamic load balancing is crucial.
4. **DeepSeek R1 Configuration**
   - **Question**: Describe how you might configure a **TaskManager** to use the "auction" algorithm. What metadata do agents need to provide for this to work effectively?
5. **Monitoring and Adaptation**
   - **Question**: Name two key metrics you might monitor to decide if tasks should be reallocated among agents.
6. **Case Study**
   - **Question**: From the smart factory case, why might a purely centralized approach be insufficient, and how does a hybrid approach address that?
7. **Short Coding Prompt**
   - **Question**: Write a pseudocode snippet to perform a **round-robin** assignment of tasks to a list of agents.

Answer Key (Suggested):

1. **Time-sensitive vs. Flexible**:
   - Time-sensitive: Emergency response to a sensor alarm, must be handled immediately.
   - Flexible: Backlog data analysis, which can run in the background. The difference guides scheduling priorities.
2. **Centralized Strategy**:

- o   Advantage: Simple to implement and monitor.
- o   Disadvantage: Single point of failure, potential bottleneck for large MAS.
3. **Static vs. Dynamic Load Balancing**:
   - o   Static: Allocations made upfront, not adapted during runtime.
   - o   Dynamic: Adjusts in real-time, vital for systems with unpredictable workloads (e.g., e-commerce spikes).
4. **Auction Algorithm**:
   - o   Agents must provide **bids** (e.g., cost, time, specialized capabilities).
   - o   **TaskManager** collects and evaluates bids, awarding tasks to the best bidder.
5. **Key Metrics**:
   - o   CPU usage, queue length, memory usage, or task completion rate.
6. **Smart Factory Case**:
   - o   A purely centralized system might be overloaded or fail if the central coordinator goes offline.
   - o   A hybrid approach distributes decision-making to local clusters, maintaining efficiency and resilience.
7. **Round-Robin Example**:

```python
python

agents = [Agent1, Agent2, Agent3]
current_index = 0

for task in task_list:
    assigned_agent = agents[current_index]
    assigned_agent.receive_task(task)
    current_index = (current_index + 1) % len(agents)
```

This chapter has provided a **comprehensive** look at **task allocation** and **load balancing** in **DeepSeek R1**, covering:

- Fundamental **task characteristics** and **allocation strategies**.
- **Load balancing** approaches (static vs. dynamic) and **common algorithms** (round robin, least loaded, market-based).
- **DeepSeek R1** configuration and implementation details, ensuring tasks are **efficiently** assigned to the **right** agents.
- Real-time **monitoring**, **adaptive** reallocation, and a **case study** demonstrating how these principles apply in a **smart factory** context.

- A **hands-on project** to help you explore **dynamic allocation** in your own environment.

Armed with this knowledge, you can now design multi-agent systems that **handle tasks effectively**, **balance workloads**, and adapt to changing conditions—all while maintaining high performance and reliability.

Chapter 8: Conflict Resolution and Robustness in MAS

In any **Multi-Agent System (MAS)**, multiple agents operate concurrently, often sharing resources or goals. This environment can lead to **conflicts**—situations where agent actions or objectives are at odds, jeopardizing the system's effectiveness or stability. In **DeepSeek R1**, conflict resolution and overall robustness are key design objectives. This chapter explores common **sources of conflicts**, outlines various **resolution strategies**, and explains how to **implement** these solutions in DeepSeek R1. It also covers **robustness** measures like fault tolerance and redundancy to ensure that the system remains resilient under stress or agent failures. By the end of this chapter, you will have a firm understanding of how to handle and test conflict resolution in a MAS, along with techniques to maintain reliability.

---

1. Sources of Conflicts in MAS

1.1. Resource Contention

One of the most frequent sources of conflict in an MAS is **resource contention**. Multiple agents may need **simultaneous access** to limited resources, such as:

- **Physical Resources**: Robots vying for the same pathway or conveyor belt space in a factory.
- **Computational Resources**: Agents competing for CPU, memory, or specialized hardware (e.g., GPUs).
- **Data Locks**: Concurrent writes to a shared database, risking data corruption or race conditions.

Example: If two manufacturing robots each try to grab the same piece of equipment, a physical collision or system deadlock could occur.

1.2. Priority Inversion

Priority inversion happens when a lower-priority task or agent holds a resource needed by a higher-priority agent, causing the higher-priority agent to be **blocked** indefinitely or for an extended period.

- **Scenario**:
    - Agent A (low priority) has locked a shared file. Agent B (high priority) needs to access that file.
    - If Agent A is not preempted or prompted to release the resource, Agent B remains blocked, causing a possible system bottleneck.

1.3. Communication Breakdowns

Agents coordinate through messages and signals. Conflicts can arise when **communication** fails or is delayed:

- **Lost Messages**: Network disruptions, leading to incomplete or erroneous task coordination.
- **Misinterpretation**: Agent A interprets a message differently than Agent B intended (e.g., ambiguous formats).
- **Timing Issues**: In real-time systems, delayed messages can cause agents to take actions based on **outdated** information, resulting in conflicts with other agents.

Table: Common Sources of Conflict in MAS

Conflict Type	Description	Example
Resource Contention	Multiple agents need the same limited resource	Two warehouse robots reaching for one product bin
Priority Inversion	A high-priority agent waits on a low-priority one	A safety-critical process blocked by a non-critical maintenance
Communication Issues	Missing, delayed, or misinterpreted messages	Agents scheduling tasks based on outdated status information

2. Conflict Resolution Strategies

2.1. Negotiation-Based Approaches

Negotiation is a collaborative strategy where agents **communicate** to find a **mutually acceptable** solution:

1. **Auction or Market-Based Negotiation**: Agents bid for resources or tasks, and the highest bidder wins. Useful for resource allocation when each agent has a "budget" or utility function.
2. **Contract Net Protocol**: A manager agent broadcasts a task (call for proposals), and worker agents bid with time/cost estimates. The manager selects the best bid.
3. **Multi-Round Negotiation**: Agents may propose counteroffers, gradually converging on a compromise.

Advantages:

- Agents can factor in local preferences or constraints.
- Encourages fair resource sharing if well-designed.

Disadvantages:

- Potential overhead in complex negotiations.
- Risk of no agreement if agents' objectives strongly conflict.

2.2. Arbitration and Mediation Techniques

In arbitration or mediation, a **neutral party** or a **dedicated mechanism** resolves disputes:

1. **Arbitrator Agent**: An agent (or system module) with authority to impose decisions.
2. **Mediation**: The mediator helps agents clarify needs and propose compromises, but final decisions remain in agent hands.
3. **Escalation Hierarchy**: If agents cannot resolve a conflict at one level, the issue escalates to a higher authority, such as a senior manager agent or a global coordinator.

Pros/Cons:

- **Pro**: Swift resolution, especially in high-stakes conflicts requiring a definitive outcome.

- **Con**: Agents may depend too heavily on an external authority, reducing system decentralization.

2.3. Priority Scheduling

Assigning **priorities** to agents or tasks can avoid some conflicts:

1. **Preemption**: Higher-priority agents preempt resource usage or lock acquisition.
2. **Priority Ceiling**: A resource (e.g., a shared lock) is given the highest priority of any agent that may need it, preventing lower-priority usage that could cause inversion.
3. **Priority Inheritance**: A lower-priority agent holding a resource temporarily **inherits** the higher priority of a blocked agent, ensuring it completes and releases the resource quickly.

Use Cases:

- Real-time systems needing to guarantee that critical tasks are never unduly delayed.
- Manufacturing lines where safety or time-critical tasks must always take precedence.

---

3. Implementing Conflict Resolution in DeepSeek R1

3.1. Configuring Conflict Handlers

DeepSeek R1 allows developers to define **conflict handlers**, which are specialized modules or callbacks that automatically manage conflict scenarios:

1. **Handler Registration**
   o During agent or TaskManager setup, specify how conflicts (e.g., resource locks, scheduling overlaps) should be handled.
2. **Handler Types**:
   o **Locking Handlers**: Manage resource locks with priority ceilings or inheritance.

o **Negotiation Handlers**: Initiate a negotiation process when a collision or contention is detected.

Example Pseudocode:

```python
# conflict_config.py
conflict_handler_config = {
    "type": "priority_inheritance",
    "max_retries": 3,
    "escalation_agent": "GlobalArbitrator"
}
```

3.2. Automating Conflict Detection and Resolution

Agents can automatically **detect** conflicts by monitoring state changes:

1. **Detecting Resource Collisions**
   o If two or more agents attempt to lock the same resource, the conflict handler is invoked.
2. **Escalation**
   o If local attempts (e.g., priority inheritance) fail, the system calls the **GlobalArbitrator** to impose a resolution.
3. **Communication Conflicts**
   o A conflict might arise if agent **A** expects a response from **B** by a certain time and does not receive it. The system triggers a fallback or re-send routine.

Code Snippet:

```python
# conflict_manager.py
from deepseek_r1_sdk import ConflictManager

class ResourceLockConflictHandler:
    def handle_conflict(self, resource_id, agents_involved):
        # Example: use priority inheritance logic
        highest_priority_agent = max(agents_involved,
key=lambda a: a.priority)
        for agent in agents_involved:
            if agent != highest_priority_agent:
                agent.priority =
highest_priority_agent.priority
```

```
        # Force lower-priority agent(s) to release the
resource quickly
        # ... resolution logic here ...

conflict_manager = ConflictManager()
conflict_manager.register_handler("ResourceLock",
ResourceLockConflictHandler())
```

- **Explanation**:
  - o A `ResourceLockConflictHandler` manages collisions by boosting the priority of the agent that needs immediate access, thus resolving the conflict faster.

---

4. Ensuring System Robustness

4.1. Fault Tolerance Mechanisms

A robust MAS remains **operational** despite failures:

1. **Agent-Level Fault Tolerance**
   - o Each agent detects and recovers from local faults (e.g., re-initializing state or rolling back incomplete tasks).
2. **System-Level Fault Tolerance**
   - o A supervisor agent or module monitors agent health. If an agent fails, tasks are reassigned to a backup agent.

4.2. Redundancy and Failover Strategies

Redundancy ensures that if one component fails, another can take over:

1. **Agent Redundancy**
   - o Maintain **multiple agents** with identical or overlapping capabilities.
   - o If one agent crashes, others continue the work, reducing downtime.
2. **Failover**
   - o Define how the system detects failures and **switches** to a standby resource or agent.
   - o **Hot Failover**: A standby agent runs in parallel, ready to take over instantly.

o **Cold Failover**: A standby agent starts up only after the active agent fails, which may introduce delay.

Example: In a **smart grid** MAS, multiple grid management agents can monitor power distribution. If the primary agent fails, a secondary takes over without interrupting electricity supply.

---

5. Testing and Validating Conflict Resolution Mechanisms

Thorough **testing** ensures conflict resolution works as intended:

1. **Simulation of Conflict Scenarios**
   o Introduce **artificial resource contention** or **communication failures** to see how the system responds.
2. **Stress Testing**
   o Overload the system with high task volumes or simultaneous lock requests to evaluate performance and identify bottlenecks.
3. **Recovery Drills**
   o Force agent failures or network outages. Confirm that fallback agents or reallocation processes function properly.
4. **Performance Metrics**
   o Record the time taken to detect and resolve conflicts, agent downtime, and the throughput of completed tasks.

---

6. End-of-Chapter Projects

Project 8: Designing Conflict Resolution Mechanisms

Objective: Implement a simple resource contention scenario in **DeepSeek R1** and design a conflict resolution strategy using **priority inheritance** or **arbitration**.

Project Outline

1. **Resource Model**
   o A single resource (e.g., a robotic arm) that can only be operated by one agent at a time.
2. **Agents**
   o **HighPriorityAgent**: Has critical tasks.
   o **LowPriorityAgent**: Handles routine tasks.
3. **Conflict Handler**
   o When both agents request the robotic arm simultaneously, the **HighPriorityAgent** should get priority or the system should negotiate a schedule.
4. **Monitoring**
   o Log the conflict events, how they were resolved, and the final outcomes.

Sample Code (Pseudocode)

```python
# conflict_resolution_project.py
from deepseek_r1_sdk import AgentBase, ConflictManager,
ResourceLock

class HighPriorityAgent(AgentBase):
    def on_start(self):
        self.priority = 10   # Higher than default
        self.request_resource()

    def request_resource(self):
        try:
            ResourceLock.acquire("RoboticArm", agent=self)
            print(f"[{self.agent_id}] Acquired RoboticArm.")
            # Perform critical task
            self.perform_task()
        finally:
            ResourceLock.release("RoboticArm", agent=self)

    def perform_task(self):
        # Simulate work
        import time
        time.sleep(3)
        print(f"[{self.agent_id}] Completed critical task.")

class LowPriorityAgent(AgentBase):
    def on_start(self):
        self.priority = 5
```

```python
        self.request_resource()

    def request_resource(self):
        try:
            ResourceLock.acquire("RoboticArm", agent=self)
            print(f"[{self.agent_id}] Acquired RoboticArm.")
            # Perform routine task
            self.perform_task()
        finally:
            ResourceLock.release("RoboticArm", agent=self)

    def perform_task(self):
        import time
        time.sleep(3)
        print(f"[{self.agent_id}] Completed routine task.")

class PriorityInheritanceHandler:
    def handle_conflict(self, resource_id, agents_involved):
        # Identify agent with highest priority
        highest_priority_agent = max(agents_involved,
key=lambda a: a.priority)
        for agent in agents_involved:
            if agent != highest_priority_agent:
                agent.priority =
highest_priority_agent.priority
        print(f"Priority Inheritance: Boosted priorities to
match {highest_priority_agent.agent_id}")

if __name__ == "__main__":
    conflict_manager = ConflictManager()
    conflict_manager.register_handler("ResourceLock",
PriorityInheritanceHandler())

    high_agent = HighPriorityAgent(agent_id="HighAgent1")
    low_agent = LowPriorityAgent(agent_id="LowAgent1")

    high_agent.start()
    low_agent.start()
```

Explanation:

- **HighPriorityAgent** and **LowPriorityAgent** both **acquire** the "RoboticArm" resource.
- If they request it at the same time, the **PriorityInheritanceHandler** is triggered, boosting the lower agent's priority so it can release the resource promptly.
- This ensures the **HighPriorityAgent** does not experience prolonged blocking.

7. Quizzes and Self-Assessments

Quiz 8: Conflict Resolution Techniques

Use the following questions to test your understanding of conflict resolution and system robustness. Refer to code examples and earlier sections as needed.

1. **Conflict Sources**
   - **Question**: Provide one example of resource contention and one example of communication breakdown in an MAS.
2. **Negotiation vs. Arbitration**
   - **Question**: How do negotiation-based methods differ from arbitration-based methods for resolving conflicts?
3. **Priority Inversion**
   - **Question**: What is priority inversion, and how does priority inheritance help solve it?
4. **Robustness**
   - **Question**: Define **redundancy** and **failover**. In which scenario would a **hot failover** mechanism be preferable?
5. **Testing**
   - **Question**: Name two critical tests for validating conflict resolution systems in a MAS.
6. **Short Coding Prompt**
   - **Question**: Write pseudocode for a "CommunicationConflictHandler" that triggers if an agent does not receive a required response within 5 seconds, escalating the issue to a "GlobalMediator" agent.

Answer Key (Suggested):

1. **Resource Contention**: Two robots accessing the same item in a warehouse. **Communication Breakdown**: Agent A's message to Agent B is lost, causing out-of-sync scheduling.
2. **Negotiation vs. Arbitration**:
   - **Negotiation**: Agents discuss and reach a mutually agreeable solution (e.g., bidding, multi-round proposals).
   - **Arbitration**: A neutral authority or mechanism imposes a decision on conflicting parties.

3. **Priority Inversion**: A higher-priority agent is blocked by a lower-priority agent holding a shared resource. **Priority Inheritance**: Temporarily boosts the lower-priority agent to the higher priority, ensuring it completes its work quickly and frees the resource.
4. **Redundancy and Failover**:
   o **Redundancy**: Having multiple identical components (agents or resources) to cover failures.
   o **Failover**: Mechanism to switch to a standby resource when the primary fails. **Hot Failover** is best for critical systems needing instant recovery (e.g., emergency monitoring).
5. **Testing**:
   o **Conflict Scenario Simulation** (artificial resource locks, forced message loss) and **Stress Testing** (load tests to ensure system handles surges).
6. **CommunicationConflictHandler** (Pseudocode):

```python
python

class CommunicationConflictHandler:
    def handle_communication_timeout(self,
sender_agent, receiver_agent, message):
        # If a response is not received in 5 seconds
        if not message.responded_within(5):
            print(f"Escalating conflict to
GlobalMediator due to missed response.")

global_mediator.resolve_communication_conflict(sender_a
gent, receiver_agent, message)
```

In this chapter, we have covered:

- **Common Conflict Sources**: Resource contention, priority inversion, and communication breakdowns.
- **Resolution Strategies**: Negotiation, arbitration, and priority scheduling to address conflicts in multi-agent systems.
- **DeepSeek R1 Implementation**: How to configure conflict handlers, automate detection, and apply resolution tactics like priority inheritance.
- **Ensuring Robustness**: Fault tolerance, redundancy, and failover strategies that keep MAS operational under stress or partial failures.
- **Testing and Validation**: Key methods to verify that conflict resolution is effective and that the system remains stable.

By following these principles and experimenting with the **end-of-chapter project**, you will be well-prepared to handle **conflicts** in diverse MAS applications and ensure that your systems are **resilient**, **efficient**, and **robust** even in unpredictable real-world conditions.

Chapter 9: Testing and Validation in MAS

In **multi-agent systems (MAS)**, rigorous **testing and validation** play a critical role in ensuring reliability, stability, and correctness. Because MAS typically involve multiple autonomous entities interacting with each other and with shared resources, the complexity and potential for bugs are higher than in single-agent or traditional software systems. In this chapter, we discuss the **importance of testing** in MAS, explore **testing methodologies** at different levels, explain **validation techniques**, and demonstrate how to set up automated testing within **DeepSeek R1**. We also provide **best practices** to maintain a reliable MAS, followed by a **case study** showcasing how to validate a multi-agent financial trading system.

---

1. Importance of Testing in MAS

1.1. Ensuring Reliability and Stability

Multi-agent systems often handle **mission-critical** tasks, ranging from industrial automation to financial market decisions. A malfunction in one agent or a breakdown in communication can cascade throughout the system, causing:

- **Unpredictable Behavior**: Agents may fail to coordinate or take conflicting actions.
- **System Downtime**: Critical services could go offline if agents crash or lock shared resources.
- **Safety Hazards**: In physical environments (e.g., robotics, healthcare), stability is paramount to prevent accidents or harm.

Thorough testing helps identify these vulnerabilities early and ensures that each agent—and the system as a whole—functions reliably under a wide range of conditions.

1.2. Identifying and Fixing Bugs

MAS introduces unique challenges compared to single-agent systems. Agents operate **concurrently** and often react to **dynamic** changes in the environment. Common issues include:

- **Race Conditions**: Multiple agents simultaneously accessing or modifying shared data.
- **Deadlocks and Starvation**: Agents waiting on each other's resources indefinitely or lower-priority tasks never getting served.
- **Communication Failures**: Messages lost, delayed, or misinterpreted.

Testing provides a **structured** approach to uncover such bugs, enabling developers to **fix** them before deployment or during continuous improvement cycles.

---

2. Testing Methodologies for MAS

Testing methodologies can be categorized into **three main levels**:

2.1. Unit Testing for Agents

- **Definition**: **Unit tests** focus on **individual agents** or even smaller code segments (e.g., functions, methods) within an agent.
- **Purpose**:
  - o Verify that each **internal component** of an agent behaves as expected.
  - o Ensure that data processing, rule evaluation, or local decision-making works correctly in isolation.
- **Example**:
  - o A test that checks if a **WarehouseAgent** correctly increments or decrements inventory counts upon receiving messages like `"ITEM_PICKED"` or `"ITEM_RECEIVED"`.

Table: Sample Unit Test Cases

Agent / Method	Test Scenario	Expected Outcome
`WarehouseAgent.update_inventory`	Inventory update with valid item count	Inventory count changes accurately

Agent / Method	Test Scenario	Expected Outcome
`SchedulerAgent.validate_task`	Task with missing fields	Returns error or rejects task
`FinanceAgent.calculate_profit`	Negative revenue scenario	Returns correct negative or zero profit value

Benefits:

- Easier to **isolate issues** since each agent or component is tested in a controlled environment.
- Faster test execution and **immediate feedback**.

2.2. Integration Testing for Multi-agent Interactions

- **Definition**: **Integration testing** focuses on **interactions** between **two or more** agents to ensure they **communicate** and **coordinate** correctly.
- **Purpose**:
  - o Validate that message formats, protocols, and data flows function as intended.
  - o Check that agent cooperation or negotiation algorithms produce expected outcomes.
- **Examples**:
  - o A test verifying that when a **PackagingAgent** requests item locations from an **InventoryAgent**, it receives correct data within the expected time frame.

Possible Integration Issues:

- **Mismatch** in message formats or fields.
- **Inconsistent** state updates between agents (one agent thinks an order is complete while another is still processing it).

2.3. System Testing for Overall MAS Performance

- **Definition**: **System testing** evaluates the entire MAS as a **unified** application under **realistic** or **simulated** operating conditions.

- **Purpose**:
  - Ensure the system meets **end-to-end requirements**, such as throughput, latency, and overall reliability.
  - Simulate **real-world usage** patterns or edge cases, like sudden spikes in tasks or partial network outages.
- **Examples**:
  - A **stress test** where hundreds of tasks are submitted simultaneously to measure how quickly the MAS processes them and if any agents crash.

Key Metrics:

- **Response Time**: How quickly the MAS processes requests or tasks.
- **Throughput**: Volume of tasks or messages handled per unit time.
- **Error Rates**: Frequency of agent crashes, message losses, or resource contention events.

3. Validation Techniques

While testing generally checks for **defects** and **performance** issues, **validation** ensures that the MAS **meets its design goals** and **behaves** as intended under realistic scenarios.

3.1. Simulation-based Validation

- **Definition**: Create a **virtual environment** or **simulator** that mimics the real-world context in which agents operate.
- **Uses**:
  - Evaluate how agents respond to various inputs (e.g., sensor data, user commands) without risking real systems or physical equipment.
  - Test agent decision-making strategies under diverse or extreme conditions (e.g., random failures).
- **Example**:
  - A **drone swarm** simulation testing collision avoidance before real flight.
  - A **smart traffic** simulation assessing how well agents manage changing traffic patterns over time.

3.2. Real-world Scenario Testing

- **Definition**: Deploy the MAS or subsets of it in a **controlled production** or **pilot** environment, observing real interactions with minimal risk.
- **Goals**:
  - Confirm that all **hardware-software** integrations function correctly.
  - Gather actual performance data (latency, resource usage, user satisfaction).
- **Example**:
  - A **smart factory** pilot line running a limited production batch to verify agent coordination with actual robots and conveyors.

---

4. Automated Testing with DeepSeek R1

4.1. Setting Up Automated Test Suites

DeepSeek R1 offers tools and APIs for automating the testing process. Key steps include:

1. **Test Environment Configuration**
   - Establish **test-specific** settings, such as mock data sources, simulated time, or virtual sensors.
   - Use a **separate** environment (or containerized setup) to avoid conflicts with production data.
2. **Test Case Definitions**
   - Create structured **test scripts** or **scenarios** describing agent behaviors, input data, and expected outputs.
   - For example, a YAML or JSON file specifying tasks to be submitted and the correct system responses.
3. **Execution and Reporting**
   - Run the test suite using either the **DeepSeek R1 CLI** or an external tool like **pytest** or **JUnit** (depending on your language ecosystem).
   - Collect and analyze logs to see if the system's actual outcomes match the expected results.

Code Example (Pseudocode):

```python
python

# test_warehouse.py
from deepseek_r1_sdk import AgentManager, TaskManager
from my_agents import WarehouseAgent

def test_warehouse_inventory_update():
    manager = AgentManager()
    warehouse_agent = WarehouseAgent(agent_id="Warehouse1")
    manager.register_agent(warehouse_agent)

    # Submit a task to update inventory
    task = {"task_id": "UpdateInv", "type":
"INVENTORY_UPDATE", "item_count": 10}
    TaskManager.submit_task(task)

    # Check the agent's internal state or logs after some
time
    assert warehouse_agent.get_item_count() == 10, "Inventory
count should be updated to 10"
```

4.2. Continuous Testing Integration

For **continuous integration (CI)** and **continuous delivery (CD)**, you can set up a **pipeline** that automatically:

1. **Pulls** the latest code changes from version control (e.g., Git).
2. **Builds** the MAS artifacts or Docker images.
3. **Runs** the entire test suite (unit, integration, system) in a **staging** environment.
4. **Reports** any failures or performance regressions to the development team.

Benefits:

- Ensures that **new code** does not break existing functionalities.
- Provides **fast feedback** on changes, promoting iterative improvement.

5. Best Practices for Reliable MAS

5.1. Test-Driven Development (TDD)

TDD means writing **failing** tests **before** implementing new agent features:

1. **Write a Test**: Define a scenario, expected outcome, or function signature.
2. **Run the Test**: Confirm it fails initially because the feature is not yet implemented.
3. **Implement the Feature**: Write the minimal code to pass the test.
4. **Refactor**: Clean up the code while keeping tests green.

Advantages:

- Guides **design** by clarifying requirements from the start.
- Encourages **modular, testable code** in agents.

5.2. Code Reviews and Quality Assurance

Besides automated tests, **peer reviews** and **code inspections** are essential:

- **Code Reviews**: Another developer or team member examines the agent's logic, communication protocols, or resource handling.
- **Pair Programming**: Two developers alternate roles (typing vs. reviewing) to spot issues early.
- **Static Analysis Tools**: Check for code smells, unused variables, or concurrency hazards, especially relevant in concurrent MAS code.

Table: Quality Assurance Methods

Method	Focus Area	Benefits
Code Reviews	High-level logic, best practices	Catches design flaws, fosters team knowledge
Pair Programming	Real-time development and oversight	Immediate feedback, knowledge sharing
Static Analysis	Syntax, concurrency, memory usage	Early detection of potential runtime errors

6. Case Study: Validating a Multi-agent Financial Trading System

6.1. System Overview

A **multi-agent financial trading system** uses multiple **TraderAgents** to:

- **Monitor** stock prices in real-time.
- **Execute** trades based on market indicators or predictive models.
- **Coordinate** to avoid placing contradictory orders or saturating liquidity.

6.2. Potential Issues

1. **Race Conditions**: Multiple agents attempt to buy or sell the same asset, resulting in partial fills or pricing anomalies.
2. **Communication Delays**: Sudden market fluctuations might not propagate to all TraderAgents in time, causing uncoordinated decisions.
3. **Overload**: High-volume data streams can overwhelm the system, leading to missed trading opportunities or system lags.

6.3. Testing Approach

1. **Unit Tests**
   - Validate each **TraderAgent**'s logic for analyzing indicators (e.g., moving averages, RSI).
   - Confirm correct order creation or cancellation.
2. **Integration Tests**
   - Check agent interactions with the **OrderBookAgent** and **MarketDataAgent** for timely updates and order executions.
3. **System Tests**
   - Use **simulation** to emulate rapid price changes or large volumes of trades.
   - Observe how the system balances concurrency and performance.
4. **Validation**
   - **Simulation-based**: Over a historical dataset, ensuring agents produce consistent profits or minimize losses.
   - **Real-world**: Deploy a pilot on a **paper trading** platform or sandbox environment, logging all trades for verification.

6.4. Outcomes

- **Early detection** of concurrency bugs: One agent discovered to be placing duplicate orders if the network was slow.
- **Improved** overall performance: Fine-tuned communication intervals and order batch processing to reduce overhead.
- **Regulatory compliance**: Logging and replay tools validated that the system followed market rules (e.g., no insider trading or manipulative patterns).

7. End-of-Chapter Projects

Project 9: Implementing Automated Testing

Objective: Build a **basic automated testing pipeline** for a multi-agent scenario in DeepSeek R1, incorporating **unit**, **integration**, and **system** tests.

Outline

1. **Agent Development**
   o Create two or more agents with distinct roles (e.g., `OrderAgent`, `PaymentAgent` in an e-commerce domain).
2. **Unit Tests**
   o Write tests ensuring each agent's data-processing functions produce correct results.
3. **Integration Tests**
   o Validate inter-agent messaging under typical and edge-case scenarios (e.g., incomplete message fields).
4. **System Test**
   o Simulate multiple concurrent orders, verifying correct system behavior and performance.
5. **Pipeline Setup**
   o Use a CI tool (e.g., **GitHub Actions**, **Jenkins**) to run the entire suite upon each code commit.

Sample Code (Pseudocode)

```python
# unit_tests/test_order_agent.py
import unittest
from my_agents import OrderAgent
```

```python
class TestOrderAgent(unittest.TestCase):
    def test_calculate_total_cost(self):
        agent = OrderAgent(agent_id="Order1")
        total =
agent.calculate_total_cost(items=[{"price":10, "qty":2},
{"price":5, "qty":1}])
        self.assertEqual(total, 25, "Expected total cost to
be 25")

# integration_tests/test_agent_interaction.py
import unittest
from deepseek_r1_sdk import AgentManager
from my_agents import OrderAgent, PaymentAgent

class TestAgentInteraction(unittest.TestCase):
    def test_order_to_payment_flow(self):
        manager = AgentManager()
        order_agent = OrderAgent(agent_id="OrderAgent")
        payment_agent = PaymentAgent(agent_id="PaymentAgent")
        manager.register_agent(order_agent)
        manager.register_agent(payment_agent)

        # Create an order message
        order_message = {
            "sender": "Customer",
            "content_type": "ORDER_PLACED",
            "payload": {"order_id": 123, "amount": 30}
        }
        order_agent.handle_message(order_message)

        # Check if PaymentAgent eventually receives the
payment request
        # Logic to wait or mock message flow
        # Assert PaymentAgent state or logs

if __name__ == "__main__":
    unittest.main()
```

Goal:

- Develop each layer of tests and **run** them automatically, ensuring continuous feedback on system correctness.

---

8. Quizzes and Self-Assessments

Quiz 9: Testing and Validation Methods

1. **Importance of Testing**
   - **Question**: Why are testing and validation especially critical in MAS compared to single-agent or traditional software systems?

2. **Unit vs. Integration Testing**
   - **Question**: Distinguish between **unit testing** and **integration testing**. What unique challenges does integration testing address in MAS?

3. **Validation Techniques**
   - **Question**: Compare **simulation-based validation** to **real-world scenario testing**. Provide one advantage of each.

4. **Automated Testing**
   - **Question**: In a CI/CD pipeline for DeepSeek R1, name two benefits of running automated test suites on every commit.

5. **Best Practices**
   - **Question**: How does **test-driven development** (TDD) help improve the reliability and maintainability of multi-agent systems?

6. **Case Study**
   - **Question**: In the multi-agent financial trading system example, what type of concurrency issue might arise if multiple agents place orders for the same asset simultaneously?

7. **Short Coding Prompt**
   - **Question**: Write a brief pseudocode snippet for a system test that simulates a surge in tasks (e.g., 100 tasks submitted at once) to observe how the MAS handles the load.

Answer Key (Suggested):

1. **Importance of Testing**: The concurrent, distributed nature of MAS makes them more prone to synchronization issues, resource contention, and communication challenges. Testing ensures these complexities are well-managed.

2. **Unit vs. Integration**:
   - **Unit Testing** checks individual agent components in isolation.
   - **Integration Testing** validates interactions between multiple agents or modules, catching interface or protocol mismatches.

3. **Simulation vs. Real-world**:

- o **Simulation**: Offers controlled, repeatable experiments without risking real-world resources.
  - o **Real-world**: Reveals actual operational performance and practical deployment issues.
4. **Automated Testing Benefits**:
  - o Immediate detection of regressions from new commits.
  - o Ensures consistent test coverage, promoting stable releases.
5. **TDD in MAS**:
  - o Defines agent behaviors and interfaces upfront, reducing guesswork.
  - o Helps maintain a clean architecture, as changes are incremental and tested from the start.
6. **Concurrency Issue**:
  - o **Race Condition**: Multiple TraderAgents might attempt to buy/sell simultaneously, leading to partially filled orders or inconsistent states if not managed properly.
7. **Pseudocode for System Test**:

```python
def system_stress_test(task_manager, agent_manager):
    # Submit 100 tasks concurrently
    for i in range(100):
        task = {"task_id": f"T{i}", "description":
"BulkTask"}
        task_manager.submit_task(task)

    # Monitor agent states, completion times, or logs
    time.sleep(10)
    # Evaluate performance metrics (throughput, error
rates)
```

Testing and validation are indispensable in **multi-agent systems**, where multiple autonomous agents engage in concurrent, sometimes complex interactions. By leveraging **unit**, **integration**, and **system** testing, combined with **simulation-based** and **real-world** validation techniques, you can significantly enhance the **reliability**, **stability**, and **performance** of your MAS.

DeepSeek R1 facilitates automated testing through dedicated APIs, supporting everything from **small-scale** unit checks to large-scale **system stress tests**. Adopting best practices such as **test-driven development**, **code reviews**, and **continuous integration** further strengthens the foundation for deploying high-quality, robust multi-agent solutions—whether in a warehouse, financial market, or any other environment that demands intelligent collaboration and adaptability.

Chapter 10: Autonomous Vehicle Fleet Coordination

Autonomous vehicles (AVs) are rapidly reshaping transportation, logistics, and mobility. In a **Multi-Agent System (MAS)** context, fleets of autonomous vehicles can **coordinate**, **communicate**, and **adapt** to real-time conditions, reducing congestion, enhancing safety, and improving operational efficiency. This chapter provides an in-depth look at **autonomous vehicle systems**, explores the **roles** of collaborative agents in their coordination, delves into **route planning** and **real-time communication** strategies, and discusses critical **safety** and **reliability** measures. We conclude with a **case study** on autonomous delivery drones, a **project** to build a coordinated vehicle fleet, and a **quiz** for self-assessment.

---

1. Overview of Autonomous Vehicle Systems

1.1. Key Components and Requirements

An autonomous vehicle system integrates **hardware** (sensors, controllers, actuators) and **software** (perception, decision-making, and control algorithms) to operate with minimal or no human intervention. Key components include:

1. **Sensors and Perception**
   - **LiDAR, Radar, and Cameras**: Collect real-time data about the vehicle's surroundings.
   - **GPS and IMU (Inertial Measurement Unit)**: Provide global positioning and orientation information.
2. **Onboard Compute and AI**
   - **Local Processing**: Runs algorithms for object detection, mapping, and trajectory planning.
   - **Machine Learning Models**: Classify road objects, predict motion of other vehicles, and adapt driving decisions.
3. **Actuation Systems**
   - **Engine Control, Steering, and Braking**: Physical interfaces to control vehicle movement.
4. **Communication Modules**

- o **Vehicle-to-Vehicle (V2V)**: Enables vehicles to share status, intent, and environment data.
- o **Vehicle-to-Infrastructure (V2I)**: Exchanges information with traffic lights or cloud-based services.
5. **User Interface** (if applicable)
   - o **Displays and Feedback Systems**: Provide operators or passengers with critical alerts or ride status.

System Requirements:

- **High Reliability**: Transportation safety demands robust hardware and software.
- **Real-time Response**: Vehicles must react quickly (often within milliseconds) to avoid collisions or hazards.
- **Scalability**: Managing a growing fleet requires efficient coordination strategies to handle thousands of vehicles.

1.2. Role of MAS in Autonomous Vehicles

Multi-agent systems bring critical advantages to autonomous vehicle fleets:

- **Distributed Decision-Making**: Each vehicle (agent) processes local data while also sharing information with other vehicles.
- **Collaboration**: Vehicles coordinate routes, speed, or lane changes to optimize traffic flow or reduce congestion.
- **Scalability**: Adding more autonomous vehicles can be managed through agent-based protocols without centralized bottlenecks.
- **Resilience**: If a single vehicle fails or goes offline, other agents can adapt their plans, maintaining overall system functionality.

2. Designing Collaborative Agents for Vehicle Coordination

2.1. Agent Roles: Navigation, Communication, Decision Making

In an autonomous vehicle fleet, agents typically fulfill **specialized roles**. Although each vehicle may have overlapping functionalities, we can conceptually separate roles as follows:

1. **Navigation Agent**
   o Handles **route planning**, path selection, and local trajectory control.
   o Uses map data, road regulations, and traffic updates to find optimal paths.
   o May incorporate advanced algorithms for lane keeping, merging, and obstacle avoidance.
2. **Communication Agent**
   o Manages **V2V** and **V2I** communications, broadcasting or receiving essential data (e.g., position, velocity, braking status).
   o Coordinates with other vehicles to avoid collisions or optimize lane usage.
   o Interfaces with cloud-based services for real-time traffic and weather updates.
3. **Decision Making Agent**
   o Combines **perception** results with traffic or environment data to make high-level driving decisions (e.g., overtaking, re-routing).
   o Employs **machine learning** or **rule-based** logic to evaluate risks and predict the behaviors of other road users.
   o Initiates commands for the **Navigation** and **Communication** layers, ensuring consistent, safe driving policies across the fleet.

Example Table: Collaborative Agent Roles

Role	Responsibilities	Key Inputs/Outputs
Navigation Agent	Plan routes, handle local path adjustments, follow waypoints	Receives map data, outputs steering & speed cmds
Communication Agent	Exchange data with other vehicles and infrastructure	Receives V2V/V2I signals, broadcasts vehicle state
Decision Agent	Assess environment, select driving maneuvers	Receives sensor data, outputs high-level actions

3. Implementing Route Planning and Optimization

3.1. Pathfinding Algorithms

In MAS for autonomous vehicles, **pathfinding** must be both **efficient** and **robust**. Common algorithms include:

1. **Graph-Based**
   - **Dijkstra's Algorithm**: Finds the shortest path in weighted graphs. Efficient for relatively static road networks.
   - **A***: Improves upon Dijkstra by using heuristics (e.g., straight-line distance) to guide the search faster.
2. **Sampling-Based**
   - **RRT (Rapidly-exploring Random Tree)**: Useful for high-dimensional or continuous spaces.
   - **PRM (Probabilistic Roadmap)**: Samples collision-free states to build a roadmap, then searches for feasible paths.
3. **Dynamic Algorithms**
   - **D*** (pronounced "D star") or **A*** variations for re-planning in dynamic environments, updating routes when road conditions or traffic states change.

Influential Factors:

- **Road Constraints**: Speed limits, traffic rules, lane boundaries.
- **Vehicle Dynamics**: Acceleration, turning radius, braking distance.
- **Traffic Conditions**: Congestion levels, accidents, temporary closures.

3.2. Traffic Management Strategies

When coordinating multiple autonomous vehicles, MAS-level strategies help optimize global traffic flow:

1. **Platooning**
   - Vehicles form tight formations ("platoons") to reduce air drag and increase road capacity.
   - Communication ensures synchronized acceleration/braking, maintaining safe gaps.

2. **Intersection Coordination**
   o Instead of relying solely on traffic lights, vehicles can negotiate intersection usage (e.g., reservation-based intersection management).
   o Reduces waiting times and potential collisions when vehicles share data about their arrival times.
3. **Dynamic Routing**
   o Vehicles periodically recalculate routes based on real-time updates from neighboring agents or a central traffic server.
   o Balances loads across different roads, preventing bottlenecks.

4. Real-time Communication and Synchronization

4.1. Vehicle-to-Vehicle (V2V) Communication

- **Definition**: Direct wireless exchange of data between vehicles, often using dedicated protocols (e.g., DSRC, C-V2X).
- **Typical Data**: Position, speed, acceleration, braking status.
- **Benefits**:
   o Increases **situational awareness**—each vehicle "sees" not only its sensors but also neighbors' states.
   o Enables cooperative maneuvers, such as merging or collision avoidance.

4.2. Ensuring Real-time Data Exchange

Low-latency networks are critical in autonomous driving scenarios:

1. **Protocol Selection**
   o **5G** or **Dedicated Short-Range Communications (DSRC)** for minimal delays.
   o **Edge Computing** to process data close to the source, reducing round-trip times to distant servers.
2. **Synchronization**
   o **Timestamping** messages to ensure consistency in position or speed data.
   o **Event-driven updates**: Vehicles broadcast changes as soon as relevant data updates (e.g., sudden braking).

3. **Fault Tolerance**
    - o Redundant communication channels or fallback strategies if the primary network fails.
    - o Encrypt and authenticate messages to prevent spoofing or malicious attacks.

5. Safety and Reliability Considerations

5.1. Collision Avoidance Mechanisms

Safety is paramount in autonomous fleets. Collision avoidance often relies on:

1. **Sensor Fusion**
    - o Combining LiDAR, radar, camera, and V2V data for robust obstacle detection.
    - o **Kalman Filters** or **Bayesian approaches** used to refine object tracking.
2. **Predictive Models**
    - o Estimating future trajectories of other vehicles, pedestrians, or cyclists.
    - o Taking preemptive actions (e.g., decelerating, lane change) to avoid collisions.
3. **Emergency Braking Protocols**
    - o Automatic override of normal driving policies if a collision is imminent.
    - o Vehicles broadcast emergency signals to neighbors, allowing them to react promptly.

5.2. Redundancy in Critical Systems

To ensure **robustness**:

1. **Sensor Redundancy**
    - o Multiple sensor types (e.g., radar + LiDAR) can detect objects if one sensor fails or is occluded.
2. **Backup Communication Paths**
    - o If a 5G link fails, vehicles switch to DSRC or an alternative network for crucial data exchange.

3. **Fail-Safe Mechanisms**
   - If an agent's control software malfunctions, a fallback system either **safely parks** the vehicle or hands over control to a remote operator.

---

6. Case Study: Coordinating a Fleet of Autonomous Delivery Drones

6.1. Scenario Overview

A logistics company deploys **autonomous drones** to deliver packages within a city. Each drone is an **agent** that:

- **Navigates** using GPS, onboard sensors, and dynamic route adjustments.
- **Communicates** with a central hub and neighboring drones for traffic avoidance and airspace sharing.
- **Makes** local decisions on flight paths, altitude levels, and battery management.

6.2. Challenges

1. **Urban Airspace Complexity**
   - Buildings, restricted zones, weather changes.
   - High risk of collisions if multiple drones converge on the same corridor.
2. **Battery Limitations**
   - Drones must frequently check battery status and plan recharging or swapping.
   - MAS-based scheduling ensures recharging stations aren't overloaded.
3. **Real-time Adjustments**
   - Unexpected obstacles (e.g., construction cranes, tall vehicles).

- On-the-fly route re-planning coordinated among multiple drones.

6.3. MAS Coordination Approach

- **Dynamic Flight Corridors**: Drones negotiate usage of certain altitude brackets and time slots to reduce congestion.
- **Fault-Tolerant Communication**: If a drone loses connection with the hub, it still exchanges data with nearby drones to maintain situational awareness.
- **Adaptive Task Allocation**: If one drone is low on battery, another is assigned to continue or finish the delivery.

6.4. Outcomes

- **Higher Efficiency**: Reduced delivery times due to optimized route planning and load balancing across the drone fleet.
- **Enhanced Safety**: Fewer near-miss incidents, thanks to real-time agent communication and collision avoidance.
- **Scalability**: As the city's delivery demand grows, additional drones integrate seamlessly using MAS protocols.

---

7. End-of-Chapter Projects

Project 10: Building a Coordinated Vehicle Fleet

Objective: Construct a **simplified MAS** for autonomous vehicle or drone coordination, focusing on **route planning**, **communication**, and **collision avoidance**.

Outline

1. **Choose a Scenario**
   - **Option A**: Ground-based autonomous cars in a simulated city grid.
   - **Option B**: Drones delivering packages in a simplified 2D airspace.
2. **Agent Roles**
   - **Navigation Agent**: Plans/updates routes.

o **Comm Agent**: Shares speed, position, and route data with neighbors.

3. **Collision Avoidance**
   o Implement a minimal algorithm (e.g., if two agents are within a certain distance, reduce speed or shift trajectory).

4. **Real-time Updates**
   o Agents recalculate or broadcast route changes periodically (e.g., every second).

5. **Monitoring**
   o Visualize agent positions in a 2D/3D grid.
   o Log collisions, near-misses, or communication disruptions.

Example Pseudocode

```python
# project_fleet_coordinator.py
from deepseek_r1_sdk import AgentBase, AgentManager

class VehicleAgent(AgentBase):
    def __init__(self, agent_id, position, route):
        super().__init__(agent_id)
        self.position = position
        self.route = route
        self.speed = 0

    def plan_route(self, destination):
        # Basic pathfinding or pre-computed route
        self.route = compute_shortest_path(self.position,
destination)

    def on_message(self, message):
        # Handle updates, e.g., traffic info or collision
warnings
        if message['content_type'] == "COLLISION_WARNING":
            self.avoid_collision(message['payload'])

    def avoid_collision(self, collision_data):
        # Simple logic: slow down or reroute
        self.speed *= 0.5

    def step(self):
        # Move along route if not at destination
        if self.route:
            next_waypoint = self.route[0]
            # Update position by step
            self.position = move_towards(self.position,
next_waypoint, self.speed)
```

```
            if self.position == next_waypoint:
                self.route.pop(0)

if __name__ == "__main__":
    manager = AgentManager()
    vehicle1 = VehicleAgent("Car1", position=(0, 0),
route=[])
    vehicle2 = VehicleAgent("Car2", position=(10, 10),
route=[])

    manager.register_agent(vehicle1)
    manager.register_agent(vehicle2)

    vehicle1.plan_route((20, 20))
    vehicle2.plan_route((0, 0))

    # Simulate or run an event loop
    while True:
        vehicle1.step()
        vehicle2.step()
        # Possibly send collision warnings or route updates
        # ...
```

Goal: Demonstrate how multiple autonomous agents can navigate, share data, and adapt to prevent collisions in real time.

8. Quizzes and Self-Assessments

Quiz 10: Autonomous Vehicle Coordination

1. **Overview**
   o **Question**: Name two primary hardware components essential for autonomous vehicle sensing, and explain their roles.
2. **Collaborative Agents**
   o **Question**: In a MAS for vehicles, what is the function of a **Communication Agent**, and why is it crucial?
3. **Route Planning**
   o **Question**: Compare **Dijkstra's Algorithm** and **A*** in the context of finding routes for autonomous vehicles. Which might be more efficient if we have a good heuristic?
4. **Real-time Communication**

- Question: Why is **low-latency** networking critical for V2V communication, and what are two potential fallback strategies if the primary network fails?
5. **Safety Considerations**
   - **Question**: Define **sensor fusion** and give one example of how it improves collision avoidance in autonomous driving.
6. **Case Study**
   - **Question**: In the autonomous drone scenario, how do drones mitigate the risk of collisions when they operate in the same airspace?
7. **Short Coding Prompt**
   - **Question**: Write a short pseudocode snippet for an agent that broadcasts an **Emergency Brake** message to nearby vehicles if it detects an imminent collision.

Answer Key (Suggested):

1. **Hardware for Sensing**:
   - **LiDAR**: Builds 3D point clouds to detect objects and measure distances accurately.
   - **Radar**: Effective in adverse weather, calculates relative velocity of objects.
2. **Communication Agent**:
   - Manages exchange of data among vehicles. Critical for coordination, enabling features like platooning or collision avoidance.
3. **Dijkstra vs. A***:
   - **Dijkstra's**: Finds shortest paths but can be slow if the search space is large.
   - **A***: More efficient with a **good heuristic**, guiding the pathfinding in the general direction of the goal.
4. **Low-latency**:
   - Vehicles must react within milliseconds to avoid collisions.
   - Fallbacks: **DSRC** if 5G fails, or local **ad-hoc** Wi-Fi networks.
5. **Sensor Fusion**:
   - Combines data from multiple sensors (e.g., LiDAR + radar) to form a unified, more accurate representation.
   - Example: Fusing LiDAR shape detection and radar speed measurements gives improved detection of an approaching vehicle.
6. **Drone Collision Risk**:

- o They coordinate flight corridors, share altitude/time slots, and reroute if another drone enters the same zone.

7. **Emergency Brake Snippet**:

```python
python

if self.detect_collision_imminent():
    message = {
        "sender": self.agent_id,
        "content_type": "EMERGENCY_BRAKE",
        "payload": {"position": self.position,
"velocity": self.velocity}
    }
    self.broadcast_message(message)
    self.apply_brakes()
```

Coordinating a fleet of autonomous vehicles—be they **cars**, **trucks**, or **drones**—is a **prime example** of how **multi-agent systems** can revolutionize real-world domains. By assigning **collaborative roles** (navigation, communication, decision making), implementing robust **route planning**, maintaining **real-time communication**, and prioritizing **safety** and **reliability**, MAS-driven fleets can tackle the complexity of modern transportation challenges. The **case study** on delivery drones illustrates how these principles scale to different contexts, while the **end-of-chapter project** offers a pathway to **hands-on experimentation** with autonomous agent fleets.

Chapter 11: Smart Manufacturing with Collaborative Robots (Cobots)

Smart manufacturing leverages advanced technologies such as **industrial IoT**, **machine learning**, and **multi-agent systems (MAS)** to optimize production processes, enhance quality control, and improve overall efficiency. In this chapter, we explore how **collaborative robots (cobots)** fit into this paradigm, discussing their design, workflow optimization, safety considerations, and predictive maintenance strategies. We then offer a real-world **case study** on optimizing an automotive assembly line, conclude with an **end-of-chapter project** on developing cobots, and provide a **quiz** for self-assessment.

---

1. Introduction to Smart Manufacturing

1.1. Industry 4.0 and the Role of MAS

Industry 4.0 marks a shift toward **digitized** and **connected** manufacturing systems:

1. **Cyber-Physical Systems (CPS)**
   o Physical machinery (e.g., robots, CNC machines) integrated with digital components (sensors, control software).
2. **Connectivity and IoT**
   o Devices within the factory floor continuously share data (e.g., production status, diagnostic info).
3. **Data-Driven Intelligence**
   o Machine learning models and analytics platforms derive insights to enhance productivity, reduce downtime, and adapt workflows in real time.
4. **Multi-Agent Systems**
   o Agents within a factory—machines, robots, or software modules—act autonomously while coordinating with each other.

MAS in Smart Manufacturing:

- **Distributed Control**: No single point of failure, as each robot or station makes local decisions, guided by shared goals.
- **Flexibility**: Agents can reconfigure themselves for different production tasks with minimal downtime.
- **Scalability**: Adding or removing production lines or robots is straightforward when each agent can integrate into an existing communication framework.

2. Designing Collaborative Robot Agents

2.1. Specialization of Cobots: Assembly, Quality Control, Inventory Management

Collaborative robots (cobots) are built to work alongside humans or with other robots, sharing tasks in a **cooperative** environment. Common specializations include:

1. **Assembly Cobots**
   - Perform **precision assembly** tasks (e.g., attaching screws, placing circuit boards).
   - Use **end-effectors** such as grippers or welding tools.
2. **Quality Control (QC) Cobots**
   - Inspect products or components using **vision systems** (cameras), force sensors, or ultrasonic testing.
   - Identify defects in real time and flag them for rework or disposal.
3. **Inventory Management Cobots**
   - Move materials or parts between stations, maintaining **stock levels** in real time.
   - Integrate with warehouse management systems to track incoming/outgoing items.

Table: Common Cobots and Their Roles

Cobot Type	Primary Function	Key Tools / Sensors	Example Task
Assembly Cobot	Performs assembly operations	Gripper, welding tool, torque sensors	Screwing components onto a circuit board
QC Cobot	Inspects and tests products	Cameras, force/torque sensors, ultrasonic probes	Checking weld seams for imperfections
Inventory Cobot	Manages material flow	LIDAR for navigation, RFID readers	Transporting boxes from storage to production

3. Implementing Workflow Optimization

3.1. Task Sequencing and Scheduling

In **smart manufacturing**, the order in which tasks are executed significantly impacts **efficiency**. By treating **each task** as an **agent-assignable** job, you can apply **MAS** scheduling:

1. **Centralized Scheduling**
   o A **master scheduler** or **TaskManager** allocates tasks to cobots based on real-time data about their capabilities and workload.
2. **Distributed Negotiation**
   o Cobots **bid** or **negotiate** for tasks. E.g., a packaging job that matches a certain robot's location and skill set is offered to that robot, and the best "bidder" wins.

Examples of Sequencing Tactics:

- **Just-in-Time (JIT)**: Tasks are scheduled to arrive at workstations right before they're needed, minimizing inventory or idle time.
- **Batch Processing**: Certain tasks (e.g., painting) are grouped for efficiency, ensuring the cobot doesn't need to switch tools frequently.

3.2. Resource Allocation and Utilization

Efficient resource utilization involves allocating **machines**, **parts**, and **cobots** optimally:

1. **Machine-Agnostic** Cobots
   o Cobots can seamlessly switch between different machines or stations if trained to handle multiple operations.
2. **Material Flow Optimization**
   o Agents continuously monitor storage levels. If a particular station is running low on parts, a cobot is directed to replenish them.

Code Example (Pseudocode) for Simple Scheduling:

```python
# simple_scheduler.py
from deepseek_r1_sdk import TaskManager, AgentManager

class AssemblyCobot:
    def __init__(self, cobot_id, skillset):
        self.cobot_id = cobot_id
        self.skillset = skillset  # e.g., {"drilling": True,
"welding": False}
        self.current_task = None

    def can_handle(self, task):
        return self.skillset.get(task["type"], False)

    def perform_task(self, task):
        print(f"{self.cobot_id} performing {task['type']} on
item {task['item_id']}")
        # simulate work
        # ...
        print(f"{self.cobot_id} completed task
{task['task_id']}")

class SimpleTaskManager(TaskManager):
    def assign_task(self, task, available_cobots):
        for cobot in available_cobots:
            if cobot.can_handle(task):
                cobot.perform_task(task)
                return

if __name__ == "__main__":
    # Setup
    manager = AgentManager()
    cobot1 = AssemblyCobot(cobot_id="CobotA1",
skillset={"drilling": True})
```

```
    cobot2 = AssemblyCobot(cobot_id="CobotA2",
skillset={"welding": True})

    # Define tasks
    task1 = {"task_id": "T001", "type": "drilling",
"item_id": "PartX1"}
    task2 = {"task_id": "T002", "type": "welding", "item_id":
"PartX2"}

    # Assign tasks
    st_manager = SimpleTaskManager()
    st_manager.assign_task(task1, [cobot1, cobot2])
    st_manager.assign_task(task2, [cobot1, cobot2])
```

Explanation:

- A **SimpleTaskManager** assigns tasks to the **first** capable cobot.
- This can be extended with more advanced scheduling or negotiation algorithms.

---

4. Ensuring Safe Collaboration

4.1. Human-Robot Interaction Protocols

When cobots **collaborate with humans** on the factory floor, safety is paramount:

1. **Safety Zones**
   o **Light curtains** or sensors stop the cobot's motion if a human enters a restricted zone.
2. **Force Limiting**
   o Cobots with **torque sensors** detect collisions or excessive force, pausing movement to avoid harm.
3. **Augmented Reality Interfaces**
   o Humans can visualize robot intentions or paths via AR headsets, improving situational awareness.

4.2. Safety Standards and Compliance

ISO and **ANSI** standards provide guidelines for **robotic safety**:

1. **ISO 10218**: Addresses industrial robot safety and protective measures.
2. **ISO/TS 15066**: Specifies safety requirements for **collaborative robot** operations, including maximum permissible contact forces.
3. **Compliance**
   - o Manufacturers must meet or exceed these standards, ensuring safe robot motion planning, fail-safes, and emergency stops.

5. Predictive Maintenance and Monitoring

5.1. Agent-Based Monitoring Systems

In a **MAS**, monitoring agents track **robot health**, **performance**, and **environmental** conditions:

1. **Sensors on Cobots**
   - o Temperature, vibration, motor torque readings.
   - o Real-time analysis can detect anomalies (e.g., unusual motor heat).
2. **Dashboard Aggregation**
   - o Central or distributed dashboards collect data across all cobots, enabling quick diagnosis or alert generation.

5.2. Predictive Analytics for Maintenance

Predictive maintenance uses **historical data** and **machine learning** to predict equipment failures:

1. **Feature Extraction**
   - o Convert raw sensor data into meaningful metrics (e.g., torque variance over time).
2. **ML Models**
   - o **Random Forest**, **LSTM**, or **Bayesian** models to estimate the remaining useful life of critical components.
3. **Maintenance Scheduling**
   - o Agents coordinate downtime or maintenance tasks, ensuring minimal impact on production lines.

Example:

```python
python

# predictive_maintenance.py
import random
def predict_failure_probability(sensor_data):
    # A placeholder ML model returning random probability
    return random.uniform(0, 1)

class MaintenanceAgent:
    def on_sensor_update(self, cobot_id, sensor_data):
        prob_failure =
predict_failure_probability(sensor_data)
        if prob_failure > 0.8:
            print(f"[ALERT] High failure risk for {cobot_id},
scheduling maintenance.")
```

Explanation:

- In practice, you'd replace `random.uniform(0,1)` with an actual trained model.
- If the predicted failure risk surpasses a threshold, the system schedules maintenance before catastrophic breakdown occurs.

---

6. Case Study: Optimizing an Automotive Assembly Line with Cobots

6.1. Background

An automotive manufacturer integrates a **cobot fleet** into its assembly line to improve throughput and flexibility:

1. **Assembly Cobots** install components such as doors and electronics.
2. **QC Cobots** perform real-time inspections, ensuring consistent part tolerances.
3. **Inventory Cobots** manage just-in-time part deliveries to workstations.

6.2. Implementation Steps

1. **MAS Design**

- o Each station is an **agent** that requests tasks from the main scheduler. Cobots handle specialized tasks, pulling required parts from inventory.
2. **Real-time Data Exchange**
   - o Cobots share status with a central **MES (Manufacturing Execution System)**, which orchestrates workflows and automatically triggers reorder points or maintenance alerts.
3. **Safety Integration**
   - o Cobots operate in close proximity to human workers. Force sensors and vision-based obstacle detection ensure no collisions with personnel.

6.3. Results

- **Increased Efficiency**: Through intelligent scheduling, idle time decreased by **15%**, boosting overall throughput.
- **Reduced Defects**: QC cobots detected faults early, preventing downstream rework.
- **Improved Worker Satisfaction**: Workers entrusted with higher-level tasks, while cobots handled repetitive, ergonomically challenging activities.

Table: Measured Improvements

Metric	Pre-Integration	Post-Integration	Gain
Throughput (units/hour)	100	115	+15%
Defect Rate (%)	2.5	1.8	-28% relative decrease
Worker Injuries (per year)	5	2	-60%

7. End-of-Chapter Projects

Project 11: Developing Collaborative Robots for Manufacturing

Objective: Create a **simplified MAS** that includes assembly, QC, and inventory cobots, demonstrating **task allocation**, **safety considerations**, and **predictive maintenance**.

Outline

1. **Agent Setup**
   - **AssemblyCobots**: Skilled in various operations (e.g., drilling, fastening).
   - **QCCobots**: Vision-based quality checks.
   - **InventoryCobots**: Transport parts to each station.
2. **Task Workflows**
   - Multiple tasks (e.g., "Fasten X screws," "Deliver Part Y to Station Z") queued in a **TaskManager**.
   - Agents accept tasks if they match their skill set and availability.
3. **Safety Simulation**
   - If a QCCobot's sensor detects a human's proximity, it halts or slows the cobot.
   - Basic collision avoidance logic for InventoryCobots moving in shared aisles.
4. **Predictive Maintenance**
   - Agent simulating sensor data for each cobot's joint motors.
   - If a motor vibration reading exceeds a threshold, schedule maintenance.

Example Code (Pseudocode)

python

```
# manufacturing_project.py
from deepseek_r1_sdk import AgentManager, TaskManager

class AssemblyCobot:
    def __init__(self, agent_id, capabilities):
        self.agent_id = agent_id
        self.capabilities = capabilities   # e.g.
{"fastening": True, "drilling": True}
        self.health = 100  # pretend measure of maintenance
state

    def on_task_assigned(self, task):
        if task["type"] in self.capabilities:
            print(f"{self.agent_id} performing {task['type']}
on {task['item']}")
```

```
            self.health -= 0.1  # degrade health
        else:
            print(f"{self.agent_id} cannot handle
{task['type']}")

    def monitor_health(self):
        if self.health < 50:
            print(f"[Alert] {self.agent_id} requires
maintenance soon.")

class QCCobot:
    def inspect(self, item):
        # random inspection outcome
        pass

# etc.

if __name__ == "__main__":
    manager = AgentManager()
    a_cobot1 = AssemblyCobot(agent_id="Assembly1",
capabilities={"fastening": True})
    # ... additional cobots

    # Simulate tasks, health checks
    task1 = {"task_id": "T001", "type": "fastening", "item":
"PanelA"}
    a_cobot1.on_task_assigned(task1)
    a_cobot1.monitor_health()
```

Goal: Illustrate how multiple cobot types collaborate to complete tasks safely and efficiently.

---

8. Quizzes and Self-Assessments

Quiz 11: Smart Manufacturing Concepts

1. **Industry 4.0**
   - Question: Briefly define **Industry 4.0** and describe one key role MAS play within it.
2. **Collaborative Robots**
   - Question: Name two specialized cobot roles in manufacturing and give an example task for each.
3. **Workflow Optimization**

- o **Question**: Differentiate between **centralized** and **distributed** scheduling of tasks for cobots. What are the main advantages of each?
4. **Safety**
   - o **Question**: Explain **force-limiting** in cobots and why it's essential for human-robot collaboration.
5. **Predictive Maintenance**
   - o **Question**: How do **agent-based monitoring** and **machine learning** techniques help reduce unplanned downtime?
6. **Case Study**
   - o **Question**: In the automotive assembly line example, what were two measurable improvements realized by integrating cobots?
7. **Short Coding Prompt**
   - o **Question**: Write a pseudocode snippet for a **QCCobot** that performs a vision check on a part, and if a defect is found, sends a "REWORK_NEEDED" message to a `RepairAgent`.

Answer Key (Suggested):

1. **Industry 4.0**: A shift to fully **connected**, **data-driven** factories where **MAS** enable distributed decision-making and real-time coordination.
2. **Cobot Roles**:
   - o **Assembly Cobot**: Installs screws or welds components.
   - o **QC Cobot**: Scans products for defects (e.g., using camera-based inspections).
3. **Workflow Optimization**:
   - o **Centralized Scheduling**: A single scheduler decides all allocations (simple to manage but can become a bottleneck).
   - o **Distributed**: Cobots negotiate or bid for tasks (more scalable, reduces single points of failure).
4. **Force-Limiting**: Cobots detect and **limit** force or torque exerted, stopping quickly if they collide with a human to prevent injuries.
5. **Predictive Maintenance**: Agents collect sensor data (e.g., vibration, temperature) and **ML models** predict failures. **Early alerts** help schedule maintenance before breakdowns occur, minimizing downtime.
6. **Case Study Improvements**:
   - o **Increased Throughput** (+15%), **Reduced Defect Rate** (-28% relative decrease).
7. **QC Cobot Pseudocode**:

```python
python

class QCCobot:
    def vision_check(self, part):
        defect_detected = analyze_image(part.image)
        if defect_detected:
            message = {
                "sender": self.agent_id,
                "receiver": "RepairAgent",
                "content_type": "REWORK_NEEDED",
                "payload": {"part_id": part.id}
            }
            self.send_message(message)
```

Smart manufacturing merges **collaborative robots**, **intelligent systems**, and **real-time data** to create highly **adaptive** and **efficient** production lines. **MAS** principles allow cobots to **specialize**, share tasks, maintain safe interactions with humans, and optimize workflows via effective scheduling and resource management. Predictive maintenance and continuous monitoring further reduce downtime, enhancing profitability and agility.

By following the **guidelines** and **examples** in this chapter, you can design systems where multiple cobots work **safely** and **productively**, addressing a wide variety of manufacturing tasks. The **case study** in automotive assembly line optimization demonstrates tangible benefits, including **throughput** improvement, **defect** reduction, and better **worker conditions**—all hallmarks of a successful **Industry 4.0** transformation.

Chapter 12: AI-Driven Customer Service Systems

In the digital era, **customer service** is often the **first point of contact** that shapes a customer's perception of a brand. **AI-driven** approaches, especially through **multi-agent systems (MAS)**, have revolutionized how companies handle **inquiries**, **transactions**, and **personalized recommendations**. This chapter provides an **overview** of AI's role in customer service, explores how to **design and integrate** virtual assistant agents with **DeepSeek R1**, covers **personalization** strategies, discusses **scalability**, and showcases a **case study** of building a multi-agent support platform for an e-commerce business.

---

1. Overview of AI in Customer Service

1.1. Benefits and Challenges

AI-driven customer service offers transformative benefits:

1. **24/7 Availability**
   - Virtual assistants and chatbots provide **always-on** support, handling queries even outside business hours.
2. **Cost Efficiency**
   - Automation reduces the load on human agents, cutting operational expenses.
3. **Scalability**
   - AI agents can handle **thousands** of concurrent inquiries without significant degradation in service quality.
4. **Personalized Experiences**
   - Machine learning models can tailor responses or suggestions based on user profiles.

However, there are also challenges:

- **Complex Queries**: AI systems may struggle with unusual or ambiguous questions.

- **Maintaining Empathy**: Emotional intelligence and nuanced understanding of context remain difficult for AI.
- **Security and Privacy**: Dealing with sensitive customer data demands robust encryption and compliance (e.g., GDPR).
- **Integration**: Seamless collaboration between AI agents, human agents, and backend systems can be non-trivial.

1.2. Role of MAS in Enhancing Customer Experience

Multi-agent systems significantly enhance **customer experience** in the following ways:

1. **Distributed Expertise**: Different agents specialize in tasks like billing, tech support, or order tracking, routing customers to the most relevant resource.
2. **Parallel Processing**: Multiple agents handle simultaneous user requests, ensuring minimal wait times.
3. **Collaborative Problem-Solving**: Agents share context and data, enabling quick escalation or transfer when needed.
4. **Adaptive Learning**: Agents can learn from interactions, improving their conversation flows or recommended solutions over time.

2. Designing Virtual Assistant Agents

2.1. Defining Agent Roles: Inquiry Handling, Transaction Processing, Personalized Recommendations

To implement a **virtual assistant**, you can break down its functionalities into **agent roles**:

1. **Inquiry Handling Agent**
   - Addresses **frequently asked questions** (FAQs), providing straightforward or knowledge-base-based answers.
   - Escalates complex queries to specialized or human agents if necessary.
2. **Transaction Processing Agent**
   - Securely handles **orders**, **refunds**, or **bill payments**.
   - Integrates with payment gateways or inventory systems for real-time transactions.

3. **Recommendation Agent**
   - o Analyzes user preferences, purchase history, and browsing patterns to suggest **relevant products** or content.
   - o Helps drive **upselling** or cross-selling in e-commerce.

Table: Common Virtual Assistant Agent Types and Responsibilities

Agent Type	Key Functions	Typical Integrations
Inquiry Handling Agent	Answer FAQs, escalate complex cases	Knowledge base, ticketing system
Transaction Processing Agent	Payment handling, order creation, refunds processing	Payment gateways, CRM
Recommendation Agent	Suggest products/content, personalize interactions	Recommender systems, user profile database

3. Implementing Natural Language Processing (NLP)

3.1. Integrating NLP with DeepSeek R1

DeepSeek R1 can be extended with **NLP** capabilities:

1. **Language Understanding Modules**
   - o Convert **unstructured user text** into structured intent and entity data.
   - o Tools/libraries: **spaCy**, **NLTK**, **Hugging Face Transformers** for advanced language models (e.g., BERT, GPT).
2. **API Integration**
   - o Use DeepSeek R1's **AgentManager** or **Messaging Layer** to funnel text queries into NLP pipelines.
   - o Parse user inputs before routing them to appropriate agents.

Example (Pseudocode):

```python
# nlp_integration.py
from deepseek_r1_sdk import AgentBase
from some_nlp_lib import parse_user_message
```

```
class InquiryHandlingAgent(AgentBase):
    def handle_message(self, message):
        user_input = message["payload"]["text"]
        intent, entities = parse_user_message(user_input)
        # Based on intent, respond or escalate

        if intent == "billing_question":
            self.respond_billing(entities)
        elif intent == "product_inquiry":
            self.respond_product_info(entities)
        else:
            self.escalate_to_human()
```

- **Explanation**:
  - o The agent uses an NLP library to extract **intent** and **entities** from user text.
  - o Logic flows accordingly: respond to "billing_question," or provide "product_inquiry" details.

3.2. Enhancing Agent Communication Capabilities

Once NLP is integrated:

1. **Context Maintenance**
   - o Agents store conversation context (e.g., user's previous queries) to provide **coherent, continuous** assistance.
2. **Context Switching**
   - o If a user shifts topics mid-conversation, the system gracefully adapts without confusion.
3. **Knowledge Graph**
   - o Linking recognized entities (e.g., product names, account IDs) to internal data for richer responses.

4. Personalization and User Profiling

4.1. Building and Utilizing Customer Profiles

Personalization greatly enhances user satisfaction. Key steps:

1. **Data Collection**

- Gather user data: purchase history, browsing patterns, demographic info, feedback logs.
- Compliance with privacy regulations (e.g., GDPR) is crucial.
2. **Profile Construction**
   - Create or update a **user profile** each time a user interacts.
   - Track preferences (e.g., favorite categories, loyalty status, complaint history).
3. **Agent Access**
   - Agents retrieve profile data to tailor responses or recommendations.
   - E.g., a returning user sees custom suggestions based on past orders or inquiries.

4.2. Context-Aware Interactions

Context refers to the **situational** or **historical** details surrounding a user's session:

1. **Session Context**
   - If the user asked about a delayed shipment earlier, subsequent queries about shipping times might not need repeated details.
2. **Omni-channel Consistency**
   - Users switching from chat to phone or email find the conversation picks up seamlessly, because the same context is shared across agents.
3. **Adaptive Recommendations**
   - Agents update suggestions if the user's behavior changes mid-session (e.g., toggling from men's clothing to electronics).

5. Scalability and Load Management

5.1. Handling High Volumes of Customer Interactions

When user traffic spikes (e.g., during sales or promotions), **scalability** is vital:

1. **Agent Clustering**

- o Deploy multiple instances of virtual assistant agents, each handling a subset of incoming requests.
- o A **load balancer** routes new interactions to the least busy agent instance.

2. **Auto-scaling**
   - o If certain agents (like billing queries) experience high load, the system spins up additional copies of that agent type.

3. **Caching**
   - o Frequently accessed data (e.g., product info) is cached to reduce database queries, improving response times.

5.2. Ensuring Consistent Service Quality

Even as load increases:

1. **Performance Monitoring**
   - o Track **response times, throughput, error rates**.
   - o If average response time grows, add agent capacity or optimize code.

2. **Fallback Strategies**
   - o In worst-case scenarios, fallback to minimal-service chat flow or quick FAQ responses, and escalate complex cases to humans.

3. **Prioritization**
   - o High-value customers or urgent issues (e.g., payment failure) jump to the front of the queue.
   - o MAS-based scheduling ensures critical tasks remain prompt.

6. Case Study: Building a Multi-agent Customer Support Platform for an E-commerce Business

6.1. Problem Statement

An e-commerce retailer faces **thousands** of daily customer inquiries about products, deliveries, returns, and technical questions. Relying solely on human agents becomes **expensive** and leads to **long wait times**.

6.2. MAS-Driven Solution

1. **Agent Roles**
   o **Inquiry Handling**: Basic FAQs, returns procedures, product availability.
   o **Order Processing**: Secure checkout, refunds, shipping status.
   o **Recommendation Agent**: Suggesting relevant products based on purchase or browsing history.
2. **NLP Integration**
   o The platform uses a **natural language model** to parse user queries, identify key topics, and route them to the correct agent.
3. **Personalization**
   o A **user profile** system ties into each interaction, enabling personalized greetings or tailor-made product suggestions.
4. **Scalability & Load Balancing**
   o Agents scale horizontally on cloud infrastructure. During peak sales, additional agent instances handle the surge in queries.

6.3. Results

- **Reduced Wait Times**: Average response time dropped from **2 minutes** to under **20 seconds**.
- **Cost Savings**: 40% fewer escalations to human staff.
- **Improved User Satisfaction**: Customer feedback indicated higher overall approval, citing quick, relevant responses.

Table: Key Performance Metrics (Before vs. After MAS Implementation)

Metric	Before MAS	After MAS	Improvement
Avg. Response Time	2 min	20 sec	-83.3%
Human Escalation Rate	60% of queries	20% of queries	-66.7%
Customer Satisfaction (CSAT)	75%	88%	+13 percentage points

7. End-of-Chapter Projects

Project 12: Creating a Virtual Customer Assistant

Objective: Develop a **simple multi-agent** customer service system capable of handling basic inquiries, processing transactions, and recommending items using DeepSeek R1.

Outline

1. **Agent Setup**
   o **InquiryAgent**: Fields FAQs, escalates complex queries.
   o **PaymentAgent**: Manages orders, billing, refunds.
   o **RecommendationAgent**: Generates product suggestions based on user profile data.
2. **NLP Integration**
   o Use an NLP library or mock parser to identify user intents.
   o Route user input to the correct agent via **DeepSeek R1** messaging.
3. **Personalization**
   o Implement a minimal user profile structure.
   o Display custom recommendations or greetings if the user is recognized.
4. **Scalability Simulation**
   o Simulate multiple concurrent user sessions, verifying performance and agent load distribution.

Example Code (Pseudocode)

python

```python
# project_customer_assistant.py
from deepseek_r1_sdk import AgentManager, AgentBase

class InquiryAgent(AgentBase):
    def handle_message(self, message):
        user_intent = message["payload"]["intent"]
        if user_intent == "faq":
            self.respond_faq()
        else:
            self.escalate_to_human_agent()

    def respond_faq(self):
        print("Here are some helpful FAQs...")

class PaymentAgent(AgentBase):
    def handle_message(self, message):
        if message["payload"]["action"] == "process_payment":
            self.process_payment(message["payload"])
        else:
```

```
                print("Unsupported payment action.")

    def process_payment(self, details):
        # Validate payment method, total cost, etc.
        print(f"Processing payment for order
{details['order_id']}")

class RecommendationAgent(AgentBase):
    def handle_message(self, message):
        if message["payload"]["intent"] == "recommend":
            user_profile =
self.load_user_profile(message["sender"])
            self.suggest_products(user_profile)

    def suggest_products(self, profile):
        # Simple logic or ML-based approach
        print("Suggesting items based on user profile
preferences...")

if __name__ == "__main__":
    manager = AgentManager()
    inq_agent = InquiryAgent(agent_id="InquiryAgent")
    pay_agent = PaymentAgent(agent_id="PaymentAgent")
    rec_agent = RecommendationAgent(agent_id="RecAgent")

    manager.register_agent(inq_agent)
    manager.register_agent(pay_agent)
    manager.register_agent(rec_agent)

    # Simulate user message
    test_message = {
        "sender": "User123",
        "payload": {
            "intent": "recommend"
        }
    }
    rec_agent.handle_message(test_message)
```

Goal: Illustrate a basic **multi-agent** customer service architecture integrating inquiry, payment, and recommendation functionalities.

8. Quizzes and Self-Assessments

Quiz 12: AI in Customer Service

1. **Overview**

    ○ **Question**: What are two major challenges in implementing an AI-driven customer service system?

2. **Virtual Assistant Agents**
    ○ **Question**: How does a **Transaction Processing Agent** differ from an **Inquiry Handling Agent** in terms of required integrations and functions?

3. **NLP**
    ○ **Question**: Describe one benefit of **integrating NLP** with DeepSeek R1's agents, especially regarding user queries.

4. **Personalization**
    ○ **Question**: Why is **context-awareness** crucial for delivering a personalized customer experience?

5. **Scalability**
    ○ **Question**: Name one technique to manage high volumes of customer interactions without sacrificing response quality or speed.

6. **Case Study**
    ○ **Question**: From the e-commerce platform example, mention one key metric that improved significantly after deploying the MAS-driven solution.

7. **Short Coding Prompt**
    ○ **Question**: Write a pseudocode snippet where an **InquiryAgent** detects a "shipping_delay" intent from user input and escalates it to a specialized **LogisticsAgent**.

Answer Key (Suggested):

1. **Challenges**: Handling **complex or ambiguous** queries, ensuring **security/privacy** for sensitive user data.

2. **Agent Roles**:
    ○ **Transaction Processing** requires integration with payment gateways, while **Inquiry Handling** primarily focuses on knowledge bases or FAQ data.

3. **NLP Integration Benefit**: Agents can **interpret** natural language user input, identify **intents** or **entities**, and route the request to the correct module automatically.

4. **Context-Awareness**: Prevents users from repeatedly providing the same info, delivering a **continuous conversation** flow and tailored responses.

5. **Scalability Technique**: Auto-scaling agent instances during peak loads, or employing a **load balancer** to distribute traffic.

6. **Metric Improvement**: Average response time dropped from **2 minutes** to **20 seconds**, drastically boosting user satisfaction.
7. **Pseudocode**:

```python
python

if intent == "shipping_delay":
    message = {
        "sender": self.agent_id,
        "receiver": "LogisticsAgent",
        "content_type": "ESCALATION",
        "payload": {"user_query": user_input}
    }
    self.send_message(message)
else:
    self.handle_general_inquiry(user_input)
```

AI-driven customer service systems **transform** how businesses handle **inquiries**, **transactions**, and **recommendations** by providing **24/7** availability, **personalized** interactions, and **fast** response times. **MAS** architectures distribute workloads among specialized agents, ensuring **scalability** and **collaboration**. By integrating **NLP** to parse user queries, harnessing **user profiles** for personalization, and managing high volumes effectively, organizations can **significantly** enhance customer satisfaction. The **case study** on e-commerce demonstrates tangible benefits—drastically reduced response times, cost savings via reduced human escalations, and an improved overall experience.

Chapter 13: Smart Grids and Energy Management Systems

Smart Grids represent the next-generation power infrastructure, integrating **information technology** and **multi-agent systems (MAS)** to optimize energy distribution, consumption, and reliability. By coordinating **renewable energy sources**, **storage solutions**, and **real-time monitoring**, smart grids address modern energy challenges such as fluctuating demand, renewable variability, and grid stability. In this chapter, we explore the **components** and **architecture** of smart grids, design **energy management agents**, implement **distributed energy resource (DER) management**, discuss **real-time monitoring**, and review strategies for **grid stability**. We conclude with a **case study** and **projects** for practical experience, followed by a **quiz** for self-assessment.

---

1. Introduction to Smart Grids

1.1. Components and Architecture

A **smart grid** is a **digitally enhanced** power grid that leverages **two-way communication**, **monitoring**, and **automation** technologies. Key components include:

1. **Power Generation**
   - Conventional sources (coal, gas, nuclear) and **renewables** (solar, wind, hydro).
2. **Transmission and Distribution**
   - High-voltage lines transport electricity over long distances; distribution networks deliver power to end users.
3. **Consumers / Prosumer Nodes**
   - Households, industries, or businesses can be both consumers and producers (e.g., rooftop solar).
4. **Communication Infrastructure**
   - Smart meters, sensors, and networked control systems enabling real-time data exchange.
5. **Control Centers / Cloud Services**

     ○   Central or distributed intelligence analyzing data, optimizing grid operation, and coordinating agents.

Architecture:

```lua
    +-----------------------+
    |      Power Sources    |
    |   (Conventional, RE)  |
    +-----------+-----------+
                |
                v
    +-----------+-----------+         +-----------------------
  -+
    | Transmission Network  |<----->  | Real-time Data &
Control|
    +-----------+-----------+         |      (Control Center, AI)
  |
                |
                v
    +-----------+-----------+
    | Distribution Network  |
    +-----------+-----------+
                |
            (Smart Meters, Sensors)
                |
                v
    +-----------+-----------+
    |  Consumers / Prosumers |
    +-----------------------+
```

1.2. Importance of MAS in Energy Management

Multi-agent systems (MAS) excel in **distributed control** and **decision-making**, key traits for:

1. **Scalability**: Agents handle local grids, coordinating with neighboring grids when necessary.
2. **Flexibility**: Changing demand, generation patterns, or storage capacities are managed by adaptive agent behaviors.
3. **Robustness**: If one agent fails, others can compensate, ensuring continued grid functionality.
4. **Local Optimization**: Agents optimize consumption, generation, or storage within their jurisdiction, improving overall efficiency and reliability.

2. Designing Energy Management Agents

2.1. Roles: Energy Distribution, Consumption Monitoring, Demand Forecasting

Energy management agents typically specialize in the following roles:

1. **Distribution Agent**
   - **Manages** power flows across transmission/distribution lines.
   - **Allocates** or throttles power to different regions, preventing overloads.
2. **Consumption Monitoring Agent**
   - Collects **real-time usage** data (e.g., from smart meters).
   - Identifies patterns (peak/off-peak hours) and alerts Distribution Agents to supply more or less power.
3. **Demand Forecasting Agent**
   - Uses **historical consumption** and external data (weather, holidays, events) to **predict** future load.
   - Informs generation or distribution strategies to ensure adequate supply.

Table: Common Energy Management Agents

Agent Type	Primary Function	Data Inputs	Outputs/Decisions
Distribution Agent	Balance loads, route power across networks	Line capacity, real-time usage, generator status	Power dispatch schedules, load shedding instructions
Consumption Monitoring Agent	Track end-user or industrial consumption patterns	Smart meter readings, local sensor data	Usage reports, load alerts
Demand Forecasting Agent	Predict future energy requirements	Historical usage, weather data,	Demand curves, recommended generation or storage actions

Agent Type	Primary Function	Data Inputs	Outputs/Decisions
		event calendars	

3. Implementing Distributed Energy Resources (DER) Management

3.1. Coordinating Renewable Energy Sources

Modern grids often incorporate **renewable energy** (solar, wind, hydro) distributed across multiple sites. MAS approaches can:

1. **Aggregate** small-scale producers (e.g., solar rooftops) into a virtual power plant.
2. **Balance** intermittent sources (wind/solar vary with weather conditions) by adjusting loads or tapping storage.
3. **Negotiate** contracts or price signals: Agents respond to dynamic tariffs, encouraging generation or consumption when beneficial.

3.2. Optimizing Energy Storage and Distribution

Energy storage (batteries, pumped hydro) plays a crucial role in balancing supply and demand:

1. **Charge/Discharge Logic**
   o **Storage Agents** decide when to charge (e.g., during off-peak or high renewable output) vs. discharge (peak demand times).
2. **Location-aware Optimization**
   o Minimizes line losses by using localized storage solutions near high-demand areas.
3. **Market Mechanisms**
   o Agents trade surplus energy in local or regional markets, adjusting prices in near real-time.

Code Example (Pseudocode):

```
python
```

```python
# DER_management.py
from deepseek_r1_sdk import AgentBase

class SolarFarmAgent(AgentBase):
    def __init__(self, agent_id):
        super().__init__(agent_id)
        self.current_generation = 0

    def update_generation(self, solar_irradiance):
        self.current_generation = solar_irradiance * 100  # simplistic model
        self.broadcast_generation()

    def broadcast_generation(self):
        message = {
            "sender": self.agent_id,
            "content_type": "GENERATION_UPDATE",
            "payload": {"power": self.current_generation}
        }
        self.send_message(message)
```

- **Explanation**: A simple agent computing generation from a solar irradiance input. In a real system, the agent would coordinate with storage or distribution agents to handle excess power.

---

4. Real-time Monitoring and Control

4.1. Agent-Based Monitoring Systems

Smart grids rely on comprehensive **monitoring** to identify faults or deviations:

1. **Data Collection**
   - Sensors measure **voltage**, **frequency**, **temperature** at critical points.
   - Agents compile data for local or global analysis.
2. **Diagnostic Agents**
   - Use **machine learning** or **rule-based** methods to detect anomalies (e.g., line overload, voltage sag).
   - Alert operators or automatically trigger corrective actions.

4.2. Implementing Real-time Control Mechanisms

Real-time control ensures the grid maintains **stable** operation:

1. **Demand Response**
   o   Agents adjust large customers' loads when supply is limited (e.g., briefly turning off HVAC systems).
2. **Generation Ramping**
   o   Increase or decrease power plants' output to match predicted demand curves.
3. **Automated Switching**
   o   Reconfigure distribution lines to isolate faults and reroute power.

MAS Approach:

- Each agent has local control logic but also **communicates** with neighboring agents for global optimization.

5. Ensuring Grid Stability and Reliability

5.1. Balancing Supply and Demand

A stable grid depends on **continuous** balance between supply (generation) and demand (consumption):

1. **Frequency Regulation**
   o   If demand > supply, frequency drops; if supply > demand, frequency rises. Agents coordinate generators or loads to keep frequency near nominal (50 or 60 Hz).
2. **Load Shedding**
   o   In emergencies, certain loads are **shed** (disconnected) to prevent widespread blackouts. MAS decide which segments are least critical, preserving essential services.

5.2. Implementing Failover and Recovery Strategies

Robust **failover** ensures the grid remains operational even under component failures:

1. **Redundant Agents**

- Multiple distribution or substation agents can handle the same tasks; if one agent fails, another takes over.
2. **Island Mode**
   - If a region is **isolated** from the main grid, local generation and storage agents form a **microgrid** to keep local supply stable.
3. **Automated Restoration**
   - Fault-detection agents quickly **locate** line failures, triggering reconfiguration or repair teams.

6. Case Study: Managing a Microgrid with DeepSeek R1-Powered Agents

6.1. Scenario

A rural community installs a **microgrid** with **solar panels**, **battery storage**, and **diesel backup**. The microgrid must operate independently or connect to the main utility grid.

6.2. Agent Architecture

1. **SolarAgent**: Measures irradiance, forecasts daily generation.
2. **BatteryAgent**: Decides charging/discharging strategy.
3. **LoadAgent**: Aggregates local household demands.
4. **GridAgent**: Coordinates with the main grid, deciding when to import or export power.

6.3. MAS Coordination

- **BatteryAgent** receives generation updates from SolarAgent and consumption updates from LoadAgent, adjusting battery charge accordingly.
- **GridAgent** requests excess power from SolarAgent or BatteryAgent if the main grid experiences a shortfall.
- **Demand Response**: If total consumption is too high, LoadAgent orchestrates demand response or dynamic pricing signals.

6.4. Results

- **Improved Autonomy**: The microgrid meets 80% of local demand from solar + storage, reducing main-grid dependence.
- **Reduced Diesel Use**: Diesel backup usage dropped by 50%.
- **Enhanced Reliability**: Outages in the main grid cause minimal disruption, as the microgrid's MAS quickly reconfigures to island mode.

Table: Measured Improvements

Metric	Before (No MAS)	After (MAS)	Gain
Diesel Backup Usage	40 hours/month	20 hours/month	-50% usage
Renewable Energy Penetration	60%	80%	+20 percentage points
Outage Duration (per event)	3 hours	0.5 hours	-83% shorter outages

7. End-of-Chapter Projects

Project 13: Developing an Energy Management System

Objective: Implement a **simplified** MAS-based energy management system using **DeepSeek R1**, featuring **renewable** generation, **battery storage**, and **demand** agents.

Outline

1. **Agent Definition**
   - **SolarAgent**: Simulate varying generation based on a random "solar irradiance" input.
   - **BatteryAgent**: Decide when to charge/discharge.
   - **LoadAgent**: Represent consumption patterns (peak/off-peak).
2. **Real-time Coordination**
   - Agents communicate generation, demand, and battery state changes every "time step."

o BatteryAgent ensures grid balance by matching generation with consumption, drawing from storage as needed.

3. **Monitoring**
   o Log each agent's state (power in/out).
   o Alert if supply-demand mismatch exceeds a threshold.

Sample Code (Pseudocode)

python

```python
# energy_management_project.py
import random
from deepseek_r1_sdk import AgentBase, AgentManager

class SolarAgent(AgentBase):
    def __init__(self, agent_id):
        super().__init__(agent_id)
        self.current_power = 0

    def generate_power(self):
        # Simple random irradiance model
        irradiance = random.uniform(0.3, 1.0)
        self.current_power = irradiance * 100   # in kW
        self.broadcast_generation()

    def broadcast_generation(self):
        msg = {
            "sender": self.agent_id,
            "content_type": "SOLAR_GEN",
            "payload": {"power": self.current_power}
        }
        self.send_message(msg)

class BatteryAgent(AgentBase):
    def __init__(self, agent_id):
        super().__init__(agent_id)
        self.capacity = 500   # kWh
        self.soc = 250        # state of charge

    def on_message(self, msg):
        if msg["content_type"] == "SOLAR_GEN":
            solar_power = msg["payload"]["power"]
            self.handle_power_in(solar_power)

        elif msg["content_type"] == "LOAD_DEMAND":
            load_power = msg["payload"]["power"]
            self.handle_demand(load_power)

    def handle_power_in(self, power_in):
```

```python
        # Charge if not full
        available_capacity = self.capacity - self.soc
        if power_in > available_capacity:
            power_in -= available_capacity
            self.soc = self.capacity
            print(f"{self.agent_id}: Battery full, leftover
power = {power_in} kW exported to grid.")
        else:
            self.soc += power_in
            power_in = 0
            print(f"{self.agent_id}: Charged battery to
{self.soc} / {self.capacity} kWh.")

    def handle_demand(self, load_power):
        if self.soc >= load_power:
            self.soc -= load_power
            print(f"{self.agent_id}: Covered load
{load_power} kW from battery.")
        else:
            shortfall = load_power - self.soc
            self.soc = 0
            print(f"{self.agent_id}: Battery depleted.
{shortfall} kW not covered, request from main grid.")

class LoadAgent(AgentBase):
    def generate_demand(self):
        # Random load demand (kW)
        demand_power = random.uniform(10, 50)
        msg = {
            "sender": self.agent_id,
            "content_type": "LOAD_DEMAND",
            "payload": {"power": demand_power}
        }
        self.send_message(msg)

if __name__ == "__main__":
    manager = AgentManager()
    solar = SolarAgent("SolarAgent1")
    battery = BatteryAgent("BatteryAgent1")
    load = LoadAgent("LoadAgent1")

    manager.register_agent(solar)
    manager.register_agent(battery)
    manager.register_agent(load)

    # Simulate time steps
    for t in range(10):
        solar.generate_power()
        load.generate_demand()
```

Goal: Show how **solar** generation, a **battery** agent, and a **load** agent can coordinate in a simple energy management environment, highlighting **charging**, **discharging**, and **shortfalls**.

---

8. Quizzes and Self-Assessments

Quiz 13: Smart Grids and Energy Management

1. **Introduction**
   - **Question**: Name two essential components of a **smart grid** and briefly describe their roles.
2. **Energy Management Agents**
   - **Question**: What are the main functions of a **Demand Forecasting Agent**, and how does it support the grid?
3. **DER Management**
   - **Question**: Why is **coordinating** renewable energy sources with energy storage critical for modern grids?
4. **Real-time Monitoring**
   - **Question**: Provide one example of how agent-based monitoring helps detect or respond to grid anomalies.
5. **Grid Stability**
   - **Question**: Explain how **load shedding** prevents large-scale blackouts.
6. **Case Study**
   - **Question**: In the microgrid scenario, mention one key advantage gained by MAS-based coordination.
7. **Short Coding Prompt**
   - **Question**: Write pseudocode for an **AlarmAgent** that listens for "VOLTAGE_DROP" messages and triggers a fallback strategy if voltage remains too low for more than 3 consecutive checks.

Answer Key (Suggested):

1. **Smart Grid Components**:
   - **Communication Infrastructure** (smart meters, sensors) for real-time data.
   - **Control Centers** that orchestrate or analyze data to maintain efficient, stable operation.

2. **Demand Forecasting Agent**:
   - Predicts future usage patterns, enabling the grid to **preemptively** ramp up/down generation or storage.
3. **DER Coordination**:
   - Renewables can be **intermittent**. Coordinating with storage ensures the grid continues to meet demand even if wind or sun fluctuates.
4. **Agent-Based Monitoring**:
   - A **Diagnostic Agent** that sees an unusual voltage spike can isolate lines or alert operators, preventing equipment damage.
5. **Load Shedding**:
   - Temporarily **disconnects** certain loads so that total consumption does not exceed supply, preventing grid collapse.
6. **Case Study Benefit**:
   - **Reduced** diesel backup usage and increased self-sufficiency through local solar + battery synergy.
7. **Pseudocode**:

```python
class AlarmAgent(AgentBase):
    def __init__(self):
        super().__init__()
        self.low_voltage_count = 0

    def on_message(self, msg):
        if msg["content_type"] == "VOLTAGE_DROP":
            self.low_voltage_count += 1
            if self.low_voltage_count > 3:
                self.trigger_fallback()
        else:
            self.low_voltage_count = 0

    def trigger_fallback(self):
        print("Voltage remains too low. Activating
fallback strategy.")
        # e.g., request load shedding, dispatch
battery, or isolate subnetwork
```

Smart grids harness **multi-agent systems** to **optimize** power distribution, **monitor** real-time conditions, and **integrate** renewable resources effectively. **Energy management agents** handle tasks like distribution, consumption monitoring, and demand forecasting, while **DER management** ensures balanced renewable generation and storage. Real-time **monitoring** and **control** keep the grid stable, with fallback mechanisms ready if failures occur. The **microgrid** case study highlights how **DeepSeek R1-powered** agents manage a localized energy network, showcasing the tangible benefits of MAS—**reduced** diesel usage, enhanced reliability, and improved operational autonomy. Through the provided **end-of-chapter project**, you can experiment with building a basic **energy management** system, reinforcing the concepts of **distributed** intelligence in the energy sector.

Chapter 14: Scalability and Performance Optimization in MAS

Scalability and **performance** are crucial in **multi-agent systems (MAS)** where the number of agents, the volume of data, and the complexity of interactions can grow significantly. Ensuring that the system can handle increasing load without compromising efficiency or responsiveness is a core challenge. In this chapter, we delve into **scalability challenges**, explore **architecture design** choices, discuss ways to **optimize communication overhead**, outline **performance tuning** techniques, and address **load testing** strategies. A **case study** on scaling a financial trading MAS illustrates real-world considerations, and we conclude with projects and a quiz to reinforce the concepts.

1. Scalability Challenges in MAS

1.1. Managing Large Numbers of Agents

When a MAS grows to include **hundreds** or **thousands** of agents, challenges emerge:

1. **Coordination Overhead**
   - Increased messaging between agents can lead to **network congestion** or higher latency.
   - Identifying the right balance between local autonomy and centralized decision-making becomes harder.
2. **Computational Load**
   - Each agent may run **logic** (reasoning, learning, decision-making) that can strain CPU or memory resources.
   - Synchronous updates or large-scale simulations consume significant computing power.
3. **Agent Lifecycle Management**
   - Dynamically **adding** or **removing** agents requires robust lifecycle controls—agents must register and deregister cleanly.
   - Resource leaks (unreleased memory, stale connections) become major pitfalls.

1.2. Ensuring Efficient Resource Utilization

MAS must optimize **CPU**, **memory**, and **network** usage:

1. **Dynamic Allocation**
   - Provision more compute or scale back as agent workload fluctuates.
   - Deploy additional agent instances in a **cloud-based** environment if a specific agent type becomes a bottleneck.
2. **Prioritizing Critical Agents**
   - Some agents (e.g., safety-critical or real-time) get higher priority threads or dedicated resources to maintain responsiveness.
3. **Monitoring Tools**
   - Agents track their own **resource consumption**, reporting anomalies so the system can adapt or alert operators.

2. Scalable Architecture Design

2.1. Distributed vs. Centralized Architectures

1. **Centralized**
   - A **master node** or manager agent coordinates tasks or resources.
   - **Advantages**: Simpler logic, single point for system overview.
   - **Disadvantages**: Bottleneck risk, single point of failure, limited scalability.
2. **Distributed**
   - Agents **autonomously** coordinate, using protocols (e.g., contract net, negotiation).
   - **Advantages**: High scalability, no single point of failure.
   - **Disadvantages**: Increased complexity of communication protocols, potential for conflicts or duplication.

Table: Centralized vs. Distributed Architectures

Aspect	Centralized Architecture	Distributed Architecture
Single Point of Control	Yes, one master node	No, decisions spread across multiple agents
Scalability	Limited by master node's capacity	Typically more scalable
Failure Impact	Master node failure can halt system	Redundancy among agents mitigates this risk
Communication Complexity	Lower (simple requests to master)	Higher (peer-to-peer or multi-party)

2.2. Microservices and Modular Design

MAS solutions can adopt **microservices** principles:

1. **Service Separation**
   o Each agent or agent group runs as an independent service (e.g., Docker containers).
   o Scales horizontally by adding more container instances for high-demand agents.
2. **API Contracts**
   o Agents communicate via well-defined endpoints or messaging interfaces, ensuring low coupling.
   o Facilitates incremental updates or replacements of specific agent services without disrupting the entire system.
3. **Monitoring and Logging**
   o Each microservice logs and reports metrics individually; centralized dashboards compile performance data.

Example:

```
text

+---------------------+                    +----------------------
-+
| Agent-based Service: |   msgs/rpc |   Agent-based Service:
|
|    TradingAgentPool  |----------->|   RiskAssessmentPool
|
+---------------------+                    +----------------------
-+
     ^              |                              ^
```

```
   |  logs   | metrics               |  logs
   |         v                        |
   +---------------+                  +--------------+
   | Monitoring &  |                  | Data Storage |
   |  Dashboard    |                  +--------------+
   +---------------+
```

- **Explanation**: TradingAgentPool and RiskAssessmentPool run independently, scaled as needed. They exchange data via a message bus or RPC calls, logging metrics to a monitoring solution.

3. Optimizing Communication Overheads

3.1. Efficient Messaging Protocols

As agent numbers grow, **messaging** can dominate overhead:

1. **Publish/Subscribe**
   - Agents **subscribe** to relevant topics, avoiding direct peer-to-peer chatter for each message.
   - Reduces **unnecessary** message duplication if multiple agents need the same data.
2. **Message Batching**
   - Combine multiple small messages into **larger** but fewer transmissions, lowering overhead.
   - Carefully handle latency implications to ensure timely agent reactions.
3. **Compression and Serialization**
   - Use lightweight or **binary** formats (e.g., Protocol Buffers, Cap'n Proto) for messages, cutting bandwidth usage.

3.2. Reducing Latency and Bandwidth Usage

1. **Local Caching**
   - Agents can cache repeated data (like static environment info or system states) for quick lookups.
2. **Adaptive Update Rates**
   - Agents only broadcast changes if the difference is above a threshold or occurs after certain intervals (e.g., event-triggered rather than continuous streaming).

3. **Network Topology**
    o Agents physically or logically close can communicate via **LAN** or local brokers, minimizing wide-area network delays.

Code Example (Pseudocode):

```python
# messaging_optimization.py
from deepseek_r1_sdk import AgentBase

class PubSubAgent(AgentBase):
    def on_message(self, message):
        # If the content hasn't changed significantly, ignore
further updates
        if self.is_redundant_update(message):
            return
        else:
            self.process_message(message)

    def is_redundant_update(self, msg):
        # Check if the new value differs from old by a
threshold
        # e.g. only process if difference > 2% or time since
last update > 10s
        pass
```

- **Explanation**: An example agent applying a threshold-based approach to manage data updates.

4. Performance Tuning Techniques

4.1. Profiling and Benchmarking MAS

Profiling identifies where **time**, **memory**, or **network resources** are heavily used:

1. **Agent-Level Profiling**
    o Each agent logs **CPU** time, **memory** usage, and message processing durations.
    o Tools (e.g., **Python cProfile**, **JVM Flight Recorder**) reveal function-level hotspots.
2. **System-Wide Benchmarking**

o Evaluate MAS throughput: **number of tasks** completed or **messages** processed per second.
o Observe latencies at each **communication** step or agent action.

4.2. Identifying and Mitigating Bottlenecks

Common performance bottlenecks include:

1. **Central Manager Overload**
   o If too many tasks or messages flow through a single manager.
   o **Solution**: Distribute management or shard tasks among multiple managers.
2. **Excessive Synchronous Calls**
   o Agents waiting on blocking calls hamper concurrency.
   o **Solution**: Use asynchronous or event-driven messaging patterns.
3. **Contention for Shared Resources**
   o Data stores or locks cause queueing delays.
   o **Solution**: Partition data, apply concurrency-safe structures or reduce lock granularity.

Example:

```
text

1. Identify -> AgentManager CPU usage 90%, queue backlog
2. Mitigation -> Deploy additional AgentManager instances or
switch to distributed coordinator approach
3. Verify -> Post-optimization, CPU usage ~50%, backlog
cleared
```

5. Load Testing and Stress Testing

5.1. Simulating High-load Scenarios

Load testing subjects the MAS to expected or **peak** loads:

1. **Test Tools**
   o Custom scripts generating **mass agent interactions** or user requests.

- Frameworks like **Locust**, **JMeter** (for HTTP-based systems), or custom concurrency harness for message-based MAS.

2. **Key Metrics**
   - Response times, agent throughput, error rates, memory usage, CPU usage under rising load.

3. **Scenarios**
   - **Spike Tests**: Sudden large load to see if the system auto-scales or collapses.
   - **Soak Tests**: Prolonged normal-high load to reveal memory leaks or slowly accumulating overhead.

5.2. Ensuring System Stability Under Stress

During **stress testing**:

1. **Degradation Handling**
   - If the system exceeds normal capacity, degrade gracefully (e.g., lower-priority tasks queued, best-effort response for non-critical queries).

2. **Auto-recovery**
   - Agents detect failures or performance drops, re-spawning or shifting tasks to healthy nodes.
   - Monitoring triggers alerts, enabling operators to react quickly.

3. **Result Analysis**
   - Compare actual throughput and latency to **SLAs** (service-level agreements).
   - Identify tipping points where performance significantly deteriorates or errors spike.

6. Case Study: Scaling a Multi-agent Financial Trading System

6.1. Initial Setup

A **financial trading** platform uses **TraderAgents** (executing orders), **MarketDataAgents** (streaming price updates), and **RiskAgents** (managing portfolio risks). Initially, the system handles a moderate load of **5,000** orders/day.

6.2. Scalability Challenges

1. **Trade Volume Growth**
   - o Orders ramp up to **50,000/day** during market volatility, saturating the central TraderManager.
2. **Real-time Market Data**
   - o Bursts of price updates cause **messaging** spikes, leading to delayed TraderAgents reacting to stale data.
3. **Risk Bottleneck**
   - o RiskAgents evaluate every trade for margin and limit checks, forming a CPU bottleneck.

6.3. Optimization Steps

1. **Distributed Architecture**
   - o Replaced a single TraderManager with **multiple** manager instances, each handling a subset of TraderAgents.
2. **Efficient Messaging**
   - o Implemented **publish/subscribe** for MarketDataAgents, letting TraderAgents subscribe to only relevant instruments.
   - o Used a **binary** protocol to reduce message size.
3. **Performance Tuning**
   - o Profiled RiskAgents: identified heavy CPU usage in a repeated margin calculation function.
   - o Cached repeated computations and parallelized risk checks across multiple nodes.

6.4. Outcomes

- **Throughput** improved from **5,000** to **60,000** orders/day without saturating CPU.
- **Latency** for trade confirmations dropped from **1s** to **200ms**.
- **System** sustained **peak** loads during major market events with no downtime.

Table: Key Metric Improvements (Before vs. After)

Metric	Before Optimization	After Optimization	Improvement
Max Orders/Day	5,000	60,000	+1100%

Metric	Before Optimization	After Optimization	Improvement
Avg Trade Latency	1 second	200 ms	-80%
System Uptime during Peak	Frequent slowdowns	Zero downtime	Sustained performance

7. End-of-Chapter Projects

Project 14: Optimizing MAS Performance

Objective: Create a **prototype MAS** under **high load**, apply **performance tuning** techniques, and measure **improvements**.

Outline

1. **Baseline System**
   - Implement a simple MAS with multiple agents performing tasks (e.g., data processing or simulated trading).
   - Central manager or aggregator coordinates tasks.
2. **Load Generation**
   - Write a script generating **thousands** of tasks or requests concurrently.
   - Log system metrics (CPU, memory, response times) to gauge baseline performance.
3. **Optimizations**
   - Move from centralized to partially distributed coordination.
   - Introduce **message batching** or publish/subscribe to reduce overhead.
   - Profile the system, fix the biggest bottleneck, and re-measure performance.
4. **Reporting**
   - Graph changes in throughput or latency before/after each optimization step.
   - Summarize lessons learned.

8. Quizzes and Self-Assessments

Quiz 14: Scalability and Optimization

1. **Scalability Challenges**
   o **Question**: Mention one difficulty that arises from managing **large numbers** of agents in a MAS.
2. **Architecture Design**
   o **Question**: How does **distributed** architecture mitigate the risk of a **single point of failure** compared to a **centralized** approach?
3. **Communication Overheads**
   o **Question**: Give an example of how **publish/subscribe** can lower message volume in a MAS with many agents.
4. **Performance Tuning**
   o **Question**: Why is **profiling** crucial before making any performance optimizations?
5. **Load & Stress Testing**
   o **Question**: Define the difference between a **load test** and a **stress test** in the context of MAS.
6. **Case Study**
   o **Question**: In the financial trading system example, what was one main technique used to reduce **message** overhead for market data?
7. **Short Coding Prompt**
   o **Question**: Write pseudocode for a utility function `batch_messages(agent_list, max_batch_size)` that batches outgoing messages from a list of agents if the total message count exceeds `max_batch_size`.

Answer Key (Suggested):

1. **Scalability Challenge**: **Coordination** overhead grows significantly, leading to potential network or CPU saturation as agent count increases.
2. **Distributed Architecture**: By spreading responsibilities among multiple agents, if one agent or node fails, others continue the system's operation, removing the single choke point.
3. **Pub/Sub Example**: Instead of each agent sending updates to all others, they **publish** to a topic. Only agents **subscribed** to that topic receive the data, avoiding duplication.
4. **Importance of Profiling**: It identifies **true** bottlenecks, preventing time wasted optimizing parts of the code that don't significantly impact performance.

5. **Load vs. Stress Test**:
   - o **Load Test**: Involves normal or peak load levels expected in production.
   - o **Stress Test**: Pushes the system beyond normal capacity to see how it degrades or fails.
6. **Case Study**: Implementing **publish/subscribe** with **binary** messages for market data drastically reduced overhead.
7. **Pseudocode**:

```python
def batch_messages(agent_list, max_batch_size):
    batched_messages = []
    for agent in agent_list:
        for msg in agent.outgoing_messages:
            batched_messages.append(msg)
            if len(batched_messages) >= max_batch_size:
                send_batch(batched_messages)
                batched_messages = []
    # Send any leftover messages
    if batched_messages:
        send_batch(batched_messages)
```

Scalability and performance optimization are fundamental for **multi-agent systems** dealing with **increasing load** or **large-scale** deployments. **Distributed architectures**, **microservices**, and **efficient communication** protocols help handle the strain of large agent populations. Profiling and tuning ensure resource usage remains optimal, while **load testing** and **stress testing** validate system resilience under extreme conditions. The **financial trading** case study highlights real-world benefits—significant throughput gains and lower latency once bottlenecks are addressed. By applying these techniques, MAS developers can confidently deploy robust, high-performing solutions.

Chapter 15: Integration with Other AI Technologies

Multi-agent systems (MAS) can achieve far greater functionality and intelligence when combined with **other AI technologies**, such as **Natural Language Processing (NLP)**, **Reinforcement Learning (RL)**, **Knowledge Graphs**, **Computer Vision**, and **Big Data analytics**. By leveraging these complementary technologies, agents in a MAS can engage in natural conversations, learn from interactions, reason with rich knowledge structures, perceive their environment more effectively, and make data-driven decisions in real-time. This chapter explores each of these integration points with **DeepSeek R1**, concluding with a **case study** on predictive maintenance and a set of **projects** and **quizzes** to reinforce the concepts.

---

1. Natural Language Processing (NLP) Integration

1.1. Enhancing Agent Communication with NLP

Natural Language Processing (NLP) enables agents to **understand** and **generate** human language, making interactions more intuitive:

1. **Intent Recognition**
   - Extract user **intent** (e.g., "buy product," "check order status") from text.
   - Helps route messages to the right agent or domain.
2. **Entity Extraction**
   - Identify **key items** (e.g., product IDs, customer names, locations) for further processing.
   - Speeds up workflows by automating data entry or lookups.
3. **Context Maintenance**
   - Maintain conversation history so that follow-up questions do not start from scratch.
   - Manage pronouns, references, or incomplete queries effectively.

MAS Benefit:

- Agents can **parse** natural language instructions from users or other agents, reducing friction in human–machine interactions.
- MAS can funnel requests from an **NLP** input pipeline to specialized agents.

1.2. Implementing Conversational Agents

A **conversational agent** extends NLP integration:

1. **Dialogue Management**
   - Keeps track of the **conversation state**, deciding how to respond based on user queries and system context.
2. **Response Generation**
   - Simple rule-based templates or advanced language models (e.g., GPT-like transformers) craft replies.
3. **Multi-turn Conversations**
   - Agents clarify ambiguous user input, gather additional details, or provide step-by-step guidance.

Code Example (Pseudocode):

```python
# nlp_conversational_agent.py
from deepseek_r1_sdk import AgentBase

class ConversationalAgent(AgentBase):
    def __init__(self, agent_id, nlp_model):
        super().__init__(agent_id)
        self.nlp_model = nlp_model
        self.conversation_history = {}

    def on_message(self, message):
        user_id = message["sender"]
        user_input = message["payload"]["text"]
        intent, entities = self.nlp_model.analyze(user_input)

        response = self.generate_response(user_id, intent, entities)
        self.send_message({
            "sender": self.agent_id,
            "receiver": user_id,
            "content_type": "CHAT_RESPONSE",
            "payload": {"text": response}
        })
```

```
def generate_response(self, user_id, intent, entities):
    # Logic to decide best response using conversation
history
    # Possibly delegating tasks to specialized agents
    return "Here is your requested information..."
```

- **Explanation**:
  - The agent uses an **NLP** pipeline to interpret user input, maintaining conversation context.
  - Complex logic can route tasks to other agents or apply advanced response generation.

2. Reinforcement Learning (RL) in MAS

2.1. Applying RL for Agent Training

In **Reinforcement Learning (RL)**, agents learn through **trial and error**:

1. **Reward Signal**
   - Agents receive **positive** or **negative** feedback based on actions and outcomes (e.g., successful task completion).
2. **Policy Learning**
   - Over time, agents refine their **policy** (mapping states to actions) to maximize cumulative reward.
3. **Exploration vs. Exploitation**
   - Agents must **explore** new actions to discover better strategies while **exploiting** known successful actions.

MAS Impact:

- Multi-agent RL scenarios can emerge when multiple agents simultaneously learn to cooperate or compete, shaping each other's reward environment.

2.2. Implementing Reward-Based Learning Mechanisms

Typical RL pipeline:

1. **State Representation**
   - Agents observe partial or full environment states (e.g., resource levels, positions).
2. **Actions**
   - Discrete or continuous movements, decisions, or communications.
3. **Rewards**
   - Immediate or delayed returns. Could be **shared** among agents for cooperative tasks or individual for competitive tasks.
4. **Algorithmic Approaches**
   - **Q-learning** or **Deep Q Networks (DQN)** for discrete actions; **Policy Gradient** or **Actor-Critic** methods for continuous or complex spaces.

Example:

```python
# rl_example.py

class RLAgent:
    def __init__(self, agent_id, action_space):
        self.agent_id = agent_id
        self.action_space = action_space
        self.q_table = {}
        # Or load a neural network

    def choose_action(self, state):
        # e.g., epsilon-greedy approach
        pass

    def receive_reward(self, state, action, reward,
new_state):
        # Update Q-table or neural net
        pass
```

- **Explanation**:
  - The agent implements **Q-learning** or a policy-based approach to improve decisions over repeated episodes.

3. Knowledge Graphs and Semantic Web Technologies

3.1. Integrating Knowledge Graphs for Enhanced Reasoning

Knowledge Graphs store relationships in a graph-like structure:

1. **Nodes**: Entities (people, products, concepts).
2. **Edges**: Relations ("is part of," "owned by," "located in").
3. **Properties**: Node or edge attributes (dates, numerical values, categories).

Benefits:

- Agents can perform **semantic queries** (e.g., SPARQL) to find relevant data or infer new facts.
- Enhanced reasoning by linking related concepts (e.g., "User X likes brand Y, so recommend product Z.")

3.2. Semantic Data Interchange Between Agents

Semantic Web standards (RDF, OWL, JSON-LD) enable:

1. **Common Vocabulary**
   o Agents share a consistent **ontology**, reducing misunderstandings about data fields or relationships.
2. **Inference Rules**
   o Agents can infer additional facts from known relations (e.g., if A is a subclass of B, properties apply).
3. **Distributed Knowledge**
   o Each agent manages a piece of the knowledge graph, linking data from remote graphs in a **federated** manner.

4. Computer Vision and Sensor Integration

4.1. Enabling Perception Capabilities in Agents

Computer Vision provides agents the ability to **see** and **interpret** images or video:

1. **Object Detection**

o Identifying objects within an image (e.g., bounding boxes for cars, humans, products).
2. **Semantic Segmentation**
   o Classifying each pixel, enabling precise environment understanding for tasks like robotics or surveillance.
3. **Facial Recognition**
   o Recognizing user identities or expressions, supporting security or personalized interactions.

4.2. Integrating Sensor Data for Real-time Decision Making

Beyond vision, agents incorporate data from other sensors:

1. **LIDAR/Radar** for distance measurements or velocity detection.
2. **Temperature, Pressure** sensors in industrial settings.
3. **IoT** data streams for environment or machine status updates.

MAS Perspective:

- Agents adapt decisions (e.g., route changes, production line adjustments) immediately when sensor readings deviate from the norm.

Code Example (Pseudocode):

python

```
# cv_sensor_integration.py
from deepseek_r1_sdk import AgentBase

class VisionAgent(AgentBase):
    def on_image_received(self, image_data):
        objects = self.detect_objects(image_data)
        for obj in objects:
            self.handle_detected_object(obj)

    def detect_objects(self, image_data):
        # e.g., YOLO or another detection model
        pass

    def handle_detected_object(self, obj):
        # Possibly send message to relevant agent
        pass
```

- **Explanation**:

o The agent processes **image_data** using a detection model, then interacts with other system components based on recognized objects.

5. Big Data and Analytics

5.1. Leveraging Big Data for Informed Decision Making

Big Data tools manage vast amounts of structured or unstructured data:

1. **Data Lakes**
   o Store raw data from agent logs, sensor events, user interactions in scalable repositories (HDFS, cloud storage).
2. **Analytics Engines**
   o Spark, Flink, or custom HPC solutions process large datasets for pattern discovery or advanced ML model training.
3. **Predictive Models**
   o Agents access predictive insights (e.g., next best action, anomaly detection) derived from historical analysis.

5.2. Implementing Real-time Analytics in MAS

Real-time analytics involves **stream processing**:

1. **Event Stream**
   o Data arrives continuously (sensor data, user events).
   o Agents handle or route these streams to real-time analytics pipelines (e.g., Kafka + Spark Streaming).
2. **Online Learning**
   o Models update incrementally as new data arrives, refining agent decision strategies.
   o Minimizes staleness in predictions or recommendations.

MAS Impact:

- Agents remain up-to-date on evolving trends, environment changes, or user behaviors, consistently making **data-driven** decisions.

6. Case Study: Integrating DeepSeek R1 with Machine Learning Models for Predictive Maintenance

6.1. Scenario

An industrial facility wants to **reduce unplanned downtime** by detecting machine faults early. They combine **DeepSeek R1** multi-agent coordination with advanced **ML** models for predictive maintenance.

6.2. System Architecture

1. **SensorAgent**
   - Collects temperature, vibration, voltage from machines, streaming data to other agents.
2. **MLInferenceAgent**
   - Loads a **predictive** model (trained offline on historical machine failures).
   - Receives sensor data, outputs a **probability** of failure or recommended maintenance windows.
3. **MaintenanceSchedulerAgent**
   - If predicted failure risk is high, schedules maintenance tasks, coordinating with production schedules to minimize disruption.

6.3. Implementation

- **DeepSeek R1** serves as the **messaging backbone**:
  - SensorAgent broadcasts sensor readings.
  - MLInferenceAgent listens, runs the ML model, sends alerts.
  - MaintenanceSchedulerAgent finalizes maintenance tasks and notifies technicians.
- Real-time analytics ensures an **alert** is triggered within seconds of anomaly detection, preventing machine breakdown.

6.4. Results

1. **Downtime Reduction**: Unplanned outages fell by **30%**.
2. **Cost Savings**: Fewer emergency repairs and production halts.

3. **Data-driven Culture**: Operators trust the system to proactively catch faults, leading to better resource allocation.

7. End-of-Chapter Projects

Project 15: Integrating NLP and Computer Vision with MAS

Objective: Combine **NLP** for user interactions and **Computer Vision** for environment sensing into a multi-agent application that uses **DeepSeek R1**.

Outline

1. **NLP Integration**
    o   A **ConversationalAgent** that accepts textual commands from users, interprets them via an NLP library, and delegates tasks.
2. **Computer Vision**
    o   A **VisionAgent** that processes images or video feeds. E.g., detecting objects or QR codes in a warehouse environment.
3. **Collaboration**
    o   ConversationalAgent can handle a request: "Find item X in the warehouse." It delegates to VisionAgent, which identifies item locations in camera feeds.
4. **Advanced Project Extensions**
    o   RL for navigation tasks, Knowledge Graph for linking item metadata, or Big Data analytics for user preferences.

8. Quizzes and Self-Assessments

Quiz 15: AI Technology Integration

1. **NLP**
    o   **Question**: How does **intent recognition** benefit multi-agent communication in a customer service scenario?
2. **Reinforcement Learning**
    o   **Question**: Define **reward** in the context of RL and explain how it guides agent behavior.

3. **Knowledge Graphs**
   - ○ **Question**: Why might integrating a **knowledge graph** improve the reasoning capabilities of MAS agents?
4. **Computer Vision**
   - ○ **Question**: Name two ways an agent could use vision data for real-time decision making.
5. **Big Data**
   - ○ **Question**: Outline a scenario where a **real-time analytics** pipeline helps MAS adapt to changing conditions on the fly.
6. **Case Study**
   - ○ **Question**: In the predictive maintenance example, which agents are responsible for data collection and for making maintenance decisions?
7. **Short Coding Prompt**
   - ○ **Question**: Write a pseudocode snippet for an **MLInferenceAgent** that loads a predictive model, receives sensor data, and broadcasts an "ALERT" message if the failure probability exceeds 0.7.

Answer Key (Suggested):

1. **Intent Recognition**: It routes user requests accurately to the correct agent, reducing confusion and speeding up resolution.
2. **RL Reward**: A numerical signal that conveys how good or bad an action's outcome was, shaping agent learning for better future decisions.
3. **Knowledge Graph**: Agents can derive new facts or relationships from the graph, leading to richer context and advanced inferential capabilities.
4. **Computer Vision**: Agents might **detect** obstacles in a robot's path or **identify** objects in a warehouse to fulfill picking tasks.
5. **Big Data + Real-time Analytics**: An MAS for traffic management adjusts signal timings on-the-fly when traffic surges are detected in live data streams.
6. **Case Study**: **SensorAgent** collects data, while **MaintenanceSchedulerAgent** decides on maintenance scheduling based on alerts from **MLInferenceAgent**.
7. **Pseudocode**:

```python
class MLInferenceAgent(AgentBase):
    def __init__(self, model):
```

```
        super().__init__("MLInferenceAgent")
        self.model = model  # e.g., loaded pre-trained
model

    def on_message(self, msg):
        if msg["content_type"] == "SENSOR_UPDATE":
            prob_failure =
self.model.predict(msg["payload"]["sensor_values"])
            if prob_failure > 0.7:
                self.send_message({
                    "sender": self.agent_id,
                    "receiver":
"MaintenanceSchedulerAgent",
                    "content_type": "ALERT",
                    "payload": {"risk": prob_failure}
                })
```

Integrating **Natural Language Processing**, **Reinforcement Learning**, **Knowledge Graphs**, **Computer Vision**, and **Big Data analytics** with **multi-agent systems** (MAS) expands the **capabilities** of agents, allowing them to handle more sophisticated tasks, learn from experience, reason about complex relationships, perceive their environment, and make informed, data-driven decisions. **DeepSeek R1** serves as a robust foundation for combining these AI technologies, as illustrated in the **predictive maintenance case study**. By exploring and experimenting with the examples and projects in this chapter, you can design MAS that truly embody **intelligent, adaptive, and context-aware** behavior across diverse domains.

Chapter 16: Security and Privacy in Multi-agent Systems

As **multi-agent systems (MAS)** become increasingly central to critical applications—from healthcare to financial services—ensuring **security** and **privacy** is paramount. MAS architectures inherently involve multiple autonomous agents communicating and exchanging data. This presents unique attack surfaces and privacy concerns. In this chapter, we explore the **threats** facing MAS, discuss **secure communication** mechanisms, examine **authentication** and **authorization** approaches, delve into **privacy-preserving** techniques, and present strategies for **intrusion detection**. We conclude with a **case study** on securing a healthcare MAS, followed by projects and quizzes to reinforce key concepts.

---

1. Security Threats in MAS

1.1. Types of Threats: Unauthorized Access, Data Breaches, Agent Hijacking

1. **Unauthorized Access**
   - Attackers may gain entry to an agent's internal logic or data, using it for malicious purposes (e.g., injecting false commands or stealing sensitive info).
   - Exploits can stem from weak passwords, open network ports, or outdated software libraries.
2. **Data Breaches**
   - MAS often handle large volumes of information—personal records, financial data, or operational analytics.
   - A single agent compromise can lead to broad leakage if systems are overly interconnected or lack strong segmentation.
3. **Agent Hijacking**
   - Attackers can "take over" an agent's identity or logic to sabotage tasks (e.g., sending erroneous instructions to other agents).
   - Could lead to critical disruptions in production lines, energy grids, or financial trading processes.

1.2. Vulnerabilities in MAS Architectures

1. **Distributed Communication**
   o Multi-agent collaboration relies on message exchange, which might be insecure if protocols are unencrypted or unverified.
   o Complex distributed interactions can obscure standard security boundaries, leaving blind spots in monitoring.
2. **Dynamic Agent Discovery**
   o Agents may join or leave the system at runtime. If identity checks are insufficient, malicious agents can pose as legitimate participants.
3. **Third-Party Integrations**
   o MAS often integrate external services (e.g., cloud ML, third-party APIs). Each integration expands the attack surface if not properly vetted or sandboxed.

Table: Common Security Threats in MAS

Threat Type	Description	Potential Impact
Unauthorized Access	Attacker gains undue entry to an agent's functions	Manipulation of tasks, stolen data
Data Breaches	Large-scale exfiltration of sensitive information	Regulatory fines, reputational damage
Agent Hijacking	Malware or impersonation seizes an agent's identity	System sabotage, erroneous decisions
Weak Integrations	Insecure third-party or plugin usage	Indirect compromise, supply chain attacks

2. Implementing Secure Communication

2.1. Encryption Techniques

Encryption ensures data in transit and at rest cannot be easily intercepted or tampered with:

1. **Symmetric Encryption**
   o A shared secret key encrypts/decrypts messages (e.g., AES-256).

- o Efficient but requires secure key distribution among agents.
2. **Asymmetric Encryption**
   - o Uses a **public** key for encryption and a **private** key for decryption (e.g., RSA, ECC).
   - o Simplifies key exchange but can be slower.
3. **Hybrid Approaches**
   - o Combine asymmetric methods for key exchange with symmetric ciphers for bulk data encryption, balancing security and speed.

2.2. Secure Messaging Protocols

To secure agent-to-agent communication:

1. **TLS/SSL**
   - o Transport Layer Security ensures end-to-end encryption over common protocols (e.g., HTTPS or secure WebSockets).
2. **Message-Level Encryption**
   - o Each message is individually encrypted before sending, preventing any intermediary from reading its contents.
   - o **S/MIME** or custom solutions using JSON Web Encryption (JWE) are possible.
3. **Digital Signatures**
   - o Agents sign messages with private keys, ensuring authenticity and integrity.
   - o Recipients verify signatures using public keys, confirming the sender's identity.

Code Example (Pseudocode):

```python
# secure_message.py
from cryptography.fernet import Fernet

class SecureAgent:
    def __init__(self, agent_id, shared_key):
        self.agent_id = agent_id
        self.cipher = Fernet(shared_key)  # Symmetric encryption

    def send_encrypted(self, payload, receiver):
        encrypted_msg = self.cipher.encrypt(payload.encode('utf-8'))
```

```
        message = {
            "sender": self.agent_id,
            "receiver": receiver,
            "content_type": "ENCRYPTED",
            "payload": encrypted_msg
        }
        # send message over MAS framework

    def on_message(self, message):
        if message["content_type"] == "ENCRYPTED":
            decrypted_data =
self.cipher.decrypt(message["payload"]).decode('utf-8')
            self.handle_decrypted(decrypted_data)

    def handle_decrypted(self, text):
        print(f"Decrypted content for {self.agent_id}:
{text}")
```

- **Explanation**:
  - o Illustrates a **simple** symmetric encryption approach. Real-world scenarios might add key management or digital signatures for authenticity.

---

3. Authentication and Authorization

3.1. Agent Identity Management

Authentication verifies an agent is who it claims to be:

1. **Certificates and PKI**
   - o Agents hold digital certificates signed by a trusted CA, verifying their identities.
   - o The system checks certificate validity before granting agent privileges.
2. **Username/Password** or **Token**
   - o Less common in MAS, but feasible if each agent must supply credentials to a directory service or identity provider.
3. **Hardware/Software Keys**
   - o Secure enclaves or hardware security modules (HSMs) store agent private keys.

3.2. Access Control Mechanisms

Once an agent is authenticated, define what resources or actions it can access:

1. **Role-Based Access Control (RBAC)**
   - Agents assigned roles (e.g., "DataProcessor," "Supervisor").
   - Each role has predefined permissions or resource scopes.
2. **Attribute-Based Access Control (ABAC)**
   - Agents' attributes (location, time, role, security clearance) are evaluated in real-time for authorization decisions.
3. **Policy Enforcement**
   - Central or distributed policy engines intercept requests to resources, verifying if the agent's privileges suffice.

Example:

```text
Policy: "Only agents with role=DataProcessor can update the
'SensorData' database table between 6 AM - 10 PM."
```

4. Data Privacy in MAS

4.1. Ensuring Compliance with Privacy Regulations (e.g., GDPR)

GDPR and similar laws mandate how personal data is handled:

1. **Consent**
   - Agents collecting user info must ensure explicit user consent.
2. **Right to Erasure**
   - Users can request agent-held data be deleted, requiring data lifecycle management.
3. **Data Minimization**
   - Agents store only data relevant to their functions, reducing exposure risk.

4.2. Implementing Privacy-Preserving Techniques

1. **Data Anonymization**
   - Remove or mask personally identifiable information (PII) before distribution among agents.

2. **Differential Privacy**
    o   Agents add noise to aggregated statistics, preventing re-identification of individuals.
3. **Secure Multi-Party Computation**
    o   Multiple agents compute a joint function over data without revealing their inputs to each other, maintaining data confidentiality.

Table: Privacy-Preserving Methods in MAS

Technique	Use Case	Drawback
Data Anonymization	Sharing user datasets for analytics	May lose detail if overly anonymized
Differential Privacy	Generating summary stats without PII leakage	Tuning noise for acceptable accuracy
Secure Multi-Party Computation	Collaborative computations among untrusted parties	Higher computational overhead

5. Intrusion Detection and Prevention

5.1. Monitoring Agent Activities

Intrusion Detection Systems (IDS):

1. **Behavioral Analysis**
    o   Agents exhibit normal patterns (message frequency, action sequences). Deviations may signal infiltration or compromised code.
2. **Log Aggregation**
    o   Collect agent logs centrally to run pattern analysis or anomaly detection models (e.g., suspicious consecutive failed tasks).
3. **Real-time Alerts**
    o   If an agent's actions appear malicious, the system quarantines or restricts that agent pending investigation.

5.2. Detecting and Mitigating Security Breaches

Once a breach is suspected:

1. **Isolation**
   - o Immediately sever the compromised agent from the network, limiting damage to other agents.
2. **Forensic Analysis**
   - o Inspect the agent's code, logs, and communications for the attack vector used.
3. **Recovery/Failover**
   - o Restore normal operation with backups or redundant agents.
   - o Patch vulnerabilities (e.g., fix code flaws, revoke compromised keys).

Code Example (Pseudocode):

```python
# ids_agent.py

class IDSAgent(AgentBase):
    def __init__(self, threshold):
        super().__init__("IDSAgent")
        self.anomaly_threshold = threshold

    def on_message(self, message):
        # track message metrics
        if self.detect_anomaly(message):
            self.raise_alert(message["sender"])

    def detect_anomaly(self, message):
        # simple heuristic: if sender spams too many messages
in short time
        pass

    def raise_alert(self, agent_id):
        print(f"[ALERT] Potential intrusion from
{agent_id}.")
        # possibly isolate or revoke agent credentials
```

- • **Explanation**:
   - o This **IDSAgent** monitors message patterns, triggers alerts upon suspicious spikes or unusual behavior.

6. Case Study: Securing a Multi-agent Healthcare Management System

6.1. Scenario

A hospital deploys **DeepSeek R1** to coordinate patient records, appointment scheduling, prescription management, and real-time vital monitoring through a network of agents. These systems handle **sensitive** personal health information (PHI).

6.2. Security Measures

1. **Encrypted Communication**
   o   Agents exchange PHI via TLS. Record updates are signed with digital signatures to ensure data integrity.
2. **RBAC**
   o   Care providers have read/write access to patient records, while administrative agents manage scheduling and billing.
   o   Pharmacist agents can only view prescription data relevant to medication dispensing.
3. **Privacy Compliance**
   o   The system scrubs identifying info from aggregated analytics.
   o   Patients can request data removal or portability under HIPAA/GDPR frameworks.
4. **Intrusion Detection**
   o   A specialized **SecurityAgent** monitors logs, flags any agent with abnormal queries (e.g., accessing data from unrelated wards).
5. **Failover**
   o   If the central appointment manager fails or is compromised, a backup system ensures minimal disruption to patient scheduling.

6.3. Outcomes

- **Reduced Risk**: Data breaches prevented by strong encryption and strict access controls.
- **Regulatory Adherence**: Auditing features demonstrate compliance with health privacy laws.
- **Resilient Operations**: Backup agents maintain scheduling or prescription services even when primary agents are offline for updates or incident response.

Table: Implemented Security Features and Benefits

Security Feature	Benefit
End-to-End Encryption	Protected PHI during agent communication
Role-Based Access Control (RBAC)	Restricted unauthorized data access
IDS Monitoring	Quick detection of suspicious agent activities
Failover Mechanisms	Continuity of critical healthcare services

7. End-of-Chapter Projects

Project 16: Enhancing Security in MAS

Objective: Strengthen the security of a basic **DeepSeek R1** multi-agent application, integrating **encryption**, **authentication**, and **intrusion detection**.

Outline

1. **Baseline MAS**
   o A set of agents exchanging tasks or data in plaintext.
   o Minimal authentication—any agent can join with an ID.
2. **Implement Secure Communication**
   o Introduce symmetrical or asymmetrical keys.
   o Encrypt messages.
3. **Agent Authentication**
   o Incorporate a simple PKI or token-based approach for verifying agent identities.
4. **Intrusion Detection**
   o Create an **IDSAgent** that monitors logs, alerting on suspicious behaviors (e.g., repeated unauthorized resource requests).
5. **Testing & Validation**
   o Attempt unauthorized resource queries; verify if agents or IDS blocks them.
   o Confirm that normal operations remain unaffected.

8. Quizzes and Self-Assessments

Quiz 16: Security and Privacy

1. **Security Threats**
   - **Question**: Provide one example of how **agent hijacking** could disrupt a multi-agent manufacturing system.
2. **Secure Communication**
   - **Question**: Why might a **hybrid encryption** approach (asymmetric for key exchange, symmetric for data) be preferred in MAS?
3. **Authentication & Authorization**
   - **Question**: Describe **Role-Based Access Control (RBAC)** and how it confines agent privileges in MAS.
4. **Data Privacy**
   - **Question**: How do **differential privacy** techniques help protect individual data within aggregated MAS analytics?
5. **Intrusion Detection**
   - **Question**: Mention a basic sign of suspicious agent activity that an **IDSAgent** might watch for.
6. **Case Study**
   - **Question**: In the healthcare MAS, what was one privacy compliance measure ensuring patient data remains confidential?
7. **Short Coding Prompt**
   - **Question**: Write pseudocode for an **AccessControlAgent** that checks if an agent's role is allowed to perform a specific action on a resource.

Answer Key (Suggested):

1. **Agent Hijacking**: An attacker controlling a **manufacturing robot** might disrupt assembly steps or sabotage product quality.
2. **Hybrid Encryption**: Asymmetric keys securely **exchange** a session key, while symmetric encryption is **fast** for bulk data.
3. **RBAC**: Agents get assigned **roles** (e.g., 'Admin', 'Viewer') with **fixed permissions**. This prevents them from accessing resources beyond their role's scope.
4. **Differential Privacy**: Introduces **noise** in aggregate computations so that individual data points cannot be re-identified, protecting personal privacy.

5. **Suspicious Activity**: E.g., an agent making **unusually frequent** or repetitive resource requests in a short timeframe.
6. **Case Study**: **Anonymizing** or partially **de-identifying** patient records in analytics or ensuring requests adhere to role-based restrictions.
7. **Pseudocode**:

```python
class AccessControlAgent(AgentBase):
    def __init__(self, policy):
        super().__init__("AccessControlAgent")
        self.policy = policy  # e.g., mapping of roles
-> permitted actions

    def can_perform_action(self, agent_role, resource,
action):
        allowed_actions = self.policy.get(agent_role,
[])
        return (resource, action) in allowed_actions

    def on_access_request(self, request):
        # request = {"role": "DataProcessor",
"resource": "UserRecords", "action": "UPDATE"}
        if self.can_perform_action(request["role"],
request["resource"], request["action"]):
            return "ACCESS_GRANTED"
        else:
            return "ACCESS_DENIED"
```

Security and privacy are **foundational** for multi-agent systems entrusted with critical data and operations. By **encrypting** communications, **authenticating** agents, controlling **access** to resources, and ensuring **privacy** regulations are met, MAS maintain users' trust and resilience against cyber threats. Tools like **IDS** further help detect anomalies, isolating compromised agents before damage spreads. The **healthcare** case study illustrates how integrated security measures keep sensitive information safe while preserving system functionality. Adopting these best practices and methods fosters a robust, **secure** multi-agent ecosystem in any domain.

Chapter 17: Ethical Considerations and Responsible AI in MAS

As **multi-agent systems (MAS)** continue to integrate into critical areas of society—healthcare, finance, governance, military applications—they raise profound **ethical**, **social**, and **legal** questions. Responsible AI practices ensure that MAS developments align with **human values**, prioritize fairness, and respect autonomy. This chapter examines the **ethical challenges** in MAS, proposes methods for **designing ethical agents**, reviews **regulatory standards**, and explores best practices for **sustainable** and **responsible** AI. Finally, we analyze a **case study** involving autonomous weapon systems, followed by projects and a quiz to reinforce the key concepts.

---

1. Ethical Challenges in MAS

1.1. Bias and Fairness

Bias can manifest in MAS when:

1. **Training Data is Skewed**
   - Agents employing **machine learning** or **reinforcement learning** may inherit biases present in historical data (e.g., discriminatory lending records).
2. **Algorithmic Bias**
   - Hard-coded rules or heuristics inadvertently favor specific groups or outcomes.
3. **Representation Issues**
   - Underrepresented communities or use cases not well-modeled, leading to worse agent decisions for certain populations.

Consequences:

- **Unfair Treatment**: Agents might consistently disadvantage certain demographics (e.g., job applicants, borrowers).
- **Legal/Compliance Risks**: Discriminatory outcomes can violate anti-discrimination laws.

1.2. Accountability and Transparency

Accountability in MAS revolves around identifying who or what is **responsible** for an agent's actions:

1. **Distributed Decision-Making**
   - In a highly decentralized system, it can be unclear which agent (or developer) is at fault if something goes wrong.
2. **Black Box Models**
   - Advanced AI (deep learning, complex rule sets) may yield decisions not fully explainable to users or regulators.
3. **Transparency**
   - Agents should ideally provide **explanations** or **rationales** for critical decisions, especially in sensitive areas (e.g., healthcare diagnoses, financial approvals).

1.3. Impact on Employment and Society

MAS can disrupt **job markets** by automating tasks traditionally done by humans:

1. **Job Displacement**
   - Routine tasks in manufacturing, customer service, or logistics increasingly replaced by agent-driven robotics or virtual assistants.
2. **Societal Shifts**
   - Humans may shift to higher-level, creative, or supervisory roles. But certain populations might not have the resources or training to adapt.
3. **Ethical Duty**
   - Developers and policymakers should consider **reskilling** programs, **inclusive design**, and balanced deployment strategies to mitigate negative social impacts.

Table: Ethical Challenges in MAS

Category	Description	Example
Bias and Fairness	Embedded prejudices in data/algorithms	Discriminatory loan approvals
Accountability	Difficulty pinpointing responsibility in conflicts	Multi-agent trading meltdown, uncertain blame assignment

Category	Description	Example
Societal Impact	Job displacement, economic shifts	Automated warehouses reducing local employment

2. Designing Ethical Agents

2.1. Incorporating Ethical Decision-Making Frameworks

Ethical agents must **explicitly** account for moral principles in their logic:

1. **Rule-Based Ethics**
   - Agents follow set **rules** (deontological approach). For instance, a "do no harm" directive overriding other goals.
2. **Consequentialist Approaches**
   - Agents weigh **outcomes** (maximizing overall benefit or minimizing harm).
   - E.g., in an emergency scenario, an autonomous vehicle chooses the least harmful path based on utility calculations.
3. **Hybrid Models**
   - Combining rules for critical constraints (e.g., "no lethal harm to humans") with outcome-based optimization for other decisions.

2.2. Ensuring Transparency in Agent Actions

1. **Explainable AI (XAI)**
   - Agents provide **interpretable** justifications for important decisions.
   - Surrogate models or local explanation methods (e.g., LIME, SHAP) clarify black-box behaviors.
2. **Audit Trails**
   - Agents log their **reasoning** steps or data references for external review or forensics.
   - Aids compliance with industry regulations (healthcare, finance) demanding traceability.

Code Example (Pseudocode):

```
python
```

```
# ethical_agent.py
class EthicalAgent:
    def __init__(self, ethical_rules):
        self.ethical_rules = ethical_rules   # e.g. list of
constraints or moral guidelines

    def decide_action(self, situation):
        possible_actions = situation["possible_actions"]
        safe_actions = [act for act in possible_actions if
self.check_rules(act)]
        # choose best among safe_actions
        return self.select_action(safe_actions)

    def check_rules(self, action):
        for rule in self.ethical_rules:
            if not rule.is_satisfied(action):
                return False
        return True
```

- **Explanation**:
  - o The agent checks each potential action against a set of **ethical constraints**, ensuring it never violates critical rules.

3. Regulatory Compliance

3.1. Understanding Relevant Laws and Standards

Multiple frameworks and standards govern **AI ethics** and data:

1. **EU AI Act** (proposed)
   - o Classifies AI uses by risk level. High-risk systems must meet strict data governance, documentation, transparency obligations.
2. **ISO/IEC AI Standards**
   - o Ongoing development of international standards to guide AI safety, reliability, and ethics.
3. **Domain-Specific Laws**

- HIPAA for healthcare, **GDPR** for data privacy, **FINRA** or **MiFID II** for finance.

3.2. Implementing Compliance Mechanisms

Agents can incorporate **compliance** at design-time:

1. **Policy Enforcement**
   - Agents cross-check actions or data usage with relevant legal constraints, halting or logging potential violations.
2. **Auditability**
   - Provide **logs** or data lineage for regulators or auditors to verify compliance.
   - Must handle user rights (e.g., data deletion requests in GDPR).
3. **Governance Boards**
   - Larger MAS deployments might have an **Ethics/Compliance** board reviewing agent logic and updates before production release.

4. Sustainable and Responsible AI Practices

4.1. Energy-efficient Agent Designs

MAS can be heavy on computation or communications, so optimizing resource usage is crucial:

1. **Algorithmic Efficiency**
   - Use **lightweight** models or approximate methods where exact solutions are not strictly needed.
2. **Idle Management**
   - Agents enter a **low-power** or standby mode if no tasks are active. Minimizes cloud or on-prem energy consumption.
3. **Green Data Centers**
   - Host MAS on infrastructures powered by renewables or employing advanced cooling/efficiency measures.

4.2. Promoting Inclusivity and Accessibility

AI's benefits should be **equitable**:

1. **Language Accessibility**
   o MAS-based chatbots provide multi-language support or adapt to different literacy levels.
2. **Assistive Technologies**
   o Agents incorporate **screen readers**, **voice interfaces**, or translations, helping users with disabilities.
3. **Culturally Aware**
   o System designs respect local cultural norms, privacy expectations, or ethical differences.

5. Case Study: Ethical Considerations in Autonomous Weapon Systems

5.1. Overview

Autonomous weapon systems (AWS) push ethical boundaries when agents can **identify**, **select**, and **engage** targets with minimal human oversight. Governments and organizations debate regulatory and moral implications.

5.2. Ethical Dilemmas

1. **Lethal Autonomy**
   o Agents deciding to use lethal force poses fundamental moral questions—where is human oversight?
2. **Accountability**
   o If an autonomous weapon malfunctions or misidentifies a target, who is legally or ethically responsible?
3. **Proportionality and Distinction**
   o Under humanitarian law, distinguishing combatants from civilians is critical. Agents may misclassify, risking war crimes.

5.3. Guiding Principles

- **Human-in-the-Loop**: Many experts insist a human must confirm critical actions like firing.

- **Transparency**: Systems log how target decisions were reached for post-event review.
- **Fail-safes**: Agents must revert to safe or neutral states upon anomalies or sensor failures.

5.4. Outcome

Debates continue on how to apply or ban lethal AWS. Some argue for strict prohibition or advanced global treaties, while others see limited but necessary applications in defense scenarios.

6. End-of-Chapter Projects

Project 17: Designing Ethical Agents

Objective: Develop a **DeepSeek R1** multi-agent setup incorporating **ethical decision-making** and minimal **bias mitigation** strategies.

Outline

1. **Scenario**
   - A job application screening MAS with **three** agent types: **ApplicationAgent**, **DecisionAgent**, and an **EthicalReviewAgent**.
2. **EthicalReviewAgent**
   - Checks if recommended decisions contain bias (e.g., rejecting all applicants from a certain demographic).
3. **Transparency**
   - Agents log rationale for acceptance/rejection to a tamper-proof ledger.
4. **Testing**
   - Provide a dataset with potential bias. Evaluate if the system flags or corrects discriminatory patterns.

Example Code (Pseudocode)

```python
# ethical_decision_agent.py
from deepseek_r1_sdk import AgentBase
```

```
class DecisionAgent(AgentBase):
    def evaluate_applicant(self, applicant_data):
        score = self.calculate_score(applicant_data)
        if self.violates_ethics(applicant_data):
            # escalate to EthicalReviewAgent
            pass
        else:
            return "ACCEPT" if score > 70 else "REJECT"

    def violates_ethics(self, data):
        # Check for red flags: e.g. ignoring certain
demographics entirely
        pass
```

7. Quizzes and Self-Assessments

Quiz 17: Ethical AI in MAS

1. **Ethical Challenges**
   - o **Question**: How can **algorithmic bias** arise in multi-agent systems that use machine learning?
2. **Designing Ethical Agents**
   - o **Question**: Why is maintaining an **audit trail** important for accountability in MAS?
3. **Regulatory Compliance**
   - o **Question**: Name one regulation or standard relevant to AI ethics or data protection, and a key requirement it imposes.
4. **Sustainable AI**
   - o **Question**: Give an example of how **energy-efficient designs** can reduce the environmental impact of MAS.
5. **Case Study**
   - o **Question**: In autonomous weapon systems, what is one ethical concern about giving agents lethal autonomy?
6. **Short Coding Prompt**
   - o **Question**: Write pseudocode for an **EthicsAgent** that logs each agent's decision, checking if it meets a "do no harm" rule. If violated, it issues a system-wide alert.

Answer Key (Suggested):

1. **Algorithmic Bias**: Occurs if the training data or features reflect historical discrimination, causing agents to replicate or amplify biased decisions.
2. **Audit Trail**: Facilitates **post-hoc** analysis, letting organizations trace the chain of decisions to identify responsible parties or uncover potential wrongdoing.
3. **Regulation Example**: **GDPR** demands user consent for data collection and a right to be forgotten, forcing MAS to manage personal data in compliant ways.
4. **Energy Efficiency**: Agents can scale down CPU cycles when idle or batch computations, saving energy especially in large data centers.
5. **Autonomous Weapon Systems**: The concern is lack of **human oversight** for lethal decisions, risking unethical or unlawful harm if AI misidentifies targets.
6. **Pseudocode**:

```python
class EthicsAgent(AgentBase):
    def on_decision(self, decision_info):
        # decision_info = {"agent": "SomeAgent",
"action": "XYZ", "impact": "minor"}
        self.log_decision(decision_info)
        if not self.meets_do_no_harm(decision_info):
            self.alert(decision_info["agent"])

    def meets_do_no_harm(self, decision_info):
        # e.g. check if action endangers humans or
violates moral constraints
        return True   # or False

    def alert(self, agent_id):
        print(f"[ALERT] Ethical violation by
{agent_id}! Investigating...")
```

Building **ethical** and **responsible** multi-agent systems requires careful attention to **bias**, **accountability**, **privacy**, and **sustainability**. Agents must incorporate **ethical frameworks**, maintain **transparency**, and comply with **regulatory** requirements. By considering social impacts, ensuring minimal resource usage, and preventing discriminatory or harmful outcomes, MAS can serve society in a manner that respects **human dignity** and fosters **trust**. The **autonomous weapon systems** case study underscores the high stakes— where poorly governed MAS can harm lives—underscoring the importance of **ethical** and **responsible** AI.

Chapter 18: Human-Agent Interaction

Human-Agent Interaction (HAI) focuses on how people collaborate with or oversee the decisions, behaviors, and outputs of **multi-agent systems (MAS)**. As MAS expand into areas like healthcare, customer service, manufacturing, and autonomous vehicles, **user experience** and trust become as critical as algorithmic performance. This chapter examines the **importance** of HAI, explores **UI/UX** design principles for MAS, addresses **human-in-the-loop** techniques, and investigates how to **build trust** through transparency and explainability. We also highlight **evaluation** methods for HAI effectiveness and showcase a **case study** on collaborative customer support. Finally, we propose a project on human-agent interfaces and a quiz to test your understanding.

---

1. Introduction to Human-Agent Collaboration

1.1. Importance of HAI in MAS

Human-Agent Interaction ensures that **people** can effectively:

1. **Guide** agent operations: Humans set goals, constraints, and ethical parameters.
2. **Monitor** agent actions: Observing progress, safety, or correctness.
3. **Intervene** when needed: Providing corrections or halting harmful actions.

In areas like **critical infrastructure** or **healthcare**, effective HAI is essential. Agents alone might produce valuable results, but humans need to interpret or override them to avoid negative outcomes, ensure compliance, or incorporate intangible human judgment.

1.2. Current Trends and Future Directions

1. **Explainable AI (XAI)**
   o Growing emphasis on making agent decisions **transparent** or **interpretable**.

- o Regulators increasingly expect reasons for AI-driven actions.
2. **Multimodal Interaction**
   - o Beyond text-based interfaces, users now expect **voice** or **gesture** interactions.
   - o MAS might combine speech, haptics, and visual cues for more natural experiences.
3. **Adaptive Interfaces**
   - o Systems automatically adjust complexity or detail based on user skill level or context, personalizing the collaboration experience.
4. **Extended Reality (XR)**
   - o VR or AR experiences can immerse humans in agent-driven simulations or real-time data visualizations, supporting more intuitive oversight.

2. Designing User-Friendly Interfaces

2.1. Principles of User Interface (UI) Design for MAS

Creating intuitive UIs for **agent-based** systems requires:

1. **Clarity of Agent Roles**
   - o The interface should show **which agent** is responsible for which task or domain.
   - o Distinct labels or color coding help differentiate agent outputs.
2. **Minimal Cognitive Load**
   - o Present only relevant information from multiple agents, avoiding data overload.
   - o Offer summaries or highlights, with deeper drill-down options.
3. **Consistency and Familiar Patterns**
   - o Reuse common UI elements or metaphors so users easily grasp agent-based processes (e.g., chat-style or card-based layouts).
4. **Responsive Interaction**
   - o Agents should **acknowledge** user commands quickly, even if the final result arrives later.

o   Provide clear progress indicators or placeholders to reassure users.

2.2. Enhancing User Experience (UX) with Collaborative Agents

Collaborative agents often require **multi-agent** or **multi-user** perspectives:

1. **Agent Coordination Views**
   o   Show how agents communicate or share tasks, e.g., visualizing task flows or real-time coordination events.
2. **User Empowerment**
   o   Offer manual overrides or "agent suggestions" mode. Users see agent recommendations but make the final decision.
3. **Personalization**
   o   UI adapts to individual preferences: color themes, data density, or language.
   o   Agents track user contexts (previous actions, domain knowledge) to tailor interactions.

Code Example (Pseudocode):

```python
# user_interface_mock.py
class AgentInterface:
    def display_agent_output(self, agent_name, message):
        # Example of a simple console-based approach
        print(f"[{agent_name}]: {message}")

    def request_user_input(self, prompt):
        return input(prompt)

class CollaborationUI:
    def __init__(self, interface):
        self.interface = interface

    def show_recommendation(self, agent_name, recommendation):
        self.interface.display_agent_output(agent_name, recommendation)

    def get_user_decision(self):
        decision = self.interface.request_user_input("Accept recommendation? (y/n): ")
        return decision
```

- **Explanation**:
  - ○ Illustrates a simple console-based UI that displays agent outputs and gathers user input. Real systems typically use **GUI** or **web-based** dashboards.

---

3. Human-in-the-Loop Systems

3.1. Integrating Human Feedback in Agent Decision-Making

Human-in-the-loop ensures critical agent decisions or continuous improvement:

1. **Interactive Training**
   - ○ Humans label or correct agent outputs (e.g., reinforcing correct or incorrect classification).
2. **Rule Overrides**
   - ○ Agents propose an action; humans accept or modify it. Over time, agent learns user preferences or constraints.
3. **Iterative Refinement**
   - ○ Agents provide initial solutions; users refine or add constraints. The agent updates its plan accordingly.

3.2. Balancing Automation and Human Control

1. **Automation**
   - ○ Free humans from routine or time-consuming tasks.
   - ○ In high-load environments, rely heavily on agent decisions to maintain efficiency.
2. **Human Control**
   - ○ Vital for tasks requiring nuanced judgment or moral/ethical discretion.
   - ○ Ensures accountability: a user is always "in the loop" for major consequences.

Design Approaches:

- **Adjustable Autonomy**: Users can set the agent's independence level from "fully autonomous" to "suggestion-only."

- **Approval Gates**: Certain agent actions, especially high-impact ones, require explicit human approval.

4. Trust and Transparency in HAI

4.1. Building Trustworthy Agents

Trust fosters user acceptance and more effective collaboration:

1. **Reliability and Consistency**
   - Agents must produce **consistent** outputs for similar inputs, or explain any variations.
2. **Clear Error Handling**
   - Agents gracefully degrade, providing fallback or apology messages if data or logic is incomplete.
3. **Ethical Safeguards**
   - Demonstrable adherence to moral or regulatory constraints. The user sees that agents cannot infringe vital rules (e.g., no lethal actions).

4.2. Making Agent Actions Explainable

Explainability demystifies agent decisions:

1. **Rule-based Summaries**
   - If an agent uses rules, share the relevant triggered rule for each decision.
2. **Post-hoc Explanation Tools**
   - For black-box ML, use local explanation methods (e.g., LIME, SHAP) to highlight input features influencing the output.
3. **Contextual Justification**
   - Agents provide rationales in plain language. E.g., "I recommended product X because your purchase history shows interest in Y."

Table: Strategies for Agent Explainability

Method	Description	Example
Rule-based Explanation	Display triggered rules or conditions	"Rule #12 matched: Payment overdue by 30+ days"
Local Model Explanation (LIME)	Approximate black-box model locally	"80% importance from age, 20% from location for this output"
Grad-CAM or Similar (Vision)	Visual heatmaps for image-based decisions	Overlay on image to show relevant regions of interest

5. Evaluating HAI Systems

5.1. User Studies and Feedback Collection

Empirical methods gauge user satisfaction and system usability:

1. **Surveys and Questionnaires**
   - Standard tools (e.g., **System Usability Scale** or custom forms) measuring subjective ease-of-use, trust, or clarity.
2. **Focus Groups**
   - Group discussions reveal user perceptions, desired features, or frustration points.
3. **A/B Testing**
   - Compare different UI or agent configurations to see which yields better user performance or satisfaction.

5.2. Metrics for Assessing HAI Effectiveness

Possible **quantitative** and **qualitative** metrics:

1. **Task Completion Rate**
   - Percent of tasks the user completes successfully with agent help (compared to baseline).
2. **Time to Completion**
   - Efficiency measure: how long it takes a user+agent to finish a workflow.
3. **Error Rate**
   - Frequency of mistakes or miscommunications leading to incorrect or incomplete outcomes.
4. **Trust Index**

- o Survey-based or inferred from how often users override agent decisions.

Code Example (Pseudocode):

```python
# hAI_evaluation.py
def evaluate_hai(task_logs):
    completion_count = sum(1 for log in task_logs if
log["status"] == "completed")
    total_tasks = len(task_logs)
    success_rate = completion_count / total_tasks if
total_tasks else 0

    avg_time = sum(log["time_spent"] for log in task_logs) /
total_tasks if total_tasks else 0

    print(f"Task Completion Rate: {success_rate:.2%}")
    print(f"Average Time to Complete: {avg_time:.2f}
seconds")
```

- **Explanation**:
  - o Simple function analyzing logs of user–agent tasks, computing success rates and average times as basic HAI metrics.

6. Case Study: Enhancing Customer Support with Human-Agent Collaboration

6.1. Background

A large **e-commerce** platform integrates a **multi-agent** system to handle customer queries. Virtual assistants handle routine questions, but complex issues route to **human agents**. The company wants to improve user satisfaction and cut average handling times.

6.2. Implementation

1. **Combined UI**

- o Chat-based interface displays agent suggestions and a "hand over" button for real-time human agent intervention.
2. **Adaptive Assistance**
   - o Virtual assistant tries to solve user queries. If confidence is low or the user escalates, a **human support** agent joins the conversation.
   - o The system notifies the support agent with relevant conversation context and logs.
3. **Transparency**
   - o The assistant states: "Here's my suggestion based on our returns policy. A human agent can confirm or revise."

6.3. Outcomes

- **Improved Response Times**: Routine queries remain fully automated, freeing human agents for complex tasks.
- **Increased User Trust**: Transparent disclaimers about "AI assistance" build user acceptance, especially when a tricky scenario arises.
- **Higher Satisfaction**: Surveys show 15% higher rating due to quick resolution and easy escalation.

Table: Metrics Pre vs. Post HAI Enhancement

Metric	Before HAI Enhancement	After HAI Enhancement	Change
Avg. Handle Time (simple)	3 min	1 min	-67%
User Satisfaction Score	80/100	92/100	+15% (approx)
Escalation Rate	50% of queries	25% of queries	-50%

7. End-of-Chapter Projects

Project 18: Developing Human-Agent Interfaces

Objective: Build an interface that **collaboratively** involves a user and multiple agents in **DeepSeek R1**.

Outline

1. **Scenario**
   - A scheduling system where user wants to set an event. Agents handle location booking, time suggestions, participant invites.
   - The user finalizes or overrides agent suggestions.
2. **User Interface**
   - Web or desktop UI listing each agent's proposal or data in real-time.
   - The user can see "calendar constraints" from a CalendarAgent, "location availability" from a VenueAgent, etc.
3. **Interaction Flow**
   - The user interacts with the UI. The UI sends tasks or updates to relevant agents.
   - Agents respond, the UI merges or displays suggestions, and user picks the final arrangement.
4. **Evaluation**
   - Gather logs of user decisions, track which agent suggestions were accepted, time taken, user feedback.

---

8. Quizzes and Self-Assessments

Quiz 18: Human-Agent Interaction

1. **Introduction**
   - **Question**: Why is **human-in-the-loop** crucial in high-stakes MAS applications (e.g., healthcare, defense)?
2. **Designing Interfaces**
   - **Question**: Mention one principle of **UI** design that helps reduce cognitive load when multiple agents present data.
3. **Human-in-the-Loop**
   - **Question**: Describe how an **approval gate** might operate in a system that automates risk assessment for financial loans.
4. **Trust & Transparency**
   - **Question**: Define **explainable AI** (XAI) in the context of building trust with end-users.
5. **Evaluating HAI**

- o **Question**: Name one metric you might track to gauge user satisfaction and success in a human-agent collaborative environment.
6. **Case Study**
   - o **Question**: In the customer support scenario, what mechanism ensures easy escalation from an AI-driven answer to a human-led resolution?
7. **Short Coding Prompt**
   - o **Question**: Write pseudocode for a simple "collaborative UI" function that merges agent recommendations with user feedback, returning a final decision.

Answer Key (Suggested):

1. **Human-in-the-loop**: Ensures **safety**, accountability, and nuanced decision-making when agent mistakes could cause severe harm.
2. **UI Principle**: Show only **relevant** data at first, letting users expand details if needed, minimizing information overload.
3. **Approval Gate**: Agent proposes loan acceptance; a human officer must click **approve** for final issuance. The agent logs all steps, but can't finalize alone.
4. **Explainable AI**: The concept where **AI** (or agent) decisions are made **understandable** to humans, clarifying key reasoning factors or data influences.
5. **User Satisfaction Metric**: Could be **Net Promoter Score**, or a direct "satisfaction rating" collected after each collaboration session.
6. **Case Study**: The "hand over" button that instantly brings a **human agent** into the conversation, giving context for seamless transition.
7. **Pseudocode**:

```python
def collaborative_decision(agent_suggestions,
user_input):
    final_choices = []
    # Merge or compare agent suggestions with user
input
    for suggestion in agent_suggestions:
        if user_input.accepts_suggestion(suggestion):
            final_choices.append(suggestion)
        else:

final_choices.append(user_input.override(suggestion))
    return final_choices
```

Human-Agent Interaction is pivotal for ensuring that multi-agent systems remain **usable, trustworthy**, and **adaptable** to real-world complexities. By designing **user-friendly interfaces**, incorporating **human feedback** loops, and **building transparency** into agent operations, MAS can effectively collaborate with people—maximizing benefits while respecting human expertise and ethical considerations. Proper **evaluation** of HAI through metrics and user studies continuously refines the synergy between humans and agents, as demonstrated in the customer support case.

Chapter 17: Ethical Considerations and Responsible AI in MAS

As **multi-agent systems (MAS)** continue to integrate into critical areas of society—healthcare, finance, governance, military applications—they raise profound **ethical**, **social**, and **legal** questions. Responsible AI practices ensure that MAS developments align with **human values**, prioritize fairness, and respect autonomy. This chapter examines the **ethical challenges** in MAS, proposes methods for **designing ethical agents**, reviews **regulatory standards**, and explores best practices for **sustainable** and **responsible** AI. Finally, we analyze a **case study** involving autonomous weapon systems, followed by projects and a quiz to reinforce the key concepts.

---

1. Ethical Challenges in MAS

1.1. Bias and Fairness

Bias can manifest in MAS when:

1. **Training Data is Skewed**
   - Agents employing **machine learning** or **reinforcement learning** may inherit biases present in historical data (e.g., discriminatory lending records).
2. **Algorithmic Bias**
   - Hard-coded rules or heuristics inadvertently favor specific groups or outcomes.
3. **Representation Issues**
   - Underrepresented communities or use cases not well-modeled, leading to worse agent decisions for certain populations.

Consequences:

- **Unfair Treatment**: Agents might consistently disadvantage certain demographics (e.g., job applicants, borrowers).
- **Legal/Compliance Risks**: Discriminatory outcomes can violate anti-discrimination laws.

1.2. Accountability and Transparency

Accountability in MAS revolves around identifying who or what is **responsible** for an agent's actions:

1. **Distributed Decision-Making**
   - In a highly decentralized system, it can be unclear which agent (or developer) is at fault if something goes wrong.
2. **Black Box Models**
   - Advanced AI (deep learning, complex rule sets) may yield decisions not fully explainable to users or regulators.
3. **Transparency**
   - Agents should ideally provide **explanations** or **rationales** for critical decisions, especially in sensitive areas (e.g., healthcare diagnoses, financial approvals).

1.3. Impact on Employment and Society

MAS can disrupt **job markets** by automating tasks traditionally done by humans:

1. **Job Displacement**
   - Routine tasks in manufacturing, customer service, or logistics increasingly replaced by agent-driven robotics or virtual assistants.
2. **Societal Shifts**
   - Humans may shift to higher-level, creative, or supervisory roles. But certain populations might not have the resources or training to adapt.
3. **Ethical Duty**
   - Developers and policymakers should consider **reskilling** programs, **inclusive design**, and balanced deployment strategies to mitigate negative social impacts.

Table: Ethical Challenges in MAS

Category	Description	Example
Bias and Fairness	Embedded prejudices in data/algorithms	Discriminatory loan approvals
Accountability	Difficulty pinpointing responsibility in conflicts	Multi-agent trading meltdown, uncertain blame assignment

Category	Description	Example
Societal Impact	Job displacement, economic shifts	Automated warehouses reducing local employment

2. Designing Ethical Agents

2.1. Incorporating Ethical Decision-Making Frameworks

Ethical agents must **explicitly** account for moral principles in their logic:

1. **Rule-Based Ethics**
   - Agents follow set **rules** (deontological approach). For instance, a "do no harm" directive overriding other goals.
2. **Consequentialist Approaches**
   - Agents weigh **outcomes** (maximizing overall benefit or minimizing harm).
   - E.g., in an emergency scenario, an autonomous vehicle chooses the least harmful path based on utility calculations.
3. **Hybrid Models**
   - Combining rules for critical constraints (e.g., "no lethal harm to humans") with outcome-based optimization for other decisions.

2.2. Ensuring Transparency in Agent Actions

1. **Explainable AI (XAI)**
   - Agents provide **interpretable** justifications for important decisions.
   - Surrogate models or local explanation methods (e.g., LIME, SHAP) clarify black-box behaviors.
2. **Audit Trails**
   - Agents log their **reasoning** steps or data references for external review or forensics.
   - Aids compliance with industry regulations (healthcare, finance) demanding traceability.

Code Example (Pseudocode):

```python
```

```
# ethical_agent.py
class EthicalAgent:
    def __init__(self, ethical_rules):
        self.ethical_rules = ethical_rules  # e.g. list of
constraints or moral guidelines

    def decide_action(self, situation):
        possible_actions = situation["possible_actions"]
        safe_actions = [act for act in possible_actions if
self.check_rules(act)]
        # choose best among safe_actions
        return self.select_action(safe_actions)

    def check_rules(self, action):
        for rule in self.ethical_rules:
            if not rule.is_satisfied(action):
                return False
        return True
```

- **Explanation**:
  - The agent checks each potential action against a set of **ethical constraints**, ensuring it never violates critical rules.

---

3. Regulatory Compliance

3.1. Understanding Relevant Laws and Standards

Multiple frameworks and standards govern **AI ethics** and data:

1. **EU AI Act** (proposed)
   - Classifies AI uses by risk level. High-risk systems must meet strict data governance, documentation, transparency obligations.
2. **ISO/IEC AI Standards**
   - Ongoing development of international standards to guide AI safety, reliability, and ethics.
3. **Domain-Specific Laws**
   - **HIPAA** for healthcare, **GDPR** for data privacy, **FINRA** or **MiFID II** for finance.

3.2. Implementing Compliance Mechanisms

Agents can incorporate **compliance** at design-time:

1. **Policy Enforcement**
    o   Agents cross-check actions or data usage with relevant legal constraints, halting or logging potential violations.
2. **Auditability**
    o   Provide **logs** or data lineage for regulators or auditors to verify compliance.
    o   Must handle user rights (e.g., data deletion requests in GDPR).
3. **Governance Boards**
    o   Larger MAS deployments might have an **Ethics/Compliance** board reviewing agent logic and updates before production release.

4. Sustainable and Responsible AI Practices

4.1. Energy-efficient Agent Designs

MAS can be heavy on computation or communications, so optimizing resource usage is crucial:

1. **Algorithmic Efficiency**
    o   Use **lightweight** models or approximate methods where exact solutions are not strictly needed.
2. **Idle Management**
    o   Agents enter a **low-power** or standby mode if no tasks are active. Minimizes cloud or on-prem energy consumption.
3. **Green Data Centers**
    o   Host MAS on infrastructures powered by renewables or employing advanced cooling/efficiency measures.

4.2. Promoting Inclusivity and Accessibility

AI's benefits should be **equitable**:

1. **Language Accessibility**

- MAS-based chatbots provide multi-language support or adapt to different literacy levels.
2. **Assistive Technologies**
    - Agents incorporate **screen readers**, **voice interfaces**, or translations, helping users with disabilities.
3. **Culturally Aware**
    - System designs respect local cultural norms, privacy expectations, or ethical differences.

---

5. Case Study: Ethical Considerations in Autonomous Weapon Systems

5.1. Overview

Autonomous weapon systems (AWS) push ethical boundaries when agents can **identify**, **select**, and **engage** targets with minimal human oversight. Governments and organizations debate regulatory and moral implications.

5.2. Ethical Dilemmas

1. **Lethal Autonomy**
    - Agents deciding to use lethal force poses fundamental moral questions—where is human oversight?
2. **Accountability**
    - If an autonomous weapon malfunctions or misidentifies a target, who is legally or ethically responsible?
3. **Proportionality and Distinction**
    - Under humanitarian law, distinguishing combatants from civilians is critical. Agents may misclassify, risking war crimes.

5.3. Guiding Principles

- **Human-in-the-Loop**: Many experts insist a human must confirm critical actions like firing.
- **Transparency**: Systems log how target decisions were reached for post-event review.

- **Fail-safes**: Agents must revert to safe or neutral states upon anomalies or sensor failures.

5.4. Outcome

Debates continue on how to apply or ban lethal AWS. Some argue for strict prohibition or advanced global treaties, while others see limited but necessary applications in defense scenarios.

6. End-of-Chapter Projects

Project 17: Designing Ethical Agents

Objective: Develop a **DeepSeek R1** multi-agent setup incorporating **ethical decision-making** and minimal **bias mitigation** strategies.

Outline

1. **Scenario**
   - A job application screening MAS with **three** agent types: **ApplicationAgent**, **DecisionAgent**, and an **EthicalReviewAgent**.
2. **EthicalReviewAgent**
   - Checks if recommended decisions contain bias (e.g., rejecting all applicants from a certain demographic).
3. **Transparency**
   - Agents log rationale for acceptance/rejection to a tamper-proof ledger.
4. **Testing**
   - Provide a dataset with potential bias. Evaluate if the system flags or corrects discriminatory patterns.

Example Code (Pseudocode)

```python
# ethical_decision_agent.py
from deepseek_r1_sdk import AgentBase
```

```
class DecisionAgent(AgentBase):
    def evaluate_applicant(self, applicant_data):
        score = self.calculate_score(applicant_data)
        if self.violates_ethics(applicant_data):
            # escalate to EthicalReviewAgent
            pass
        else:
            return "ACCEPT" if score > 70 else "REJECT"

    def violates_ethics(self, data):
        # Check for red flags: e.g. ignoring certain
demographics entirely
        pass
```

7. Quizzes and Self-Assessments

Quiz 17: Ethical AI in MAS

1. **Ethical Challenges**
   - **Question**: How can **algorithmic bias** arise in multi-agent systems that use machine learning?
2. **Designing Ethical Agents**
   - **Question**: Why is maintaining an **audit trail** important for accountability in MAS?
3. **Regulatory Compliance**
   - **Question**: Name one regulation or standard relevant to AI ethics or data protection, and a key requirement it imposes.
4. **Sustainable AI**
   - **Question**: Give an example of how **energy-efficient designs** can reduce the environmental impact of MAS.
5. **Case Study**
   - **Question**: In autonomous weapon systems, what is one ethical concern about giving agents lethal autonomy?
6. **Short Coding Prompt**
   - **Question**: Write pseudocode for an **EthicsAgent** that logs each agent's decision, checking if it meets a "do no harm" rule. If violated, it issues a system-wide alert.

Answer Key (Suggested):

1. **Algorithmic Bias**: Occurs if the training data or features reflect historical discrimination, causing agents to replicate or amplify biased decisions.
2. **Audit Trail**: Facilitates **post-hoc** analysis, letting organizations trace the chain of decisions to identify responsible parties or uncover potential wrongdoing.
3. **Regulation Example**: **GDPR** demands user consent for data collection and a right to be forgotten, forcing MAS to manage personal data in compliant ways.
4. **Energy Efficiency**: Agents can scale down CPU cycles when idle or batch computations, saving energy especially in large data centers.
5. **Autonomous Weapon Systems**: The concern is lack of **human oversight** for lethal decisions, risking unethical or unlawful harm if AI misidentifies targets.
6. **Pseudocode**:

```python
python

class EthicsAgent(AgentBase):
    def on_decision(self, decision_info):
        # decision_info = {"agent": "SomeAgent",
"action": "XYZ", "impact": "minor"}
        self.log_decision(decision_info)
        if not self.meets_do_no_harm(decision_info):
            self.alert(decision_info["agent"])

    def meets_do_no_harm(self, decision_info):
        # e.g. check if action endangers humans or
violates moral constraints
        return True  # or False

    def alert(self, agent_id):
        print(f"[ALERT] Ethical violation by
{agent_id}! Investigating...")
```

Building **ethical** and **responsible** multi-agent systems requires careful attention to **bias**, **accountability**, **privacy**, and **sustainability**. Agents must incorporate **ethical frameworks**, maintain **transparency**, and comply with **regulatory** requirements. By considering social impacts, ensuring minimal resource usage, and preventing discriminatory or harmful outcomes, MAS can serve society in a manner that respects **human dignity** and fosters **trust**. The **autonomous weapon systems** case study underscores the high stakes— where poorly governed MAS can harm lives—underscoring the importance of **ethical** and **responsible** AI.

Chapter 19: Deployment and Maintenance of MAS

A critical phase in the lifecycle of a **multi-agent system (MAS)** is its **deployment** and **ongoing maintenance**. Whether hosting agents on-premises, in the cloud, or through a hybrid model, ensuring robust operational strategies is vital for system stability and performance. This chapter explores **deployment strategies**, **containerization** and **orchestration**, setting up **CI/CD pipelines**, **monitoring** solutions, and approaches to **maintenance** and **updates**. A **case study** illustrates deploying a multi-agent logistics system on AWS, and we provide a project and quiz to reinforce the lessons learned.

---

1. Deployment Strategies

1.1. On-Premises vs. Cloud Deployment

On-Premises

- The organization hosts **all infrastructure** (servers, networking, storage) in local data centers or private facilities.
- **Advantages**:
  - Full control over hardware and security policies.
  - Potentially lower long-term costs if the infrastructure is already available.
- **Disadvantages**:
  - High upfront capital expense for hardware.
  - Scalability might be limited by data center capacity.

Cloud Deployment

- MAS and agents are hosted on public, private, or hybrid **cloud providers** (e.g., AWS, Azure, GCP).
- **Advantages**:
  - Quick scalability up or down.
  - Reduced maintenance overhead for hardware.
- **Disadvantages**:

- o Ongoing operational costs can accumulate.
- o Must ensure data sovereignty and compliance with region-based regulations.

1.2. Hybrid Deployment Models

A **hybrid** approach combines **on-premises** infrastructure with **cloud** resources:

1. **Burst Scalability**
   - o Base workloads run locally, while peak demand is offloaded to the cloud.
2. **Secure Data On-Premises**
   - o Sensitive data remains in local data centers; agents requiring external integration or large-scale compute go to the cloud.
3. **Edge Computing**
   - o Agents near end-users (e.g., on factory floors, retail shops) process data locally, but central coordination might be in the cloud.

Table: Comparison of Deployment Models

Model	Key Feature	Pros	Cons
On-Premises	In-house hosting	Full control, no vendor lock-in	Capital expenditure, limited scaling
Cloud	Hosted by public cloud provider	Elastic resources, pay-as-you-go	Continuous costs, compliance concerns
Hybrid	Mix of local and cloud resources	Flexibility, data segmentation	Complex orchestration

2. Containerization and Virtualization

2.1. Using Docker and Kubernetes with DeepSeek R1

Containerization packages software (including MAS agents) and dependencies in lightweight units. **Docker** is widely adopted, enabling:

1. **Consistent Environments**

      o   Avoid "it works on my machine" issues by bundling agent code plus libraries.

2. **Easy Scalability**
   - Spin up multiple container instances for load balancing or high availability.
3. **Isolation**
   - Each container runs in a sandbox, preventing conflicts or security issues.

DeepSeek R1 can be containerized by:

- Creating a **Dockerfile** that sets up the agent environment (Python dependencies, environment variables).
- Defining **entry points** to start agent processes.

Kubernetes orchestrates these containers:

1. **Pods**: Group one or more containers (e.g., an agent plus sidecar for logging).
2. **Deployments**: Manage pod replicas for scaling.
3. **Services**: Provide stable network endpoints for agent discovery and load balancing.

2.2. Managing Deployments with Container Orchestration

Kubernetes (K8s) or other orchestration tools handle complex deployment tasks:

1. **Auto-scaling**
   - Horizontal Pod Autoscaler launches more agent pods under high load, scaling back when idle.
2. **Rolling Updates**
   - Deploy new agent container versions gradually, seamlessly phasing out old versions.
   - Minimizes downtime or disruptions.
3. **Configuration Management**
   - Store agent configs, secrets, or environment variables in K8s objects, ensuring consistent usage across nodes.

Code Example (Dockerfile):

```
Dockerfile
```

```
FROM python:3.9-slim

# Set up working directory
WORKDIR /app

# Copy requirements and install
COPY requirements.txt .
RUN pip install --no-cache-dir -r requirements.txt

# Copy agent code
COPY . /app

# Expose port if agent needs external inbound connections
EXPOSE 5000

# Entry point
CMD ["python", "main_agent.py"]
```

- **Explanation**: A simple Dockerfile installing Python dependencies and agent code, then launching the agent script.

---

3. Continuous Integration and Continuous Deployment (CI/CD)

3.1. Setting Up CI/CD Pipelines

CI/CD automates the building, testing, and releasing of code updates:

1. **Version Control**
   o Agents or MAS projects stored in Git. Merges or pull requests trigger pipeline runs.
2. **Automated Builds**
   o Each commit triggers a build: compiling code, running unit tests, or building Docker images.
3. **Integration Tests**
   o A staging environment spins up to test MAS interactions, ensuring no regression or breakage.

3.2. Automating Testing and Deployment Processes

CD extends from pipeline success to deploying new code:

1. **Stages**
   - o **Test** environment for thorough checks → **Production** environment if stable.
2. **Approval Gates**
   - o Human sign-off needed for critical MAS changes or major versions before production rollout.
3. **Rollback Mechanisms**
   - o If new releases degrade performance or trigger errors, revert to a previous stable version swiftly.

Table: Example CI/CD Pipeline Stages

Stage	Actions Performed	Outcome
Build & Test	Compile code, run unit tests, static analysis	Validates code correctness
Integration Test	Deploy ephemeral MAS environment, run integration tests	Verifies agent communication & system flow
Staging Deploy	Deploy to pre-production environment	User acceptance or smoke tests
Production Deploy	Rolling update or blue-green deployment on live env	Official release if no major issues

4. Monitoring and Logging

4.1. Implementing Real-time Monitoring Solutions

To maintain reliable MAS, **real-time** insights are crucial:

1. **Metrics Aggregation**
   - o Agents publish CPU, memory, and custom usage metrics to platforms like **Prometheus**, **Grafana**, or **CloudWatch**.
2. **Health Checks**
   - o Periodic agent-level checks verifying readiness (can serve requests) and liveness (not hung or crashed).
3. **Alerts and Notifications**
   - o If performance or health thresholds exceed normal bounds, triggers alerts (email, Slack, pager) for immediate ops attention.

4.2. Logging Agent Activities and System Performance

Logging helps developers and ops staff debug or track events:

1. **Structured Logs**
   o Format logs as JSON or key-value pairs for easy parsing, searching, or correlation.
2. **Centralized Log Management**
   o Tools like **ELK Stack** (Elasticsearch, Logstash, Kibana) or **Splunk** unify logs from across agents.
3. **Retention Policies**
   o Keep enough historical logs for compliance or forensics, but not so long as to bloat storage.

Code Example (Pseudocode):

```python
# agent_monitor.py
import time

class MonitoringAgent(AgentBase):
    def __init__(self, agent_id, metrics_collector):
        super().__init__(agent_id)
        self.metrics_collector = metrics_collector

    def periodic_report(self):
        usage_data = {
            "cpu": self.get_cpu_usage(),
            "mem": self.get_mem_usage()
        }
        self.metrics_collector.send_metrics(self.agent_id, usage_data)

    def run(self):
        while True:
            self.periodic_report()
            time.sleep(10)
```

- **Explanation**:
  o A monitoring agent collects resource usage every 10 seconds, sending metrics to a collector.

5. Maintenance and Updates

5.1. Strategies for System Maintenance

1. **Scheduled Downtimes**
   o For major upgrades, plan offline windows or partial agent restarts.
   o Communicate to stakeholders so they expect reduced functionality or short outages.
2. **Proactive Maintenance**
   o Reboot or refresh agent hosts periodically to free memory leaks or fragmentation.
   o Regularly rotate encryption keys or credentials for security.
3. **Scalable Support**
   o Maintain well-documented runbooks for handling common issues or agent failures, letting on-call staff respond faster.

5.2. Rolling Out Updates Without Downtime

Minimize disruption with:

1. **Rolling Updates**
   o Gradually replace agent containers or processes (e.g., one node at a time) so the system stays operational.
2. **Blue-Green Deployments**
   o Run the new version in parallel (blue) while the old version (green) is active.
   o Switch traffic to the new version if tests pass.
3. **Canary Releases**
   o Route a small fraction of traffic to updated agents, verifying stability before broader rollout.

Case:

```
text

- A single agent type, TraderAgent, needs a bug fix.
- In a rolling strategy, 1/10 TraderAgent instances updates
to v1.1.
- If stable, proceed to next instance until all are at v1.1.
```

6. Case Study: Deploying a Multi-agent Logistics Management System on AWS

6.1. Scenario

A **logistics** company builds an MAS to manage **vehicle routing**, **warehouse inventory**, and **tracking**. Initially tested on local servers, now scaled to AWS for global coverage.

6.2. Architecture and Deployment

1. **Containerization**
   o Each agent type (RoutingAgent, InventoryAgent, TrackingAgent) runs in Docker.
2. **Kubernetes on AWS (EKS)**
   o Each agent container is orchestrated by EKS, auto-scaling based on CPU/memory metrics.
3. **CI/CD Pipeline**
   o Code changes trigger GitLab CI.
   o After tests, Docker images push to Amazon ECR.
   o EKS updates deploy the new containers with rolling strategy, ensuring no downtime.

6.3. Monitoring and Maintenance

1. **CloudWatch Metrics**
   o Real-time CPU, memory for each pod, with alarms if usage spikes or container restarts frequently.
2. **Logging**
   o Agents log to CloudWatch Logs, correlated by agent name.
3. **Auto-scaling**
   o If RoutingAgent CPU surpasses 70% for 5 minutes, EKS adds more pods.
   o Reduces request queue times in peak load.

6.4. Outcomes

- **Seamless Scalability**: System gracefully handled a 300% jump in daily route requests.

- **Minimal Downtime**: Rolling updates let new features roll out daily without user disruption.
- **Global Accessibility**: Agents communicate across AWS regions, optimizing deliveries in multiple continents.

7. End-of-Chapter Projects

Project 19: Deploying MAS on Cloud Platforms

Objective: Containerize a simplified **DeepSeek R1** multi-agent application, set up a **CI/CD** pipeline, and deploy on a **cloud** service (e.g., AWS, Azure, or GCP).

Outline

1. **Agent Containerization**
   - Create Dockerfiles for each agent type.
   - Confirm they run locally, reading configuration from environment variables.
2. **Kubernetes Deployment**
   - Write **YAML** manifests (Deployment, Service) for each agent.
   - Deploy to a local Minikube or cloud-based cluster.
3. **CI/CD Setup**
   - Use GitHub Actions or GitLab CI to build images, run tests, and push to container registry.
   - Automated deployment to staging, then manual approval for production.
4. **Monitoring & Logging**
   - Integrate a minimal Prometheus/Grafana or Cloud vendor's monitoring solution.
   - Set alerts for agent resource usage or error rates.

8. Quizzes and Self-Assessments

Quiz 19: Deployment Strategies

1. **Deployment Approaches**
   - o **Question**: What is one **key difference** between on-premises and cloud-based MAS deployment in terms of scalability?
2. **Containerization**
   - o **Question**: Why might organizations choose **Docker + Kubernetes** for running a multi-agent system?
3. **CI/CD**
   - o **Question**: Describe a typical pipeline stage sequence (build → test → deploy). How does it prevent regressions?
4. **Monitoring**
   - o **Question**: Name two metrics that are critical for tracking MAS performance in production.
5. **Maintenance**
   - o **Question**: Explain how **rolling updates** help ensure minimal downtime when rolling out new agent versions.
6. **Case Study**
   - o **Question**: In the AWS-based logistics system, what triggers auto-scaling of RoutingAgent pods?
7. **Short Coding Prompt**
   - o **Question**: Provide pseudocode for a **DeployAgent** that sends a message to "update" or "roll back" specific agent containers based on a new image tag.

Answer Key (Suggested):

1. **On-Prem vs Cloud**: Cloud can easily scale up or down on demand, while on-premises scaling requires additional hardware procurement.
2. **Docker + Kubernetes**: Enables **consistent** container environments and automates **orchestration**, scaling, and rolling updates for MAS.
3. **CI/CD Pipeline**: Build (compile + unit test) → Integration test (test multi-agent interactions) → Deploy (to staging, then production). This pipeline ensures code changes pass checks before release.
4. **Monitoring Metrics**: CPU usage and **message throughput** for each agent are critical indicators of system health and performance.
5. **Rolling Updates**: Gradually updates a few instances at a time. If something fails, the system reverts quickly and unaffected instances keep running.
6. **Case Study**: CPU usage surpassing 70% for a sustained period triggers scaling new pods for the RoutingAgent.
7. **Pseudocode**:

```python
```

```python
class DeployAgent(AgentBase):
    def on_deployment_request(self, request):
        # request: {"action": "update", "agent_type":
"TraderAgent", "image_tag": "v2.1"}
        if request["action"] == "update":

self.update_containers(request["agent_type"],
request["image_tag"])
        elif request["action"] == "rollback":

self.rollback_containers(request["agent_type"],
request["image_tag"])

    def update_containers(self, agent_type, image_tag):
        print(f"Updating {agent_type} containers to
{image_tag}...")
        # Send commands to orchestrator (e.g., K8s API)

    def rollback_containers(self, agent_type,
image_tag):
        print(f"Rolling back {agent_type} containers to
{image_tag}...")
        # Revert to previous stable version
```

Deployment and **maintenance** strategies are central to ensuring multi-agent systems **operate** reliably and **scale** effectively. Whether on-premises, cloud-based, or hybrid, modern best practices incorporate **containerization** (Docker, Kubernetes), **CI/CD** pipelines for continuous testing and deployment, robust **monitoring** solutions for real-time insights, and **maintenance** techniques like rolling updates or canary releases to avoid disruptions. The **AWS logistics** case study demonstrates the practical benefits of these approaches, including simpler scaling, minimized downtime, and secure agent orchestration. By exploring the project and quiz in this chapter, you can refine your own MAS deployment, ensuring high availability and superior performance in production environments.

Chapter 20: Monitoring and Maintenance of MAS

Once a **multi-agent system (MAS)** is successfully deployed, **monitoring** and **maintenance** become essential to keep it performing at a high level, avoid outages, and quickly resolve issues when they arise. This chapter outlines **real-time monitoring tools** compatible with DeepSeek R1, discusses **defining and tracking performance metrics**, provides strategies for **troubleshooting** common MAS problems, and explores how to implement **automated maintenance** and backup/recovery plans. We also examine a **case study** on maintaining a multi-agent energy distribution system, concluding with a practical **project** and a quiz for self-assessment.

1. Real-time Monitoring Tools

1.1. Overview of Monitoring Solutions Compatible with DeepSeek R1

DeepSeek R1 integrates smoothly with various monitoring ecosystems:

1. **Prometheus + Grafana**
   - Collects time-series metrics (CPU usage, message throughput, memory).
   - **Prometheus** scrapes agent endpoints or push gateways; **Grafana** provides interactive dashboards.
2. **ELK Stack (Elasticsearch, Logstash, Kibana)**
   - Captures logs from agents, aggregates them in **Elasticsearch**, and visualizes them in **Kibana**.
   - **Logstash** or **Filebeat** feed data from multiple agent sources into Elasticsearch.
3. **Cloud-Native Services**
   - AWS CloudWatch, Azure Monitor, or GCP Operations for metrics, logs, and alerts if you deploy MAS on these clouds.
4. **Zabbix / Nagios**
   - Traditional server monitoring tools that can be adapted to track agent-based processes.

Key Considerations:

- **Resource Overhead**: Ensure that collecting detailed metrics/logs for each agent does not overly burden the system.
- **Scalability**: As agent count grows, pick a monitoring architecture that can handle increased data volume.

1.2. Setting Up Dashboards and Alerts

1. **Dashboards**
   - Visualize real-time statuses: total agent count, average CPU usage, message queues, etc.
   - Provide drill-downs for individual agents or agent groups, highlighting performance outliers.
2. **Alerts and Notifications**
   - Define conditions (e.g., CPU usage > 80%, message queue backlog > 1000).
   - Trigger alerts via email, Slack, or pager.
   - Prioritize alerts to avoid alert fatigue—only critical ones should be high-priority.

Example (Pseudocode):

```python
# agent_metrics.py
class MetricsCollector:
    def __init__(self, monitoring_service):
        self.monitoring_service = monitoring_service

    def record_cpu_usage(self, agent_id, usage):
        metric_name = f"agent.{agent_id}.cpu"
        self.monitoring_service.send_metric(metric_name,
usage)

    def record_queue_size(self, agent_id, queue_size):
        metric_name = f"agent.{agent_id}.message_queue"
        self.monitoring_service.send_metric(metric_name,
queue_size)
```

- **Explanation**:

- Each agent logs CPU usage or queue sizes to a central monitoring service, feeding dashboards and alert systems.

---

2. Performance Metrics and KPIs

2.1. Defining Key Performance Indicators for MAS

KPIs vary by system domain but typically include:

1. **Throughput**
   - How many tasks, messages, or transactions agents handle per second/minute/hour.
2. **Latency**
   - Time from request to response, e.g., how long an agent takes to complete a job.
3. **Resource Utilization**
   - CPU, memory, or bandwidth usage across agents, ensuring no single node saturates.
4. **Error/Failure Rates**
   - Frequency of agent crashes, message drops, or exceptions.

2.2. Measuring and Analyzing System Performance

Tools like **Grafana** or cloud dashboards help interpret metrics:

1. **Trend Analysis**
   - Identify usage spikes at certain times (e.g., peak business hours).
   - Preemptively scale or shift resources to avoid bottlenecks.
2. **Comparative Benchmarks**
   - Compare current metrics with historical baselines or expected SLAs.
   - If an agent's latency grows by 50% since last month, investigate resource contention or code changes.
3. **Custom Dashboard Panels**
   - E.g., a "Top 5 busiest agents" panel highlights performance hotspots.

Table: Example KPIs for MAS

KPI	Description	Measurement Approach
Throughput (tasks/min)	Tasks completed or messages processed per minute	Agent logs, aggregator metrics
Average Latency (ms)	Time from request to agent response	Timestamps in logs or distributed tracing
CPU Utilization (%)	Average CPU usage across nodes	OS-level or container metrics
Error/Failure Rate (%)	Proportion of failed tasks or agent crashes	System logs, agent exit codes

3. Troubleshooting Common Issues

3.1. Diagnosing and Resolving Communication Failures

MAS rely on **messaging**; disruptions can stall entire workflows:

1. **Network Connectivity**
   - Check if certain nodes or containers lost network routes. Firewall or DNS misconfiguration can isolate agents.
   - Tools: `ping`, `traceroute`, or container orchestration logs.
2. **Protocol Mismatch**
   - Agents might expect **JSON** but receive binary data, or version differences in message formats cause parse errors.
   - Ensure consistent agent library versions.
3. **Queue Overflows**
   - If messages queue faster than agents consume them, backlog or timeouts occur.
   - Consider increasing concurrency or queue capacity, or applying back-pressure strategies.

3.2. Handling Agent Crashes and Unexpected Behaviors

When an agent **crashes** or misbehaves:

1. **Crash Loop**
   - Repeated agent restarts, signifying memory leaks, exceptions in initialization, or missing dependencies.
   - Gather crash logs, fix root cause, and test thoroughly.

2. **Logic Flaws**
   o Agents stuck in infinite loops or contradictory logic states.
   o Insert debug statements or step through with distributed tracing to identify deadlocks or infinite recursion.
3. **Version Incompatibility**
   o Rolling upgrades might cause partial agent sets running old code, others on new code, conflicting message formats or workflows.

Code Example (Debug):

```python
def debug_agent_crash(agent_id, crash_log):
    # parse crash_log
    if "OutOfMemoryError" in crash_log:
        print(f"{agent_id} might have a memory leak or
insufficient heap.")
    elif "KeyError" in crash_log:
        print(f"{agent_id} encountered missing dictionary
key; check message fields.")
    else:
        print(f"{agent_id} generic crash: investigate
further.")
```

- **Explanation**:
   o A simplified function that inspects crash logs for known patterns, offering quick suggestions.

4. Automated Maintenance Tasks

4.1. Implementing Self-healing Mechanisms

Self-healing improves MAS resilience:

1. **Agent Restarts**
   o If an agent stops responding (failing health checks), an orchestration tool kills and restarts it.
2. **Redundancy**
   o Multiple agent replicas in active–active configurations ensure tasks continue even if one fails.

3. **Automated Failover**
   - ○ If a manager node or database agent is down, workload is reassigned to a healthy node or replica.

4.2. Automating Routine Maintenance Processes

1. **Scheduled Cleanups**
   - ○ Agents or scripts purge old logs, temp files, or partial data at set intervals.
2. **Credential Rotation**
   - ○ Periodically rotate encryption keys, tokens, or certificates.
   - ○ Automated pipeline retrieves new secrets from a vault and restarts relevant agents seamlessly.
3. **Periodic Reboots**
   - ○ Some organizations schedule off-peak reboots for memory refresh, applying OS patches or new container images.

Table: Example Self-healing Features

Mechanism	Implementation Strategy	Benefit
Health Check Restarts	Probes agent at /health endpoint	Quickly recovers from transient failures
Redundant Agent Replica	Keep 2–3 identical agent instances active	Minimizes single points of failure
Automated Failover	Orchestrator monitors node health, reassign tasks	Avoids system downtime on node crashes

5. Data Backup and Recovery

5.1. Strategies for Data Protection

Ensuring MAS data remains safe:

1. **Regular Backups**
   - ○ Database snapshots, file archives, or object storage backups.
   - ○ Schedule daily/weekly incremental backups plus monthly full backups.
2. **Replication**

- Use **multi-zone** or **multi-region** replication to mitigate localized disasters.
- Agents reading data from near replicas to reduce latency.
3. **Backup Testing**
    - Periodically **verify** backups restore successfully; partial or corrupted backups are only discovered if tested.

5.2. Implementing Recovery Plans

Disaster Recovery for MAS:

1. **Hot/Cold Standbys**
    - **Hot** standby runs continuously, can take over instantly.
    - **Cold** standby starts only when needed, slower but cheaper.
2. **Recovery Time Objective (RTO)**
    - Acceptable downtime window. E.g., <5 minutes for high-critical systems.
3. **Recovery Point Objective (RPO)**
    - Tolerable data loss window. E.g., losing last 1 hour of data is acceptable if it's lower priority.

Code Example (Pseudocode):

```python
# backup_scheduler.py
import time

class BackupScheduler:
    def __init__(self, backup_target, interval_hours):
        self.backup_target = backup_target
        self.interval = interval_hours * 3600

    def run(self):
        while True:
            self.perform_backup()
            time.sleep(self.interval)

    def perform_backup(self):
        # snapshot or archive logic
        print(f"Backing up {self.backup_target} data to
secure storage...")
```

- **Explanation**:

o   A script scheduling periodic backups of data used by MAS agents. Real-world usage includes storing in S3 or an on-prem vault.

6. Case Study: Maintaining a Multi-agent Energy Distribution System

6.1. Context

A utility company uses **MAS** (powered by **DeepSeek R1**) to coordinate **energy distribution** across multiple regions, each with renewable sources, battery storage, and consumption monitoring.

6.2. Monitoring and Alerting Implementation

1. **Metrics**
   o   CPU usage for each agent, frequency regulation actions, and load balancing decisions logged in **Prometheus**.
   o   Out-of-range frequencies trigger high-priority alerts.
2. **Dashboards**
   o   **Grafana** shows real-time supply vs. demand graphs per region.
   o   Operators see red/yellow status if certain thresholds approach critical levels.

6.3. Maintenance Processes

1. **Rolling Updates**
   o   New versions of the "DistributionAgent" tested on one region. If stable, rolled out to all.
2. **Self-healing**

- o If "RenewableAgent" fails or times out, the orchestrator restarts it. Meanwhile, battery fallback ensures no grid disruption.
3. **Disaster Recovery**
   - o If entire data center fails, a different region's MAS nodes pick up central coordination roles, ensuring the grid remains partially operational.

6.4. Results

- **Reduced Downtime**: Frequent minor updates cause almost no user-visible disruptions.
- **Improved Reliability**: Quick auto-restart of key agents prevents supply imbalances from escalating.
- **Cost Savings**: Early detection of misconfiguration or agent overload helps avoid emergency peak sourcing from external suppliers.

7. End-of-Chapter Projects

Project 20: Implementing Monitoring Solutions

Objective: Add comprehensive **monitoring** and **maintenance** features to an existing **DeepSeek R1** multi-agent system.

Outline

1. **Select or Install Monitoring Stack**
   - o For example, Prometheus + Grafana locally or a cloud monitoring service.
2. **Instrument Agents**
   - o Each agent publishes CPU/memory usage, queue lengths, error counts to the monitoring stack.
   - o Include a /health or /metrics endpoint if needed.
3. **Set Up Alert Rules**
   - o High CPU usage or repeated agent crashes trigger alarms.
   - o Low throughput might indicate communication bottlenecks or failing nodes.
4. **Maintenance Scripting**

o Implement a scheduled script rotating logs, performing data backups, or revalidating agent credentials monthly.

5. **Validate**
   o Force agent crashes or resource overuse in a test environment, ensuring system recovers or alerts.

---

8. Quizzes and Self-Assessments

Quiz 20: Monitoring and Maintenance

1. **Monitoring Tools**
   o **Question**: Name one **open-source** monitoring solution often used for collecting and visualizing MAS metrics.
2. **Performance Metrics**
   o **Question**: Why is it critical to define **KPI** thresholds for multi-agent systems, and how do they help operators?
3. **Troubleshooting**
   o **Question**: Provide an example of a **communication failure** in MAS and how you might diagnose it.
4. **Automated Maintenance**
   o **Question**: What does "self-healing" mean in the context of MAS, and give one technique to achieve it.
5. **Data Backup**
   o **Question**: Outline a simple backup strategy that ensures minimal data loss in case of unexpected failures.
6. **Case Study**
   o **Question**: In the energy distribution example, how does rolling update prevent system-wide outages?
7. **Short Coding Prompt**
   o **Question**: Write pseudocode for a "HealthCheckAgent" that periodically checks other agents' /health endpoints and restarts them if unresponsive.

Answer Key (Suggested):

1. **Monitoring Tool**: Prometheus (often paired with Grafana for dashboards).

2. **KPI Thresholds**: They define **alert** triggers and serve as operational goals (e.g., keep CPU <80%), helping operators quickly react if metrics deviate.
3. **Communication Failure**: Example: Agents cannot parse each other's messages due to format mismatch. Diagnosed by checking logs or trying a simpler handshake test.
4. **Self-healing**: MAS automatically recovers from errors or crashes (e.g., container orchestration restarts a failed agent).
5. **Backup Strategy**: Perform daily incremental backups and weekly full backups to secure storage, verifying restore capabilities each month.
6. **Rolling Update**: Upgrading one region or agent instance at a time ensures if something fails, only a small part is affected; rest remain stable.
7. **Pseudocode**:

```python
class HealthCheckAgent(AgentBase):
    def __init__(self, agent_list):
        super().__init__("HealthCheckAgent")
        self.agents_to_check = agent_list

    def run_periodically(self):
        while True:
            for agent in self.agents_to_check:
                if not self.check_health(agent):
                    self.restart_agent(agent)
            time.sleep(30)

    def check_health(self, agent):
        response =
self.http_get(f"http://{agent}/health")
        return response.status_code == 200

    def restart_agent(self, agent):
        print(f"{agent} is unresponsive; triggering
restart.")
        # or call orchestrator API to kill/recreate
container
```

Monitoring and maintaining a **multi-agent system** is an ongoing process that ensures **availability**, **performance**, and **resilience** over time. By deploying comprehensive **monitoring solutions**, defining **KPIs**, and instituting robust **maintenance** strategies—including self-healing, backups, and safe update mechanisms—organizations can keep MAS running smoothly and adapt to evolving demands. The **energy distribution** case study demonstrates how well-executed monitoring and maintenance lead to a stable, efficient system, even under rapid updates or agent restarts.

Chapter 21: Real-Time Adjustments and Adaptations

Real-time adjustments and **adaptations** are critical in **multi-agent systems (MAS)** that operate in dynamic or unpredictable environments. By reacting to new data streams, changing conditions, and user feedback, MAS can maintain optimal performance and seamlessly scale resources. This chapter explores **dynamic environment handling**, **hot swapping of agents**, **real-time data integration**, the use of **feedback loops** for continuous improvement, and **automated scaling**. We also feature a **case study** on real-time adaptation in a financial analysis system, followed by a practical **project** and a quiz for self-assessment.

---

1. Dynamic Environment Handling

1.1. Adapting to Changing Conditions

Environment in MAS can evolve due to:

1. **External Factors**
   - Weather changes affecting supply/demand in an energy grid, shifts in user traffic for e-commerce, or changing resource availability in a factory.
2. **Internal System States**
   - Agent load spikes, partial hardware failures, or evolving agent configurations.

Adaptation strategies:

- **Context-Aware Agents**: Agents maintain an internal model of the environment (e.g., current demand, resource states, or user interactions). Changes in these states trigger recalculations or re-planning.
- **Rule-Based Adaptation**: Agents follow explicit rules: "If traffic load > X, switch to high throughput mode."
- **Learning Models**: Machine learning–driven responses, where agents refine policies based on new data.

1.2. Implementing Real-time Learning and Adaptation

Real-time learning (online or incremental) updates agent decision models continuously:

1. **Incremental Training**
   - o Agents refine their models each time they receive new data or user feedback, gradually adjusting behaviors.
2. **Reinforcement Learning**
   - o Agents repeatedly experiment in the environment, receiving rewards or penalties. As conditions shift (e.g., new user behaviors), the agent updates value functions or policies accordingly.
3. **Active Learning**
   - o When uncertain, agents query users or specialized modules for clarification or labeling, ensuring models remain fresh and accurate.

Code Example (Pseudocode):

```python
# dynamic_environment_handling.py
class AdaptiveAgent:
    def __init__(self, policy_model):
        self.policy_model = policy_model  # e.g. an ML model
or rule set

    def observe(self, new_data):
        self.policy_model.update(new_data)  # incremental or
online update

    def decide_action(self, state):
        return self.policy_model.predict(state)
```

- **Explanation**:
  - o The agent updates its decision logic whenever new data arrives, ensuring continuous adaptation to changing conditions.

---

2. Hot Swapping Agents

2.1. Adding or Removing Agents Without Downtime

Hot swapping means modifying the MAS composition at runtime, crucial for:

1. **Scalability**
   o Launch new agent instances when load grows, retire them during off-peak.
2. **Modularity**
   o Switch agent versions (e.g., upgrading from v1.0 to v1.1) without halting the entire system.
3. **Fault Recovery**
   o Replace malfunctioning agents on the fly.

Techniques:

- **Orchestrator Integration**: Tools like Kubernetes gracefully add or remove containers while maintaining the rest of the system.
- **Service Registries**: Agents register to a directory. When an agent leaves, the registry updates, ensuring no stale references remain.

2.2. Ensuring System Stability During Changes

When removing or updating an agent:

1. **Drain or Migrate Tasks**
   o Ongoing tasks are completed or handed off before the agent shuts down, avoiding abrupt failures.
2. **Coordinated Protocol**
   o Agents notify neighbors of departure or version change, so no critical messages get lost or misrouted.
3. **Version Compatibility**
   o Agents should remain backward-compatible for messaging or have an interoperability strategy (e.g., fallback to older protocols until all updated).

Table: Strategies for Hot Swapping Agents

Strategy	Implementation Detail	Benefit
Rolling Upgrade	Gradually replace instances with new versions	Minimal disruption, easy rollback

Strategy	Implementation Detail	Benefit
Parallel Launch	Spin up new agent instances first, then retire old ones	No downtime, allows warm-up of new versions
Graceful Shutdown	Agents complete tasks before exit	Avoids partial tasks or data corruption

3. Real-time Data Integration

3.1. Incorporating Live Data Streams

MAS often requires **live data** to adjust decisions:

1. **Streaming Frameworks**
   - Tools like Kafka, RabbitMQ, or Apache Pulsar feed continuous event data into agents.
2. **Event-Driven Architectures**
   - Agents subscribe to relevant streams (e.g., "PriceUpdates," "SensorData"), receiving incremental updates in near-real-time.

Challenges:

- **High Throughput**: Agents must handle spikes in event volume without lag or data loss.
- **Ordering Guarantees**: Some tasks require sequential event processing. Solutions like Kafka partitions or concurrency controls help maintain order.

3.2. Ensuring Data Consistency and Integrity

As data streams in from multiple sources:

1. **Schema Evolution**
   - E.g., if new fields appear in sensor data, agents must handle it gracefully, ignoring unknown fields or updating their logic.
2. **Deduplication**
   - Streams can produce duplicate events. Agents track message IDs or timestamps to avoid repeated processing.
3. **Distributed Transactions**

o Some operations need consistent updates across agents or data stores, requiring two-phase commit or similar protocols for strong consistency.

Code Example (Pseudocode):

```python
# streaming_integration.py
class StreamConsumerAgent:
    def __init__(self, stream_source):
        self.stream_source = stream_source

    def run(self):
        for event in self.stream_source.consume():
            if not self.is_duplicate(event):
                self.handle_event(event)

    def handle_event(self, event):
        # E.g., update agent state or forward to relevant
peers
        pass

    def is_duplicate(self, event):
        # Check a cache or ID record to filter duplicates
        return False
```

- **Explanation**:
    - o Illustrates continuous consumption from a streaming source, ignoring repeated events to maintain data integrity.

4. Feedback Loops and Continuous Improvement

4.1. Implementing Feedback Mechanisms

Feedback loops refine agent performance or user satisfaction:

1. **User Feedback**
    - o Agents gather user ratings or comments on decisions (e.g., "helpful/unhelpful" for a recommendation).
2. **System Metrics**

- Agents track success/failure rates, adjusting policies. For instance, a scheduling agent sees frequent manual overrides, indicating a need to revise its constraints.
3. **Self-Assessment**
   - Agents regularly check their own predictions against real outcomes (e.g., demand forecasting vs. actual usage).

4.2. Using Feedback for System Enhancements

Feedback can drive:

1. **Model Retraining**
   - Agents fine-tune ML models with corrected labels or outcomes for better future accuracy.
2. **Rule Optimization**
   - Agents delete or revise rarely used or contradictory rules.
3. **User-Centric Prioritization**
   - If certain tasks repeatedly fail or cause user frustration, escalate them to be handled first or assigned to more capable agents.

5. Automated Scaling and Resource Management

5.1. Dynamic Resource Allocation

When load surges or new tasks arise:

1. **Load Balancers**
   - Distribute requests across multiple agent instances.
   - Agents register/deregister with balancers upon arrival or removal.
2. **Autoscalers**
   - Monitor agent metrics (CPU usage, message queue) and automatically spawn new instances or scale them down.
   - For example, if queue length remains high, double the number of WorkerAgents.

5.2. Scaling Agents Based on Demand

Scenarios:

1. **Time-based Scheduling**
   - Agents scale up during known peak hours, scale down at night.
2. **Reactive Scaling**
   - Triggered by real-time metrics crossing thresholds (e.g., TraderAgent CPU usage > 80%).
3. **Proactive Forecasting**
   - Demand forecasting agent signals upcoming spikes, prompting early scale-ups to avoid backlogs.

Table: Auto-scaling Approaches

Approach	Trigger	Benefits
Threshold-based	Metrics exceed thresholds (CPU, queue length)	Simple to configure, direct reaction
Schedule-based	Known peak times or events	Avoids overhead of continuous metric checks
Predictive/Forecasting	Agent predictions (ML-based) of future demand	Minimizes lag, more proactive scaling

6. Case Study: Real-time Adaptation in a Multi-agent Financial Analysis System

6.1. Scenario

A **finance** company runs a MAS analyzing market data for **stock recommendations**. Data arrives in real-time from multiple exchanges, and agents generate trades or alerts for clients.

6.2. Implementation

1. **Dynamic Data Integration**
   - Agents subscribe to live **price feeds**. Each agent tracks relevant symbols.

2. **On-the-fly Agent Swapping**
   o If a new analysis module emerges, the old module is **hot-swapped**; the system seamlessly transitions to the updated agent.
3. **Adaptive Learning**
   o Agents tune strategies with each market shift. If certain trades underperform, the agent reduces that strategy's weighting.

6.3. Outcome

- **Responsive Trading**: Agents adapt models within hours of emerging market patterns.
- **Minimal Disruption**: Replacing an underperforming agent instance causes no downtime; trades continue.
- **Increased Profitability**: Real-time feedback loops let the system pivot quickly, capturing opportunities or limiting losses.

Table: Measurable Adaptation Gains

Metric	Before Adaptive Strategy	After Adaptive Strategy	Improvement
Avg. Model Latency	1 second	300 ms	-70% latency
Strategy Update Cycle	Weekly retrains	Ongoing incremental	Real-time corrections
Profit Rate Variation	High swings on changes	More stable performance	Reduced volatility

7. End-of-Chapter Projects

Project 21: Developing Adaptive MAS

Objective: Build a **DeepSeek R1** multi-agent system with **real-time adaptation**. Incorporate dynamic environment handling, hot swapping of agents, and a feedback loop mechanism.

Outline

1. **Initial Setup**

o   Develop a baseline MAS (e.g., a job scheduling or data processing scenario).

2. **Dynamic Inputs**
   o   Emulate changing environment data (e.g., random load surges or new tasks).

3. **Adaptive Agents**
   o   Agents learn or reconfigure parameters based on environment shifts.
   o   Possibly incorporate a "manager" agent for partial planning adjustments.

4. **Hot Swap**
   o   Deploy an updated agent mid-run, verifying no downtime or data loss.

5. **Feedback Loop**
   o   Collect user or system feedback (success rates, satisfaction). Agents refine behavior or model accordingly.

8. Quizzes and Self-Assessments

Quiz 21: Real-Time Adaptations

1. **Dynamic Environment**
   o   **Question**: Why do multi-agent systems require **on-the-fly** adaptation when operating in complex, rapidly changing domains?

2. **Hot Swapping**
   o   **Question**: Define **hot swapping** in MAS and give one practical example of its benefit.

3. **Real-time Data**
   o   **Question**: How can **event-driven** architectures and data streaming benefit MAS performance?

4. **Feedback Loops**
   o   **Question**: Name a use case where **human feedback** directly improves agent decisions.

5. **Scaling**
   o   **Question**: What triggers might an **autoscaler** watch for to decide agent scaling in real-time?

6. **Case Study**

- ○ **Question**: In the financial analysis system, name one advantage of regularly adjusting agent strategies.
7. **Short Coding Prompt**
   - ○ **Question**: Write pseudocode for a method `replaceAgent(old_agent, new_agent)` that ensures minimal disruption when swapping out an agent.

Answer Key (Suggested):

1. **On-the-fly Adaptation**: MAS face **unpredictable** events (market shifts, user surges). Adapting in real time prevents performance degradation or missed opportunities.
2. **Hot Swapping**: Replacing or adding agent instances **without system downtime** (e.g., upgrading a data parser agent mid-day so data processing never stops).
3. **Event-driven**: Agents react instantly to changes, avoiding polling delays. They scale or alter decisions as new messages stream in.
4. **Human Feedback**: E.g., **customer support** agents learn from user satisfaction scores or corrections, refining future responses.
5. **Autoscaler Triggers**: CPU usage, message queue lengths, or response latency rising above thresholds.
6. **Case Study**: Adjusting agent strategies to match **new** market data helps maintain or improve trading gains, reducing losses from outdated models.
7. **Pseudocode**:

```python
def replaceAgent(old_agent, new_agent):
    # Step 1: gracefully stop new tasks to old_agent
    old_agent.set_accept_new_tasks(False)

    # Step 2: old_agent finishes pending tasks or
migrates them to new_agent
    while not old_agent.is_idle():
        time.sleep(1)

    # Step 3: start new_agent, register with directory
or orchestrator
    new_agent.register()

    # Step 4: deregister and shut down old_agent
    old_agent.deregister()
    old_agent.shutdown()
```

Real-time **adjustments** and **adaptations** keep multi-agent systems **responsive** and **robust** in ever-evolving environments. By **dynamically** handling environment shifts, **hot swapping** agents, integrating **live data** streams, implementing **feedback loops**, and **auto-scaling** resources, MAS remain flexible and efficient. The **financial analysis** case exemplifies how quick adaptation fosters better performance. Applying these principles in the **end-of-chapter project** will deepen your skill in designing MAS that gracefully adapt to real-time changes, ensuring continual effectiveness and stability.

Chapter 22: Testing and Validation in MAS

Testing and **validation** play a **crucial role** in ensuring multi-agent systems (MAS) are reliable, stable, and aligned with their intended purposes. Given the inherently distributed and interactive nature of MAS, thorough testing uncovers potential bugs, performance bottlenecks, and unexpected interactions that only emerge when multiple agents collaborate. This chapter delves into the **importance** of testing MAS, outlines **testing methodologies** from unit to system level, discusses **validation** (simulation vs. real-world), covers how to automate testing with **DeepSeek R1**, and highlights **best practices**. We also look at a **financial trading** case study and propose a project plus a quiz for comprehensive learning.

---

1. Importance of Testing in MAS

1.1. Ensuring Reliability and Stability

Multi-agent systems often run critical tasks—whether in healthcare, autonomous vehicles, or large-scale financial trading. Reliability ensures:

1. **Consistent Operation**
   - Agents consistently fulfill tasks, responding to requests with minimal errors.
2. **High Availability**
   - Even if some agents encounter issues, the system as a whole continues to function.
3. **Predictable Performance**
   - Reduces the risk of serious failures or unexpected downtimes.

Failing to test thoroughly can lead to:

- **Cascading failures**: One agent's bug triggers negative effects in others.
- **Unpredictable results**: Agents coordinate poorly or produce contradictory outcomes.

1.2. Identifying and Fixing Bugs

MAS bugs can be subtle:

1. **Coordination Mistakes**
   - Race conditions in message flows or incorrect synchronization among agents.
2. **Logic Errors**
   - Agents misapply rules or ML models, leading to suboptimal or destructive decisions.
3. **Communication Breakdowns**
   - If messages fail to parse or are lost at scale, the entire system's functioning can degrade.

Thorough testing isolates these problems before deployment, saving time, money, and reputational harm.

---

2. Testing Methodologies for MAS

2.1. Unit Testing for Agents

Unit tests focus on **individual agent logic** in isolation:

1. **Function-Level Checks**
   - Validate internal methods (e.g., a scheduling function's correctness).
2. **Local Data Handling**
   - Ensure an agent's data structures (queues, knowledge base) handle edge cases (empty, large volume).
3. **Mocking External Interactions**
   - Replace agent-to-agent messages with stubs or mocks to confirm the local logic alone.

Benefits:

- Quick to execute and pinpoint where failures occur.
- Encourages more modular, testable agent designs.

2.2. Integration Testing for Multi-agent Interactions

Integration tests verify **agents** can communicate and coordinate properly:

1. **Scenario-Driven**
   o Simulate typical or edge-case workflows. For example, a request passing from a CustomerAgent to a PaymentAgent to a ShippingAgent.
2. **Network Emulation**
   o Test normal message flow, delayed messages, or partial disconnections.
3. **Behavior Validation**
   o Confirm that agents collectively achieve system goals (e.g., correct transaction completion).

2.3. System Testing for Overall MAS Performance

System-level testing focuses on:

1. **End-to-End**
   o Evaluate the entire MAS flow under realistic conditions or data volumes.
2. **Performance & Scalability**
   o Tools or load generators measure how the MAS handles concurrent tasks or large message bursts.
3. **Stress & Soak Tests**
   o Push the system beyond normal limits or run it for extended periods to find memory leaks or slow degradations.

Table: Testing Levels for MAS

Level	Scope	Example
Unit Testing	Individual agent components	Checking a PricingAgent's discount calculation logic
Integration	Multi-agent communication	Verifying OrderAgent → PaymentAgent → NotificationAgent flow
System	Whole MAS performance	Load testing a supply chain MAS with thousands of simultaneous tasks

3. Validation Techniques

3.1. Simulation-based Validation

Simulation is **key** for MAS:

1. **Virtual Environments**
   - Agents run in controlled conditions with simulated external triggers (e.g., fake sensor data, user requests).
   - Minimizes risks to real infrastructure.
2. **Scenarios & Stress Conditions**
   - Emulate high load or catastrophic events (e.g., half the agents crash) to see if the system recovers gracefully.
3. **Collect Metrics**
   - Measure throughput, latency, correctness of agent responses in the scenario.

Advantages:

- Lower cost and no real-world harm if errors happen.
- Easily repeatable for regression checks.

3.2. Real-world Scenario Testing

After simulation:

1. **Pilot Environments**
   - Deploy the MAS in a smaller subset of real conditions or with volunteer users.
2. **A/B Testing**
   - Compare new MAS features or agent logic with existing systems in a partial production setting.
3. **Gradual Rollouts**
   - Deploy to a fraction of real traffic, monitoring results carefully.

Risks:

- Potential real harm if the system has critical bugs.
- Must ensure fallback options or manual overrides.

4. Automated Testing with DeepSeek R1

4.1. Setting Up Automated Test Suites

DeepSeek R1 can integrate with **CI/CD** pipelines:

1. **Agent Test Harness**
   - Scripts instantiate test environments, spin up test agents, and orchestrate messages.
   - Verifies agent outputs or state transitions match expected results.
2. **Configuration for Test**
   - Agents may load mock data or restricted functionalities in a test mode, ensuring isolation from production resources.
3. **Headless Execution**
   - Tests run **without** user interaction, reporting pass/fail to the pipeline.
   - Logs and coverage data saved for analysis.

4.2. Continuous Testing Integration

A fully automated pipeline can:

1. **Trigger** on each commit or merge request.
2. **Build** agent code and containers, run **unit tests** then **integration tests**.
3. **Deploy** to a staging environment for system-level tests.
4. Provide dashboards summarizing test coverage and performance.

Code Example (Pseudocode):

```python
# test_agent_workflow.py

def test_agent_integration():
    # Start a minimal MAS environment with 2-3 agents
    agentA, agentB = launch_agents(["AgentA", "AgentB"],
config="test_mode")

    # Send a sample message or workload
    agentA.send_message({"receiver": "AgentB", "payload":
"hello"})
```

```
# Wait for outcome, check logs or states
results = gather_logs([agentA, agentB])
assert "received: hello" in results["AgentB"], "AgentB
didn't receive message from AgentA"

teardown_agents([agentA, agentB])
```

- **Explanation**:
    - o Illustrates a simplified approach to integration testing with a minimal cluster of agents, checking if the message flow is correct.

5. Best Practices for Reliable MAS

5.1. Test-Driven Development (TDD)

TDD merges design and testing:

1. **Write Failing Tests First**
    - o Define the agent function or behavior you want. The test initially fails since the feature isn't implemented yet.
2. **Implement Minimal Code**
    - o Just enough to pass the test. Keep code focused and robust.
3. **Refactor**
    - o Clean up, ensuring no new failures.

Advantages:

- Encourages modular, testable agent architecture.
- Reduces regression issues by building a thorough suite from the start.

5.2. Code Reviews and Quality Assurance

1. **Peer Reviews**
    - o Another developer inspects agent logic, potential race conditions, or architecture decisions.
    - o Catches design flaws or oversights early.
2. **Static Analysis**

- o Automated tools (linters, security scanners) check for suspicious patterns, memory leaks, or style violations.
3. **Regression Suites**
   - o Past bug fixes must remain tested in each iteration to ensure they don't resurface.

Table: QA Methods in MAS

QA Method	Focus Area	Benefit
TDD	Start tests before writing feature code	Ensures thorough coverage, clarifies design
Peer Review	Humans validate logic, style, concurrency	Finds conceptual errors early
Static Analysis	Automated checking for code issues	Prevents memory, concurrency, or style problems
Regression Testing	Re-check past bug fixes each iteration	Guards against reintroduced defects

6. Case Study: Validating a Multi-agent Financial Trading System

6.1. Context

A financial firm's **MAS** handles real-time **trade execution**, **risk checks**, and **market data**. Speed and correctness are paramount.

6.2. Testing Approach

1. **Unit Tests**
   - o TraderAgent's price calculation, RiskAgent's margin rules tested in isolation.
2. **Integration Tests**
   - o Full workflow from new trade submission to risk approval, ensuring no miscommunication or timing issues.
3. **Stress Testing**
   - o High frequency of trades (thousands/sec) simulating **market spikes**. Agents must maintain acceptable latency with no backlog.

4. **Simulation-based Validation**
    o   Replays historical market data, verifying the MAS yields
        consistent results.
    o   Identifies anomalies in agent logic or performance
        degradations under certain market patterns.

6.3. Outcome

*   **Fewer Production Incidents**: Early detection of concurrency bugs in
    the risk module, saving potential large trading losses.
*   **Optimized Performance**: Stress tests guided code optimization,
    reducing average trade latencies by 30%.
*   **Regulatory Compliance**: Thorough logs and validated workflows
    help meet oversight requirements from financial authorities.

Table: Testing Gains

Metric	Before Testing Overhaul	After Testing Overhaul	Improvement
Trade Latency (avg)	500 ms	350 ms	-30%
Production Incidents/mo.	5	2	-60%
Bug Fix Turnaround (days)	4	1–2	Faster resolution

7. End-of-Chapter Projects

Project 22: Creating Automated Test Suites

Objective: Develop **comprehensive** automated tests for a **DeepSeek R1**
multi-agent application, covering **unit**, **integration**, and **system** testing.

Outline

1. **Define a Basic MAS**
    o   For instance, a minimal e-commerce system with OrderAgent,
        PaymentAgent, InventoryAgent.
2. **Unit Tests**

- o Test each agent's local logic, e.g., PaymentAgent's discount function, InventoryAgent's reorder logic.
3. **Integration Tests**
   - o Start all agents in a test harness. Submit end-to-end order flows. Confirm correct item stocks, payment confirmations, etc.
4. **System Tests**
   - o Introduce load or concurrency. Time the overall processing from order creation to shipping label generation.
5. **CI Pipeline**
   - o Integrate these tests so every code commit triggers them. Summaries inform pass/fail status, coverage reports.

8. Quizzes and Self-Assessments

Quiz 22: Testing and Validation

1. **Importance of Testing**
   - o **Question**: In what ways can **thorough testing** improve MAS **reliability** and **stability**?
2. **Methodologies**
   - o **Question**: Differentiate between **integration** testing and **system** testing in MAS contexts.
3. **Validation Techniques**
   - o **Question**: Give one advantage of **simulation-based** validation over real-world scenario testing.
4. **Automated Testing**
   - o **Question**: Why is it beneficial to integrate tests into a **CI/CD** pipeline for MAS?
5. **Best Practices**
   - o **Question**: Explain how **Test-Driven Development (TDD)** aligns with building robust multi-agent architectures.
6. **Case Study**
   - o **Question**: In the financial trading MAS example, what major improvement did stress testing help achieve?
7. **Short Coding Prompt**
   - o **Question**: Write pseudocode for a **system test** function that simulates multiple user purchase flows in an e-commerce MAS and checks for correct final order states.

Answer Key (Suggested):

1. **Reliability & Stability**: Testing identifies concurrency bugs, ensures correct message handling, and prevents partial system breakdowns.
2. **Integration vs System Testing**: Integration focuses on multi-agent interactions; system testing looks at the entire MAS under real or high-load conditions.
3. **Simulation-based**: Offers safer environment with no real-world risks, can replicate extremes easily, and is more controllable.
4. **CI/CD**: Ensures **every** code change is tested, catching regressions early and automating the release pipeline for faster iteration.
5. **TDD**: Forces a design approach where each agent's functionality is clearly defined and verified, reducing untested or ad-hoc code.
6. **Stress Testing Benefit**: Reduced trade latency by 30% by revealing performance bottlenecks in the risk module or message routing.
7. **Pseudocode**:

```python
def system_test_ecommerce():
    # Launch MAS: PaymentAgent, OrderAgent,
    InventoryAgent
    order_agent, payment_agent, inventory_agent =
    launch_test_environment()

    # Simulate multiple user flows
    for user_id in range(1, 101):
        item_count = random.randint(1, 5)
        order_id = order_agent.create_order(user_id,
    item_count)
        payment_result =
    payment_agent.process_payment(order_id)
        assert payment_result == "SUCCESS", "Payment
    must succeed"

        final_status =
    order_agent.get_order_status(order_id)
        assert final_status == "SHIPPED", f"Expected
    SHIPPED, got {final_status}"

    teardown_environment([order_agent, payment_agent,
    inventory_agent])
```

Testing and validation are the **foundation** of robust, high-performing multi-agent systems. By employing **unit**, **integration**, and **system** testing methodologies—bolstered by **simulation** and **real-world scenario** checks—developers can ensure MAS meet business and user expectations. **Automated** suites embedded in **CI/CD pipelines** preserve quality through every iteration, while best practices like **TDD** and **code reviews** improve reliability. The **financial trading** case demonstrates real gains in **latency** and **production stability** when testing is a priority.

Chapter 23: Legal and Regulatory Compliance in MAS Deployment

As **multi-agent systems (MAS)** expand into sensitive and high-stakes domains—ranging from healthcare to finance to autonomous vehicles—it becomes essential to **understand** and **comply** with relevant legal frameworks. Organizations must ensure data protection, address industry-specific regulations, and consider liability implications for autonomous decision-making. This chapter explores **key laws and standards** affecting MAS, details how to implement **compliance mechanisms**, discusses **intellectual property** considerations, and outlines **accountability** in operations. A **case study** featuring a healthcare MAS demonstrates how to navigate compliance effectively, concluding with **projects** and a **quiz** for self-assessment.

1. Understanding Legal Frameworks

1.1. Key Laws and Regulations Affecting MAS

Global regulatory landscapes often impact how MAS are designed and operated:

1. **Data Protection Regulations**
   - **GDPR** in the EU, **CCPA** in California, and other data privacy laws shape how agents collect, store, and process personal information.
2. **AI-specific Legislation**
   - Proposed or emerging laws (e.g., **EU AI Act**) classify AI applications by risk level, imposing stricter obligations for high-risk use cases such as critical infrastructure or healthcare.
3. **Industry Rules**
   - Financial markets or healthcare data usage might require robust auditing, robust security, and transparency in agent decisions.

1.2. International Compliance Standards

MAS can span multiple **jurisdictions**, each with unique rules:

1. **ISO/IEC Standards**
   o AI safety, cybersecurity, and quality management standards like ISO 27001 for information security.
2. **Cross-Border Data Transfer**
   o Agents exchanging data across regions must handle it according to **GDPR** or equivalent frameworks ensuring lawful data flows.
3. **Conventions and Treaties**
   o Autonomous systems in defense or cross-border e-commerce might be subject to international arms control, export regulations, or trade agreements.

Table: Examples of Legal and Compliance Domains

Domain	Primary Focus	Example Regulation
Data Privacy	Protect personal data, ensure user rights	GDPR, CCPA
AI-specific Legislation	Classify AI risk, enforce transparency	Proposed EU AI Act
Sectoral (Finance/Health)	Safeguard consumer data, ensure safety/quality	HIPAA, MiFID II, FDA guidelines (for devices)
Security Standards	Maintain information security	ISO 27001, NIST Cybersecurity Framework

2. Data Protection and Privacy Laws

2.1. GDPR, CCPA, and Other Privacy Regulations

Data privacy laws govern how MAS handle user information:

1. **GDPR (EU)**
   o Broad **data subject rights** (access, rectification, erasure).
   o Requires explicit **consent** for data processing, strict rules on data retention, breach notifications.
2. **CCPA (California)**
   o Grants consumers rights to **opt out** of data sales, request deletion.

o   Agents interacting with California residents must handle requests accordingly.
3. **Other Frameworks**
   o   **PIPEDA** in Canada, **LGPD** in Brazil, or local privacy acts in Asia/Pacific regions.

2.2. Implementing Compliance Mechanisms in MAS

1. **Data Minimization**
   o   Agents only collect or store data essential for their tasks.
   o   Automatic purging of old logs or personally identifiable information (PII) reduces risk.
2. **User Consent Management**
   o   Agents may prompt for user consent or abide by global system settings (e.g., "do not track" toggles).
   o   MAS must handle revocation of consent gracefully.
3. **Encryption and Access Control**
   o   Protect personal data at rest (database encryption) and in transit (TLS).
   o   Only authorized agents see sensitive attributes.

Code Example (Pseudocode):

```python
# privacy_compliance.py
class PrivacyAgent(AgentBase):
    def store_user_data(self, user_id, data):
        if not self.check_consent(user_id):
            raise Exception("No consent for data processing")
        sanitized_data = self.sanitize_data(data)
        # store only necessary fields
        self.database.save(user_id, sanitized_data)

    def check_consent(self, user_id):
        # query user consent records
        return self.consent_db.has_consented(user_id)

    def sanitize_data(self, data):
        # remove unnecessary PII fields
        data.pop("ssn", None)
        return data
```

• **Explanation**:

- o A minimal example demonstrating compliance checks before storing user data, removing unneeded PII.

---

3. Industry-Specific Regulations

3.1. Healthcare, Finance, Autonomous Vehicles, etc.

MAS can operate in **highly regulated** sectors:

1. **Healthcare**
   - o **HIPAA** (in the US) for patient data protection; agents must ensure restricted disclosures and maintain audit logs.
   - o Medical device software may need FDA clearances if it influences diagnosis or treatment.
2. **Finance**
   - o **MiFID II** in the EU, **FINRA** in the US require transaction logs, compliance checks, and transparency in AI-based trading.
   - o Agents must enforce anti-money laundering (AML) or "know your customer" (KYC) procedures.
3. **Autonomous Vehicles**
   - o Standards ensuring safe driving algorithms, sensor validation, and fallback strategies.
   - o Regulatory bodies may mandate liability insurance or real-time data recording for post-accident forensics.

3.2. Navigating Sector-specific Legal Requirements

Key steps to ensure compliance:

1. **Research and Consultation**
   - o Engage domain experts or lawyers to interpret how MAS functionalities intersect with existing regulations.
2. **Technical Controls**
   - o Implement mandatory logging, encryption, or event reporting as mandated by sector guidelines.
3. **Validation and Certification**

     ○ Agents requiring official certification or audits must pass recognized test suites or meet industry thresholds (e.g., certification for medical AI solutions).

Table: Examples of Industry-Specific MAS Compliance

Sector	Core Regulatory Concerns	MAS Implications
Healthcare	Patient privacy, FDA approvals for AI-driven diagnostics	HIPAA-compliant data handling, ethical decision
Finance	Transaction audits, anti-fraud, real-time trading oversight	Strict logging, KYC checks, real-time risk agent
Autonomous Vehicles	Road safety, sensor integrity, liability frameworks	Agent logs of driving decisions, fail-safes
Manufacturing	Safety standards (ISO), worker protection	Robot-human interaction, hazard detection

4. Intellectual Property Considerations

4.1. Protecting MAS Innovations

MAS solutions often represent valuable **intellectual property** (IP):

1. **Patents**
    - Innovative algorithms or agent coordination protocols might be **patentable** if they meet novelty and non-obviousness criteria.
    - However, software patents have region-specific challenges or restrictions.
2. **Trade Secrets**
    - Agents' internal decision heuristics or data structures can remain **proprietary** if kept confidential.
3. **Copyright**
    - Codebase, agent definitions, and documentation are automatically protected under copyright law.

4.2. Licensing and Open-source Compliance

Licensing clarifies usage rights:

1. **Open-source**
   - o If MAS or underlying components adopt GPL, MIT, or Apache licensing, ensure the system respects those license requirements.
   - o Some licenses require distribution of source code if derivatives are distributed.
2. **Commercial Licenses**
   - o If you integrate commercial libraries, agent usage might be restricted by seat count, hardware environment, or usage dimension.
3. **Compliance Tracking**
   - o Tools like **FOSSA** or **Black Duck** scan code for license conflicts, ensuring you don't inadvertently violate a library's terms.

5. Liability and Accountability

5.1. Defining Responsibility in MAS Operations

When a MAS error causes harm or losses:

1. **Developer Liability**
   - o If code defects or negligence in design led to issues, the developer/organization may bear responsibility.
2. **Operator Liability**
   - o The entity deploying or overseeing the MAS (hospital, finance firm, etc.) often shares accountability for outcomes.
3. **Shared Accountability**
   - o Many legal frameworks increasingly point to distributed liability: each stakeholder must demonstrate due diligence in design, monitoring, and control.

5.2. Legal Implications of Autonomous Decision-Making

As agents become more autonomous:

1. **Agency Concept**

- Legally, the agent is not a human but may perform tasks on the organization's behalf—**who** is the agent's principal, and to what degree does the principal oversee?
2. **Autonomous Vehicle Collisions**
   - If a self-driving agent decides incorrectly, does the **manufacturer**, **software provider**, or **driver** hold liability?
3. **AI Accountability**
   - Proposed laws might require that humans remain in ultimate control, especially for high-risk actions like lethal force or major financial trades.

Table: Scenarios of Agent Liability

Scenario	Potential Liable Parties
Financial MAS executes a ruinous trade	Software dev if coding error, bank if oversight lacking
Healthcare agent misdiagnoses patient	Hospital operator, software vendor, or caretaker doctors
Autonomous vehicle accident	Car manufacturer, AI module provider, vehicle owner/operator

6. Case Study: Navigating Regulatory Compliance in a Multi-agent Healthcare System

6.1. Scenario

A **hospital** deploys a **DeepSeek R1**-based MAS to handle patient scheduling, diagnosis assistance, and medication management. The system processes personal health info, triages patients to specialized modules, and updates electronic health records.

6.2. Key Compliance Measures

1. **HIPAA Alignment**
   - Agents encrypt patient data at rest and in transit. Access controls ensure only authorized roles see sensitive health info.
2. **GDPR**

- o If serving EU patients, the system supports data subject requests (e.g., a patient can request a full data download or deletion).
3. **Audit Trails**
   - o Each agent logs relevant interactions and decisions (e.g., diagnosis suggestions), enabling post-event audits by hospital compliance officers.
4. **Liability**
   - o **Human doctors** remain in final decision loops for serious diagnoses or treatment changes, limiting purely autonomous prescription or treatment decisions.

6.3. Outcome

- **Regulatory Approvals**: The system passes internal and external audits, demonstrating compliance with data privacy and healthcare guidelines.
- **Reduced Errors**: Thoroughly validated agent logic yields fewer misdiagnoses, with doctors overseeing final calls.
- **High Patient Trust**: Transparent user notifications about AI usage, data usage, and how the system obtains final approvals by medical professionals.

Table: Compliance Gains in Healthcare MAS

Compliance Aspect	Implementation Approach	Benefit
HIPAA Data Protection	Encrypted PHI, role-based agent access	Prevents unauthorized disclosure
GDPR Right to Erasure	Patient can request deletion of agent-held data	Respects EU user privacy, reduces liability
Medical Accountability	Doctors in final decision loop for critical outcomes	Maintains safety and professional oversight

7. End-of-Chapter Projects

Project 23: Ensuring Legal Compliance in MAS

Objective: Enhance an existing **DeepSeek R1** MAS for compliance with **data privacy** and **industry** regulations.

Outline

1. **Identify Applicable Regulations**
   - Suppose you build a MAS in healthcare or finance. Outline relevant laws (HIPAA, GDPR, MiFID II).
2. **Implement Security & Privacy**
   - Agents store personal data with encryption, add logs for all actions on user data.
   - Provide user consent checks for data usage, plus a method to erase user records.
3. **Audit Logging**
   - Agents record decisions that affect user outcomes (e.g., loan denial, medical triage).
   - Logs are tamper-resistant, facilitating external reviews.
4. **Liability Clarification**
   - Add comments or documentation explaining how agent responsibilities are assigned, how overrides occur, and who retains final authority.

---

8. Quizzes and Self-Assessments

Quiz 23: Legal and Regulatory Compliance

1. **Legal Frameworks**
   - **Question**: Name one **AI-specific regulation** proposed or in development that may affect how MAS must be designed.
2. **Data Protection**
   - **Question**: Why is **data minimization** important under privacy regulations like GDPR?
3. **Industry-Specific**
   - **Question**: Provide an example of a **financial** regulation that requires strict transaction logging for MAS dealing with trades.
4. **IP Considerations**
   - **Question**: Differentiate between **patents** and **trade secrets** in the context of MAS innovations.

5. **Liability**
    o **Question**: In a scenario where an MAS in manufacturing injures a worker due to an erroneous agent decision, which parties might be liable?
6. **Case Study**
    o **Question**: In the multi-agent healthcare system example, how is a patient's data protected, and how do medical professionals remain in control?
7. **Short Coding Prompt**
    o **Question**: Write a pseudocode function `checkCompliance(agent_action, policy_rules)` that verifies if a proposed agent action meets certain policy constraints (e.g., HIPAA or GDPR restrictions), returning pass/fail.

Answer Key (Suggested):

1. **AI-specific Regulation**: The proposed **EU AI Act** in Europe sets risk-based obligations for AI providers and users.
2. **Data Minimization**: Collecting **only** essential data reduces exposure risk and ensures compliance with GDPR's principle of storing minimal personal information.
3. **Financial Regulation**: **MiFID II** in the EU demands comprehensive record-keeping of trades and communications, ensuring transparency.
4. **Patents vs. Trade Secrets**: Patents publicly disclose inventions but grant a monopoly for a limited term, while trade secrets remain confidential as long as they're kept secret, offering indefinite protection if not revealed.
5. **Liability**: Could include the **MAS developer**, the **company** operating it, possibly the **hardware** manufacturer if technical failure contributed to the accident, or other involved stakeholders (depending on negligence or compliance lapses).
6. **Healthcare Case**: Patient data is **encrypted** and has role-based access. **Doctors** retain final decision authority for diagnoses or treatments, ensuring no fully autonomous prescription.
7. **Pseudocode**:

```python
def checkCompliance(agent_action, policy_rules):
    for rule in policy_rules:
        if not rule.is_compliant(agent_action):
            return "FAIL"
```

```
return "PASS"
```

Legal and regulatory compliance is an indispensable aspect of **multi-agent system** deployment, particularly in fields handling **sensitive data** or automating **critical decisions**. Understanding **privacy laws** (e.g., GDPR, CCPA), **industry-specific** mandates, and **IP** considerations helps ensure that MAS remain secure, trustworthy, and aligned with societal expectations. By **defining liability** frameworks and fostering design principles that respect data protection, logging, and ethical constraints, MAS can avoid costly legal issues while benefiting from innovative agent-driven capabilities. The **healthcare** case study demonstrates successful compliance integration, highlighting how careful engineering and oversight preserve data integrity and user trust.

Chapter 24: Community Engagement and Open-source Collaboration

Contributing to and benefiting from **open-source** communities is a powerful way to advance multi-agent systems (MAS) development. Collaborative efforts can accelerate innovation, drive adoption, and improve the overall quality and reliability of projects. This chapter highlights the **importance** of community in MAS development, discusses **best practices** for contributing to open-source projects, explains how to engage with the **MAS and DeepSeek R1** communities, and explores **collaborative development strategies**. Finally, we outline how you can create and share your own MAS projects, provide a **case study** of an open-source multi-agent platform, and offer a project and quiz to deepen your understanding.

---

1. Importance of Community in MAS Development

1.1. Benefits of Collaborative Development

Collaboration fosters:

1. **Shared Knowledge**
   - Developers and researchers worldwide exchange ideas, solutions, and best practices.
   - Community discussions reveal how others have solved specific MAS challenges.
2. **Faster Innovation**
   - Multiple contributors can implement new features or fix bugs simultaneously.
   - Time to deploy improvements shortens as collective problem-solving occurs.
3. **Reduced Costs**
   - Teams can reuse open-source libraries or agent frameworks, lowering the overhead of building from scratch.

o   Adopting well-maintained community components reduces maintenance burdens.
4. **Wider Adoption and Feedback**
   o   Open communities help test systems in varied environments.
   o   Early adopters provide feedback, revealing performance issues or missing features.

1.2. Building a Supportive Ecosystem

A **thriving** community around MAS or a platform like **DeepSeek R1**:

1. **Encourages Mentorship**
   o   Experienced contributors guide newcomers, driving consistent code quality and user satisfaction.
2. **Fosters Inclusive Culture**
   o   Welcoming new members from diverse backgrounds broadens perspectives, improving project robustness.
3. **Cultivates Shared Vision**
   o   Users and developers unite around common goals (e.g., democratizing multi-agent technologies or tackling domain-specific problems).

Table: Benefits of an Active MAS Community

Benefit	Description	Example
Collective Problem-solving	Multiple contributors tackle complex MAS challenges	Rapid bug fixes or new ML-based agent modules
Mentorship & Learning	Experienced devs guide newcomers	Code reviews, design discussions, meetups
Ecosystem Growth	More adopters, diverse use cases	MAS frameworks gain traction in new industries
Long-term Sustainability	More maintainers reduce single points of failure	Larger contributor pool, project continuity assured

2. Contributing to Open-source Projects

2.1. Finding and Selecting Projects

Choosing the right project to contribute to:

1. **Personal Interests**
   - Align with domains you enjoy: robotics, finance, e-commerce, or specialized agent frameworks.
   - Motivates consistent involvement and learning.
2. **Project Activity**
   - Check how often maintainers merge pull requests or release updates.
   - Vibrant communities typically have regular commits, active issue discussions, or a chat/forum channel.
3. **Issue Tracker**
   - Look for "good first issue" or "help wanted" labels indicating beginner-friendly tasks.
   - Evaluate the project's backlog for pressing tasks aligned with your skill set.

2.2. Best Practices for Contributions

1. **Clone and Explore**
   - **Fork** the repository, set up the environment, and compile or run basic tests before editing code.
2. **Read Contribution Guidelines**
   - Many projects have CONTRIBUTING.md explaining coding standards, commit message conventions, and review processes.
3. **Start Small**
   - Fix a minor bug, write or improve documentation, or address a single test case.
   - Build credibility and familiarity with project structures.
4. **Engage with Maintainers**
   - Open well-described pull requests, respond to feedback, and keep changes concise.
   - Offer to refine or revise if the maintainers suggest improvements.

Code Example (Pseudocode):

```python
# Example of a small fix in an open-source MAS project:

def compute_priority(task):
```

```
# Original code may have a logic flaw:
# priority = task.urgency - task.duration  # incorrectly
penalizing longer tasks
# A fix might adjust the formula:
priority = task.urgency / (task.duration + 1)
return priority
```

- **Explanation**:
    - A trivial fix in a scheduling function. Always include relevant documentation or test updates in your pull request.

3. Engaging with the MAS and DeepSeek R1 Communities

3.1. Participating in Forums, Discussion Groups, and Meetups

Community interaction can happen:

1. **Online Forums & Mailing Lists**
    - For DeepSeek R1 or general MAS, official forums or platforms like Stack Overflow, GitHub Discussions, or specialized Slack/Discord channels exist.
2. **Meetups and Conferences**
    - Local user groups, AI, or robotics conferences often host MAS sessions, letting you network and share experiences.
3. **Workshops and Hackathons**
    - Collaborative events around problem statements, e.g., agent-based solutions to city traffic.
    - Gain new insights or code solutions quickly.

Tips:

- Ask specific, well-researched questions.
- Contribute by sharing solutions or clarifications for others, building your reputation.

3.2. Leveraging Community Knowledge and Resources

Communities often offer:

1. **Tutorials and Templates**
   - o Prebuilt agent modules, code snippets, sample projects for rapid prototyping.
2. **FAQs and Best Practices**
   - o Common pitfalls or advanced tips consolidated in wikis or pinned forum threads.
3. **Mentoring and Pair Programming**
   - o Experienced members might pair program or review your code in real time.

Encourage knowledge exchange by **posting solutions** or writing blog articles detailing MAS use cases.

4. Collaborative Development Strategies

4.1. Version Control and Collaborative Tools

Git or **Mercurial** are typical version control choices:

1. **Branching Model**
   - o Use **feature** branches for new agent functionalities, **hotfix** branches for urgent bug fixes.
2. **Pull Requests (PRs)**
   - o Proposed changes undergo code review, ensuring quality merges.
3. **Git Flow**
   - o A structured naming convention for branches (e.g., `release/`, `develop/`), widely used in open-source collaborations.

Collaboration Platforms:

- **GitHub/GitLab/Bitbucket** for hosting repos, issue tracking, code reviews, wiki pages.
- Tools like **Trello**, **Jira**, or **Asana** coordinate tasks or sprints in larger MAS teams.

4.2. Managing Contributions and Feedback

1. **Clear Contribution Guidelines**

- Outline coding standards, test coverage requirements, and how to propose changes.
2. **Issue Triaging**
   - Labeling issues ("bug," "enhancement," "urgent") and assigning priorities.
3. **Continuous Communication**
   - Use chat channels or threads for design discussions, avoiding big merges without prior consensus.

Table: Key Collaborative Tools

Tool/Platform	Purpose	Example
GitHub/GitLab	Repo hosting, PR reviews, issue tracking	Public repos, integrated CI/CD pipelines
Slack/Discord/Matrix	Real-time communication for devs/users	Quick Q&A, build community synergy
Project Management	Task boards, sprint planning	Trello for small teams, Jira for enterprise-scale dev ops
Collaborative IDEs	Remote pair programming, real-time code	VS Code Live Share or JetBrains Code With Me

5. Creating and Sharing Your Own MAS Projects

5.1. Open-sourcing Your Projects

Releasing your MAS or agent libraries as **open-source**:

1. **License Choice**
   - **MIT**, **Apache 2.0**, or **GPL**—balance ease of use (permissive) vs. reciprocal requirements (copyleft).
2. **Documentation**
   - A thorough README clarifies goals, usage instructions, and contribution guidelines.
   - Add examples or quickstart guides so new users can get started easily.

3. **Community Setup**
   - o Provide issue templates, a code of conduct, and a contributor's guide to welcome external participants.
   - o Possibly create a Slack or forum for direct user engagement.

5.2. Building a Reputation within the Community

1. **Active Maintenance**
   - o Respond promptly to issues, merge PRs responsibly, keep the project fresh with regular updates.
2. **Showcasing Success Stories**
   - o Document real-world scenarios or success from other adopters, encouraging more adoption.
3. **Encourage Collaboration**
   - o Label tasks as "good first issue," host small hackathons, or outreach on social media channels.
   - o Developer evangelism fosters a growing user base and lively discussion.

6. Case Study: Collaborative Development in an Open-source Multi-agent Platform

6.1. Background

A research group starts an **open-source** multi-agent simulation toolkit for **urban traffic management**:

1. **Initial Release**
   - o Basic agent framework, minimal tutorials, free for academic and commercial use under **Apache 2.0** license.
2. **Community Growth**
   - o Grad students worldwide contributed features (e.g., new pathfinding, custom traffic signal logic).
   - o City transport agencies tested real intersections using simulation data.

6.2. Key Collaborative Practices

1. **Public Roadmap**
   - GitHub Projects tracked upcoming features (integration with real-time sensor feeds, advanced RL modules).
2. **Regular Releases**
   - Monthly stable releases with clear changelogs.
3. **Issue Triaging & Peer Reviews**
   - Maintainers swiftly labeled issues, assigned them to volunteers, and required at least one approving review for merges.
4. **Community Showcases**
   - A dedicated wiki page for case studies from different contributors' local experiments or city pilot projects.

6.3. Results

- **Rapid Feature Expansion**: Over 50 external contributors added specialized traffic simulation modules within a year.
- **Academic Adoption**: The platform became a standard for agent-based traffic research.
- **Quality & Stability**: Thorough peer reviews and broad user testing minimized regression bugs or performance bottlenecks.

7. End-of-Chapter Projects

Project 24: Launching an Open-source MAS Project

Objective: Share an existing multi-agent system or build a small MAS from scratch, open-sourcing it and fostering a community.

Outline

1. **Project Initialization**
   - Select a domain (e.g., a scheduling MAS or a game-based MAS).
   - Prepare a GitHub repository with a suitable open-source license (MIT, Apache, etc.).
2. **Documentation & Examples**
   - Write a clear README describing the system's purpose, architecture, and usage steps.

- o Include minimal examples or demos to lower the entry barrier.
3. **Contribution Guidelines**
   - o Provide `CONTRIBUTING.md` outlining code standards, PR process, and branching model.
   - o Add labels for beginner tasks in the issue tracker.
4. **Community Outreach**
   - o Post about the project on relevant forums (DeepSeek R1 user group, general MAS groups).
   - o Encourage feedback and open discussion threads.
5. **Maintenance Plan**
   - o Ensure a small core of maintainers, handle issues promptly, release stable versions regularly.

8. Quizzes and Self-Assessments

Quiz 24: Community Engagement

1. **Importance of Community**
   - o **Question**: List two **benefits** that community collaboration brings to multi-agent system projects.
2. **Open-source Contributions**
   - o **Question**: How do you find and evaluate a new open-source MAS project to potentially contribute to?
3. **Community Engagement**
   - o **Question**: Name a key advantage of **meetups** or **online forums** in building MAS expertise.
4. **Collaboration Tools**
   - o **Question**: Why is **version control** crucial when multiple contributors work on the same MAS codebase?
5. **Creating Your Own Project**
   - o **Question**: What steps ensure a new open-source MAS project is welcoming to external contributors?
6. **Case Study**
   - o **Question**: In the traffic management simulation, how did community engagement drive rapid feature expansion?
7. **Short Coding Prompt**
   - o **Question**: Write pseudocode for a function `openSourceSetup(project_name)` that automatically

initializes a repository with a license file, README, and a contributor guide.

Answer Key (Suggested):

1. **Benefits**: 1) Faster innovation via collective knowledge, 2) Decreased development costs by sharing code.
2. **Evaluating Projects**: Check **project activity** (commits, merges), existing community size, and read "help wanted" issues.
3. **Meetups/Forums**: Offer direct **peer learning**, new ideas, mentorship, and potential collaboration leads.
4. **Version Control**: Prevents conflicts, tracks changes from multiple devs, enabling merges and rollback if needed.
5. **Welcoming**: Clear docs, code of conduct, labeled issues for newcomers, open communication channels.
6. **Traffic Case**: External devs contributed specialized modules quickly, accelerating the entire platform's feature set.
7. **Pseudocode**:

```python
def openSourceSetup(project_name):
    # Step 1: Create folder structure
    create_directory(project_name)
    # Step 2: Initialize git
    run_command(f"git init {project_name}")
    # Step 3: Add LICENSE, README, CONTRIBUTING
    create_file(f"{project_name}/LICENSE",
license_template)
    create_file(f"{project_name}/README.md",
readme_content)
    create_file(f"{project_name}/CONTRIBUTING.md",
contribution_guidelines)
    # Step 4: First commit
    run_command(f"git add . && git commit -m 'Initial
open-source setup'")
    print(f"Open-source project '{project_name}'
initialized successfully.")
```

Actively engaging with **communities** and embracing **open-source** principles elevate multi-agent system projects, providing vast knowledge-sharing, faster improvements, and long-term sustainability. Through **forums**, meetups, or code repositories, MAS developers worldwide solve complex challenges, shape new features, and collectively innovate. Launching your own **open-source MAS** or contributing to established projects fosters both personal growth and broad societal benefit, as the **case study** with a collaborative traffic platform demonstrates. By following the strategies and best practices in this chapter, you can build a **supportive** and **dynamic** ecosystem around MAS, ultimately achieving greater impact and adoption.

Chapter 25: Ethical Considerations and Responsible AI in MAS

As **multi-agent systems (MAS)** become more pervasive—in healthcare, finance, autonomous vehicles, and even military applications—**ethical and responsible AI** practices are paramount. Ensuring fairness, transparency, and accountability is not only a moral imperative but often a legal and reputational necessity. This chapter explores the **ethical challenges** in MAS, outlines ways to **design ethical agents** and comply with relevant **laws and standards**, and underscores **sustainable AI** practices that promote inclusivity and minimal environmental impact. We also examine a **case study** in autonomous weapon systems, followed by **projects** and a **quiz** for application and reflection.

---

1. Ethical Challenges in MAS

1.1. Bias and Fairness

Bias occurs when MAS decisions systematically disadvantage certain individuals or groups:

1. **Data-Driven Bias**
   o Machine learning agents may inherit discrimination from historical datasets (e.g., in lending or hiring).
2. **Algorithmic Bias**
   o Hardcoded agent heuristics might reflect developers' blind spots.
3. **Representation Gaps**
   o Underrepresented demographics or lesser-known languages lead to poorer model performance for those groups.

Consequences:

- **Unfair Outcomes**: Agents systematically exclude or penalize certain segments of society.
- **Legal Ramifications**: Violations of anti-discrimination laws (e.g., in finance or hiring).

1.2. Accountability and Transparency

In a **multi-agent** environment:

1. **Distributed Decision-Making**
   - o   Harder to pinpoint blame for detrimental outcomes if no single agent "controls" the final result.
2. **Black Box Models**
   - o   Complex ML-based agents yield decisions that are difficult to interpret, undermining user trust.
3. **Transparency**
   - o   Agents should document or explain significant decisions, aiding audits and user understanding.

1.3. Impact on Employment and Society

Automation of tasks via MAS can reshape entire sectors:

1. **Job Displacement**
   - o   Factories, customer service, or logistics may lose roles to collaborative robots or chatbots.
2. **Uneven Benefits**
   - o   Efficiency gains might not be shared equitably; certain communities or skill sets become obsolete.
3. **Social Responsibilities**
   - o   Stakeholders must consider retraining programs or transitional support for affected workers.

Table: Common Ethical Challenges in MAS

Challenge	Description	Potential Impact
Bias and Fairness	Inherited or algorithmic discrimination	Unjust decisions, legal/regulatory issues
Accountability	Difficulty attributing blame in distributed systems	Lower trust, complicated liability questions
Societal Impact	Job displacement, shifts in economic structures	Widened inequality, need for new skill sets

2. Designing Ethical Agents

2.1. Incorporating Ethical Decision-Making Frameworks

Agents that **explicitly** consider moral principles:

1. **Rule-Based Ethics**
   - Hard-coded constraints (e.g., do not cause harm to humans).
   - Similar to deontological approaches ensuring certain lines are never crossed.
2. **Consequentialist Approaches**
   - Agents weigh outcomes, choosing actions that maximize overall benefit or minimize harm.
   - In ambiguous scenarios, numeric "utility" might measure risk vs. reward, balanced by ethical constraints.
3. **Hybrid**
   - Combine **unbreakable** moral rules with cost-benefit calculations where no rule is violated.

2.2. Ensuring Transparency in Agent Actions

Explainable AI (XAI) fosters user trust:

1. **Human-Readable Justifications**
   - Agents produce short textual or visual rationales for decisions (e.g., "I recommended a loan denial because your credit score is below 500 and no collateral was provided.").
2. **Audit Trails**
   - Agents log the logic or data references behind decisions, enabling post-event reviews or compliance checks.
3. **Ethical Oversight**
   - Organizations can form **ethics boards** or run periodic audits of agent logs for fairness or compliance violations.

Code Example (Pseudocode):

```python
class EthicalAgent:
    def __init__(self, moral_rules):
        self.moral_rules = moral_rules

    def propose_action(self, situation):
        possible_actions = self.derive_actions(situation)
        # filter out unethical or rule-breaking actions
```

```
        filtered = [act for act in possible_actions if
self.conforms_to_rules(act)]
        # choose best among filtered
        chosen = self.utility_maximize(filtered)
        explanation = self.create_explanation(chosen)
        return chosen, explanation

  def conforms_to_rules(self, action):
        for rule in self.moral_rules:
            if not rule(action):
                return False
        return True
```

- **Explanation**:
  - o Demonstrates an **ethical agent** approach: it screens potential actions against moral rules, picks from the safe set, and possibly provides an explanation.

3. Regulatory Compliance

3.1. Understanding Relevant Laws and Standards

MAS must abide by **general AI** or **domain-specific** regulations:

1. **Data Protection**
   - o GDPR, CCPA, or local privacy laws for data usage.
2. **AI Risk Classifications**
   - o Proposed EU AI Act segments AI by "risk level." MAS with high potential harm face strong oversight.
3. **Sectoral Mandates**
   - o Healthcare (HIPAA in US), finance (MiFID II in EU), or automotive safety laws.

3.2. Implementing Compliance Mechanisms

Mechanisms ensuring **legal** adherence:

1. **Record-Keeping**
   - o Agents log decisions or data usage for compliance audits.
2. **Consent and Access Control**

- o For user data, ensure the system obtains explicit consent, allows data erasure, or meets other privacy requests.
3. **Algorithmic Explainability**
   - o Some laws require that individuals can contest or request rationale for automated decisions.

Table: Common Regulatory Requirements for MAS

Requirement	Applicable Law/Standard	MAS Implementation Example
Data Subject Rights	GDPR, CCPA	Agents must handle user requests for data removal or export
Auditable Decision Logs	Financial or medical regs	Agents keep secure logs of main decisions
Algorithmic Transparency	EU AI Act proposed	Agents provide explanation or fallback to human overseers
Security (Encryption, RBAC)	ISO 27001, HIPAA	Agents encrypt sensitive data, use role-based restrictions

4. Sustainable and Responsible AI Practices

4.1. Energy-efficient Agent Designs

Agents and **infrastructure** can be designed to minimize environmental impact:

1. **Optimized Algorithms**
   - o Use time and memory efficient approaches, preventing wasteful computations.
2. **Dynamic Scaling**
   - o Scale down agent containers or processes when idle to reduce electricity consumption.
3. **Eco-friendly Hosting**
   - o Deploy on data centers powered by renewables or with advanced cooling solutions.

4.2. Promoting Inclusivity and Accessibility

Responsible AI fosters inclusivity:

1. **Multi-language Support**
   o Agents handle diverse user languages or dialects, ensuring no user is marginalized.
2. **Accessible Interfaces**
   o Provide screen-reader compatibility, large font options, or voice-based input for visually or physically impaired users.
3. **Fair Data Representation**
   o Collect balanced training sets for ML-driven agents, ensuring robust performance across demographic groups.

Code Example (Pseudocode):

```python
python

class GreenAgent(AgentBase):
    def __init__(self, inactivity_timeout=60):
        super().__init__()
        self.last_active_time = time.time()
        self.inactivity_timeout = inactivity_timeout

    def on_message(self, message):
        self.last_active_time = time.time()
        # process as usual

    def check_inactivity(self):
        if time.time() - self.last_active_time >
self.inactivity_timeout:
            self.go_to_sleep_mode()

    def go_to_sleep_mode(self):
        # reduce CPU usage, limit external calls
        print("Agent is sleeping to save energy.")
```

- **Explanation**:
  o This agent enters a low-power or "sleep mode" when idle, cutting resource usage.

5. Case Study: Ethical Considerations in Autonomous Weapon Systems

5.1. Overview

Autonomous weapon systems (AWS) represent an **extreme** example of MAS usage: lethal force decisions with minimal human oversight. This domain triggers profound ethical debates and potential global regulation.

5.2. Ethical Dilemmas

1. **Lethal Autonomy**
   o Agents deciding to engage a target without direct human confirmation.
2. **Accountability**
   o If an AWS erroneously strikes civilians, who's at fault: the developer, operator, or the agent's "decision"?
3. **Proportionality and Distinction**
   o Laws of armed conflict require distinguishing combatants from non-combatants. Agents must do so reliably or face war crime implications.

5.3. Safeguards

- **Human-in-the-Loop**: Many argue lethal decisions should not be fully autonomous.
- **Strict Logging**: Full record of each lethal or potential lethal decision for post-mission reviews.
- **Fail-safes**: Agents revert to safe states if sensors degrade or mission clarity fades.

5.4. Outcome

Debate continues on partial or total AWS bans, with some treaties or guidelines emerging. The existential risk of poorly governed lethal MAS raises demand for robust, verifiable constraints and external oversight.

6. End-of-Chapter Projects

Project 25: Implementing Ethical AI Practices

Objective: Enhance a multi-agent system with **ethical** considerations, implementing fairness checks, transparency features, and energy-efficient design.

Outline

1. **Define Ethical Rules**
   - Hard-coded constraints (e.g., "no discrimination by protected characteristic," "limit resource usage to X% CPU").
2. **Implement Decision Explanation**
   - Agents generate short text explaining major decisions (why a user was declined a certain service).
3. **Integrate a Consent Mechanism**
   - If personal data usage is required, ensure an agent verifies user consent. Provide data deletion methods.
4. **Sustainability**
   - Add a "sleep mode" for idle times or schedule scanning to reduce resource usage.
5. **Testing & Validation**
   - Confirm system denies unethical requests (like violating rules) and logs each decision for auditing.

7. Quizzes and Self-Assessments

Quiz 25: Ethical AI in MAS

1. **Ethical Challenges**
   - **Question**: Name two reasons why **bias** can emerge in MAS, potentially harming certain groups.
2. **Designing Ethical Agents**
   - **Question**: Why is it essential for **agents** to provide **transparent** or explainable decisions, especially in regulated domains?
3. **Regulatory Compliance**

- o **Question**: Outline how **GDPR** influences agent data collection and user rights management in an MAS.
4. **Sustainability**
   - o **Question**: Provide one strategy that reduces the **environmental impact** of agent processes.
5. **Case Study**
   - o **Question**: In the autonomous weapon systems example, what is one key moral conflict regarding lethal autonomy?
6. **Short Coding Prompt**
   - o **Question**: Write pseudocode for an **EthicsCheck** function that determines if an agent action is permissible, returning a reason if it violates a moral constraint.

Answer Key (Suggested):

1. **Bias Emergence**:
   - o
       1. Historical data may be **skewed** or incomplete,
   - o
       2. Hard-coded logic reflecting developer assumptions or stereotypes.

2. **Transparency**:
   - o Ensures **accountability** and user trust, enabling external audits or user's right to explanation, particularly in finance, healthcare, or defense.
3. **GDPR**:
   - o Agents must gain **user consent**, store minimal data, allow data deletion upon request, and log data usage for accountability.
4. **Sustainability**:
   - o e.g., shutting down idle agent containers or using energy-saving policies for on-premises servers.
5. **Autonomous Weapons**:
   - o Moral debate over letting software "decide" lethal force with minimal or no human oversight.
6. **Pseudocode**:

```python
def EthicsCheck(action, moral_rules):
    for rule in moral_rules:
```

```
        if not rule(action):
            return (False, f"Violated rule:
{rule.__name__}")
        return (True, "Action permitted")
```

Ethical considerations and **responsible AI** principles are integral to **multi-agent systems**. Issues of **bias, accountability**, and **societal impact** demand careful agent design, ongoing oversight, and compliance with evolving legal frameworks. By implementing **transparent** decision-making, ensuring **fairness** in data and logic, adopting **energy-efficient** designs, and including **human oversight** where needed, MAS can deliver positive outcomes with **minimal harm**. The **autonomous weapon systems** case underscores the high stakes of ethical lapses in MAS. Through best practices, strong policy support, and conscientious design, MAS developers can uphold a **responsible, beneficial** future for multi-agent intelligence.

Chapter 26: Emerging Trends and Future Directions in MAS

Multi-agent systems (MAS) continuously evolve as new AI paradigms, hardware breakthroughs, and societal needs arise. Innovative integration with quantum computing, edge devices, IoT environments, and ethical governance frameworks will define the next generation of intelligent, distributed solutions. This chapter surveys **emerging trends** and explores **future directions** in MAS, from **quantum computing** synergies to **advanced human-agent collaboration**, the **IoT revolution**, and **autonomous robotics**. We conclude by highlighting **AI ethics** and **governance** developments, featuring a **case study** on environmental monitoring, plus a practical **project** and quiz for comprehensive learning.

---

1. Advancements in AI and MAS

1.1. Integration of Quantum Computing

Quantum computing offers potentially massive computational speedups for certain problem types, which can impact MAS:

1. **Optimization Problems**
   o Agents tackling complex scheduling, route planning, or combinatorial tasks may benefit from quantum algorithms (like **quantum annealing**).
2. **Quantum Machine Learning**
   o Hybrid quantum-classical models might yield faster training or more robust pattern recognition in agent-based solutions.
3. **Challenges**
   o Quantum hardware remains limited in qubit count and error rates. Early integration requires specialized knowledge and constraints on problem formulation.

Potential MAS Use Cases

- **Quantum-Supported Planning**: Single agent or manager agent offloads a part of its combinatorial planning to a quantum solver.

- **Crypto and Security**: Post-quantum cryptography might be vital for agent communications if quantum computing can break classical encryption.

1.2. Edge Computing and MAS

Edge computing processes data closer to where it's generated, reducing latency:

1. **Distributed Intelligence**
   - Agents run on local devices (IoT sensors, robots), reacting quickly to local events without round-trips to the cloud.
2. **Bandwidth Efficiency**
   - Only aggregated or essential data moves to central servers, saving network costs and enabling real-time decisions.
3. **Privacy**
   - Sensitive data stays on local nodes; only anonymized or summarized info is shared globally.

Code Example (Pseudocode):

```python
# edge_agent.py
class EdgeAgent(AgentBase):
    def on_local_sensor_data(self, data):
        # immediate local decision
        action = self.decide_local_action(data)
        self.execute(action)

    def decide_local_action(self, data):
        # e.g., if temperature > 30, turn on local fan
        if data["temperature"] > 30:
            return "TURN_FAN_ON"
        return "FAN_OFF"
```

- **Explanation**:
  - Demonstrates a small edge agent that quickly decides on local sensor data, with minimal reliance on a central server.

2. Human-Agent Collaboration

2.1. Enhancing Human-Machine Interfaces

Future MAS will prioritize **seamless** human-agent interaction:

1. **Voice and Gesture**
   o   Natural inputs such as speech, gestures, or AR/VR interfaces. Agents interpret user intent contextually.
2. **Adaptive UIs**
   o   Systems adapt to user expertise. For novices, the interface is simplified; advanced users see comprehensive agent data.
3. **Emotion and Context Sensing**
   o   Agents detect user emotional states (frustration, satisfaction) to tailor responses or escalate to a human operator.

2.2. Collaborative Intelligence Models

Collaborative intelligence merges human insight and agent efficiency:

1. **Decision Support**
   o   Agents handle large data volumes or routine analysis while humans resolve ambiguous cases or moral/ethical dilemmas.
2. **Complementary Skill Sets**
   o   Humans excel at creativity, empathy, or abstract reasoning; agents handle repetitive or data-heavy tasks, ensuring synergy.
3. **Interactive AI**
   o   Co-creative environments in fields like design or writing, where agents propose ideas and humans refine or reject them.

Table: Human-Agent Collaboration Approaches

Approach	Description	Benefit
Augmented Decisions	Agents provide suggestions, humans finalize them	Humans maintain control, aided by AI
Co-creative Systems	Both agent and human iterate on solutions	Sparks innovative, combined brainstorming
Human-in-the-Loop Reviews	Agents run autonomously but require final sign-off	Balances efficiency with accountability

3. MAS in Internet of Things (IoT)

3.1. Integrating MAS with IoT Devices

IoT networks typically involve a huge number of sensors, actuators, and interconnected devices:

1. **Agent Representation**
   - Each IoT node can host a lightweight agent managing local data, decisions (e.g., temperature control, motion detection).
2. **Hierarchical MAS**
   - Edge agents handle immediate device control; higher-level aggregator agents manage cross-device coordination.
3. **Challenges**
   - Resource constraints (battery, CPU) on IoT devices, requiring efficient agent implementations.

3.2. Smart Home and Smart City Applications

1. **Smart Home**
   - Agents coordinate appliances, heating/cooling, and security. They adapt to user habits or presence for energy savings.
2. **Smart City**
   - City-wide sensors inform traffic or environmental management. MAS can optimize traffic signals, waste collection routes, or air quality monitoring.
3. **Scalability**
   - Millions of devices require robust communication protocols, agent discovery, and fault tolerance.

4. Autonomous Systems and Robotics

4.1. Trends in Autonomous Robotics

Robots employing MAS show increasing autonomy:

1. **Swarm Robotics**

- Large groups of minimal robots cooperate via simple local rules. Examples: warehouse item retrieval, search-and-rescue in hazardous zones.
2. **Multi-robot Collaboration**
   - Heterogeneous fleets (drones, ground robots) share tasks, each specialized in carrying, sensing, or assembly tasks.
3. **Resilient Operations**
   - If one robot fails, others adapt. Agents dynamically re-route or take over tasks.

4.2. Collaborative Robotics in Various Industries

Cobots or collaborative robots:

1. **Factory Assembly**
   - Robots partner with human workers to handle repetitive or heavy tasks, guided by MAS scheduling.
2. **Agriculture**
   - Drones and ground vehicles collaborate to optimize irrigation, planting, or harvest.
3. **Logistics**
   - MAS orchestrate fleets of robots for picking, packing, or last-mile delivery.

Code Example (Pseudocode):

```python
# multi_robot_coordination.py
class RobotAgent(AgentBase):
    def plan_motion(self, task):
        # plan path or schedule
        pass

    def collaborate(self, peer_agent):
        # exchange positions or load capacities
        # decide best approach to share tasks
        pass
```

- **Explanation**:
  - A basic sketch of how each robot agent might plan tasks or coordinate with peers for shared goals.

5. AI Ethics and Governance

5.1. Evolving Ethical Standards

In advanced MAS:

1. **Revisiting Ethical Principles**
   - Concepts from earlier chapters, like accountability and fairness, intensify as agent autonomy grows.
2. **Collective Decisions**
   - When multiple agents collectively decide (e.g., resource allocation for entire communities), the ethical stakes rise.
3. **Standardization**
   - Entities like **ISO/IEC JTC 1** and committees propose guidelines for safe, ethically aligned AI, affecting MAS.

5.2. Governance Frameworks for MAS

Governance ensures agent-based systems operate under accepted norms:

1. **Internal Governance Boards**
   - Companies forming committees overseeing MAS development, reviewing proposed functionalities, or potential biases.
2. **External Regulation**
   - Agencies or legislative bodies set compliance thresholds, require auditing or certifying certain classes of MAS (e.g., critical infrastructure).
3. **Oversight Tools**
   - Agents produce verifiable logs, enabling third-party or public scrutiny. Possibly adopting blockchains or secure enclaves for tamper-proof records.

Table: Governance Layers

Layer	Focus	Example
Organizational	Company boards or ethics committees	Vet new features, review potential biases
Industry	Self-regulatory bodies, best practice codes	Robo-advisors in finance conform to guidelines
Governmental	Laws/regulations, audits	EU AI Act proposals, mandatory audits

6. Case Study: Future Directions in Multi-agent Environmental Monitoring Systems

6.1. Scenario

A consortium aims to develop next-gen **environmental monitoring** MAS for oceans, forests, and urban air quality:

1. **Swarm Drones** monitor deforestation or pollution in real time.
2. **Edge Agents** analyze sensor data on-site, only sending aggregates to central servers.
3. **Quantum Tools** for optimizing routes or data fusion tasks in complex topographies.

6.2. Future-Ready Approaches

- **Edge + Cloud** synergy ensures minimal latency for local alerts (e.g., detecting illegal logging) while archiving data for global analysis.
- **Adaptive Human-Agent Collaboration**: Park rangers or environmental scientists override or refine the drone swarm's actions, guided by real-time XAI explanations.
- **Sustainability**: Systems rely on solar or kinetic energy for drones, prioritizing minimal carbon footprint.

6.3. Impact and Prospects

- **Global Monitoring**: Real-time data on biodiversity, pollution, or climate anomalies fosters swift interventions.
- **Inter-Agency Collaborations**: Multiple countries or NGOs share data and agent logic, each preserving local autonomy.

- **Innovation**: Ongoing R&D merges quantum optimization, advanced RL for route planning, ensuring detection coverage with minimal resources.

7. End-of-Chapter Projects

Project 26: Exploring Future MAS Technologies

Objective: Implement experimental **MAS features** like quantum-inspired optimization, advanced human-agent interfaces, or IoT-based edge agents.

Outline

1. **Select a Future Trend**
   - E.g., quantum-inspired scheduling, edge-based scenario, or advanced UI for collaborative intelligence.
2. **Integrate**
   - Extend an existing or new MAS with a chosen technology (e.g., partial quantum solver for route planning).
3. **Evaluation**
   - Measure performance gains (quantum optimization) or user acceptance (improved UI) against a baseline approach.
4. **Documentation**
   - Write an overview explaining limitations, next steps, and open research questions (particularly for quantum or advanced RL).

8. Quizzes and Self-Assessments

Quiz 26: Emerging Trends in MAS

1. **Quantum Computing**

- **Question**: How might quantum computing benefit certain **MAS** tasks, and what is a primary barrier to its current adoption?
2. **Edge Computing**
   - **Question**: Why is running agents **locally** (at the edge) often advantageous compared to always depending on a central server?
3. **Human-Agent Collaboration**
   - **Question**: Name a scenario where a **co-creative** approach between human and agent yields better outcomes than a fully autonomous or fully manual approach.
4. **MAS in IoT**
   - **Question**: Provide an example of how MAS can optimize **smart city** applications.
5. **Autonomous Robotics**
   - **Question**: What does **swarm robotics** entail, and why can it be beneficial for large-scale tasks?
6. **AI Ethics and Governance**
   - **Question**: In an increasingly autonomous MAS, how can a governance framework ensure accountability for high-impact decisions?
7. **Case Study**
   - **Question**: In the environmental monitoring scenario, how does the system balance **edge** processing with **cloud** analysis?
8. **Short Coding Prompt**
   - **Question**: Write pseudocode for a minimal `QuantumPlanningAgent` that simulates calling a "quantum solver" function for scheduling tasks.

Answer Key (Suggested):

1. **Quantum**: Great for **combinatorial** or optimization tasks (e.g., route planning). Barrier: limited qubits/error rates in current quantum hardware.
2. **Edge**: Minimizes **latency** and reduces bandwidth usage; local decisions are faster, and only aggregated data heads to the cloud.
3. **Co-creative**: In a design tool, an AI agent suggests creative options, a human refines them—collaboration sparks novel solutions.
4. **Smart City MAS**: Agents might coordinate traffic signals in real time to reduce congestion, incorporate sensor data from roads, and dynamically reroute.

5. **Swarm Robotics**: Many simple robots coordinate with local rules, achieving tasks like search-and-rescue or area coverage efficiently and resiliently.
6. **Governance**: Introduce oversight boards or external audits, ensuring logs exist to trace decisions, with enforced guidelines for agent autonomy.
7. **Environmental Monitoring**: Local edge analysis handles immediate detection (e.g., illegal logging alert), while big data aggregates in the cloud for broader intelligence.
8. **Pseudocode**:

```python
python

class QuantumPlanningAgent:
    def plan_tasks(self, tasks):
        # convert tasks to a quantum optimization
format
        quantum_input =
self.prepare_quantum_problem(tasks)
        solution = quantum_solver(quantum_input)
        return self.parse_solution(solution)

    def prepare_quantum_problem(self, tasks):
        # map tasks to QUBO or other quantum-friendly
structure
        pass

    def parse_solution(self, solution):
        # interpret quantum solver's output
        pass
```

Emerging trends like **quantum computing**, **edge-based agent architectures**, **advanced human-agent collaboration**, **IoT integration**, and **autonomous robotics** promise a **transformative** future for multi-agent systems. Coupled with **ethical** and **governance** considerations, these directions ensure MAS remain beneficial and aligned with societal needs. The **environmental monitoring** case illustrates how synergy between cutting-edge technology and collaborative frameworks can drive global impact. By harnessing these innovations, MAS developers can address ever more complex challenges in the years ahead, shaping a dynamic, more intelligent, and ethically guided future.

Chapter 27: Continuous Learning and Skill Development

As **multi-agent systems (MAS)** and frameworks like **DeepSeek R1** evolve rapidly, developers and researchers must stay **continuously learning** to remain at the forefront of innovation. From staying updated with official releases to building a diverse project portfolio, consistent skill development ensures you can confidently tackle new challenges in AI and MAS. This chapter details strategies for **ongoing learning**, **advanced resources**, **community engagement**, **portfolio building**, and **future pathways** in related fields, culminating in a **case study** on career growth through MAS expertise, plus a project and quiz to reinforce the material.

---

1. Staying Updated with DeepSeek R1

1.1. Following Official Updates and Releases

DeepSeek R1 consistently **improves** with new features, bug fixes, and performance tweaks:

1. **Official Website and Documentation**
   - Regularly check release notes or changelogs for the newest agent APIs, enhancements, or security patches.
   - Bookmark official doc pages for quick reference on new capabilities.
2. **Versioning and Branches**
   - Distinguish stable (LTS) releases from beta or nightly builds if you prefer reliability over cutting-edge features.
3. **Release Newsletters or RSS Feeds**
   - Some projects issue monthly newsletters with release highlights. Subscribe or follow an **RSS** feed for real-time alerts.

1.2. Participating in DeepSeek R1 Community Forums

Forums provide a dynamic space to:

1. **Ask Questions**
   - ○ Post queries about new agent configuration changes, errors you encounter, or best-practice patterns.
2. **Share Solutions**
   - ○ If you fix a tricky integration or build an extension, share steps so others can replicate or refine it.
3. **Feedback and Feature Requests**
   - ○ Influence product direction by requesting new agent modules or performance improvements.

Example:

```text
text

Forum Post Title: "DeepSeek R1 v2.0 - New Multi-Agent
Reasoning Features!"

Body:
- Summarize changes in agent reasoning architecture
- Solicit community input on advanced usage
- Provide code snippets for immediate exploration
```

- *Explanation*: A typical forum thread introducing new functionalities, inviting discussion.

2. Advanced Learning Resources

2.1. Recommended Books and Research Papers

Expanding your MAS knowledge:

1. **Key Texts**
   - ○ "**Multi-Agent Systems: Algorithmic, Game-Theoretic, and Logical Foundations**" by Yoav Shoham, Kevin Leyton-Brown.
   - ○ "**An Introduction to MultiAgent Systems**" by Michael Wooldridge.
2. **Research Papers**
   - ○ Search **ACM**, **IEEE**, or **AAAI** digital libraries for state-of-the-art MAS techniques (distributed RL, social choice in MAS, etc.).

3. **DeepSeek R1 Whitepapers**
    - Project maintainers may release official concept docs or performance studies guiding advanced usage.

2.2. Online Courses and Tutorials

Interactive platforms for **self-paced** or real-time learning:

1. **MOOCs** (e.g., Coursera, edX)
    - Courses on AI, distributed systems, or specialized MAS modules.
    - Look for robust practice assignments to solidify concepts.
2. **DeepSeek R1 Official Tutorials**
    - Step-by-step guides implementing new agent roles or advanced agent-based solutions.
    - Often includes sample repositories, test data, or configured dev environments.
3. **Conference Workshops**
    - Many AI conferences hold tutorials or short courses about cutting-edge MAS research.

3. Engaging with the MAS Community

3.1. Attending Conferences and Workshops

Conferences are hubs for knowledge exchange:

1. **AAMAS (International Conference on Autonomous Agents and Multiagent Systems)**
    - Major annual event highlighting academic and industry MAS breakthroughs.
    - Workshops, tutorials, and demos enrich your perspective.
2. **Domain-Specific**
    - If you focus on robotics, consider **ICRA**, **IROS**. For AI in finance, explore **quant** or FinTech conferences.
3. **Networking**
    - Interact with peers or potential collaborators, see real demos, meet MAS experts in person.

3.2. Contributing to Open-source MAS Projects

Participation fosters **practical** learning:

1. **Picking a Project**
   - o Search for MAS or DeepSeek R1-based repos on GitHub, sorted by language or domain.
   - o Evaluate their activity level or help-wanted issues to find your niche.
2. **Incremental Contributions**
   - o Start with documentation or minor bug fixes to gain familiarity, then tackle bigger feature branches.
3. **Community Recognition**
   - o Consistent pull requests, user support in forums, or plugin development raise your profile in MAS circles.

Table: Avenues for Community Engagement

Engagement Method	Format	Benefits
Conferences/Workshops	In-person or virtual gatherings	High-level updates, networking, potential recruits
Open-source Projects	Online collaboration on GitHub	Real-world practice, build reputation, peer reviews
Online Forums	Q&A threads, Slack/Discord	Immediate advice, knowledge sharing

4. Building a Portfolio of MAS Projects

4.1. Showcasing Your Work

A **portfolio** proves your competence:

1. **GitHub/GitLab Repos**
   - o Keep them well-structured, with clear READMEs, instructions, test coverage.
   - o Include screenshots or short demos to illustrate system operation.
2. **Demo Videos**

- o Record short video screencasts or actual robot footage demonstrating an MAS in action.
- o Highlight key features: agent collaboration, adaptability, user interface.

3. **Technical Blogs**
   - o Post articles about project challenges and solutions, referencing your code.
   - o Encourage commentary, building audience interest and feedback.

4.2. Leveraging Projects for Career Advancement

MAS skills are in demand:

1. **Resume & Interviews**
   - o Show direct examples of how your agent tackled a real problem, with performance metrics.
   - o Potential employers value proven experience in distributed AI, advanced agent orchestration, or domain-specific solutions (finance, robotics).
2. **Freelancing or Consulting**
   - o Industry clients may need specialized MAS setups or performance tuning.
   - o A portfolio speeds trust and contract negotiation.

Code Example (Portfolio snippet):

```
text

Project: "Adaptive Warehouse MAS"
- Roles: InventoryAgent, RobotAgent, OrderAgent
- Achieved 30% faster picking times vs. baseline
- Source: https://github.com/username/AdaptiveWarehouseMAS
- Demo video: https://youtu.be/demo_example
```

- **Explanation**: A brief project summary showcasing value, link to code, and demonstration.

5. Future Learning Pathways

5.1. Exploring Related Fields: Reinforcement Learning, Distributed Systems, etc.

MAS converge with multiple AI subfields:

1. **Reinforcement Learning (RL)**
   o Agents learn policies through reward signals. Multi-agent RL explores collaboration or competition among learning agents.
2. **Distributed Systems**
   o Knowledge of concurrency, reliability, and consistent data flows complements advanced MAS design.
   o Tools like Kafka, zookeeper, or Paxos-based consensus can be relevant.
3. **Game Theory**
   o Agents modeling other agents' strategies or negotiating resources often apply game-theoretic methods (Nash equilibrium, auctions).

5.2. Pursuing Advanced Degrees or Certifications

For those aiming at **academic** or **research** excellence:

1. **Master's/PhD**
   o Many universities host labs focusing on agent-based modeling, computational economics, or advanced robotics.
   o Thesis topics might revolve around MAS optimization, RL, or social simulations.
2. **Professional Certificates**
   o Platforms like edX, Coursera, or specialized institutions may offer recognized credentials in AI ethics, distributed AI, or DevOps for MAS.

Table: Additional Learning Paths

Pathway	Focus	Outcome
Reinforcement Learning	Agents learning from trial-and-error	Deeper modeling of agent autonomy, advanced strategy

Pathway	Focus	Outcome
Distributed Systems	Concurrency, fault tolerance	Robust MAS architecture, large-scale coordination
Game Theory	Strategic interactions among multiple agents	Designing negotiation, resource allocation, or auctions
Graduate Programs	Rigorous research, leading-edge AI innovation	Potential academic or R&D career, deeper theoretical grounding

6. Case Study: Career Growth through Multi-agent Systems Expertise

6.1. Background

Laura, a software engineer, started dabbling in open-source MAS while transitioning from traditional web development. Over five years, her engagements in community forums, completing advanced ML courses, and building a robust MAS portfolio drastically boosted her career.

6.2. Progression and Key Steps

1. **Early Exposure**
   - Contributed minor fixes to a DeepSeek R1 plugin, learned agent patterns.
   - Freed time to read recommended MAS books, reinforcing fundamentals.
2. **Showcasing Projects**
   - Built a multi-agent scheduling solution for e-commerce logistics. Demonstrated results at local AI meetups.
3. **Professional Leap**
   - Landed a role in a robotics startup focusing on swarm drones for agriculture. MAS domain knowledge was a major factor.
4. **Ongoing Learning**
   - Enrolled in an online RL specialization to complement MAS skillset, adopting advanced planning in swarm robotics.

6.3. Outcome

- **Leadership Role**: Now leads a small MAS team, bridging research and industrial applications.
- **Community Recognition**: Acts as a maintainer on a popular open-source MAS library, organizes local workshops.
- **Continual Advancement**: Plans to pursue a part-time PhD focusing on multi-agent RL, merging academic theory with practical demands.

---

7. End-of-Chapter Projects

Project 27: Developing Your MAS Portfolio

Objective: Build and showcase a curated set of **multi-agent system projects** that highlight your evolving skills and adaptability.

Outline

1. **Select 2–3 Distinct Domains**
   - e.g., a small RL-based MAS, a scheduling system for supply chain, and a robotics swarm simulator.
2. **Create Repos / Presentations**
   - Each project with a README, instructions, short demo, mention of any performance results.
3. **Incorporate Continuous Learning**
   - Document how you improved or refined the system over time (feedback-driven updates, new approaches).
4. **Showcase**
   - Compile them into a personal site, LinkedIn profile, or dev blog. Solicit feedback from mentors or open-source communities.

---

8. Quizzes and Self-Assessments

Quiz 27: Continuous Learning Strategies

1. **Staying Updated**

- Question: Why should developers regularly check **DeepSeek R1** release notes, and how can they stay informed?
2. **Advanced Resources**
   - Question: Mention one **MOOC** or **research paper** that can deepen your MAS knowledge.
3. **Community Engagement**
   - Question: Describe a key benefit of posting questions or solutions in **MAS user forums**.
4. **Portfolio Building**
   - Question: Provide two elements that can enhance the **professional impact** of an MAS project showcased in your portfolio.
5. **Future Pathways**
   - Question: How might studying **game theory** or **distributed systems** further improve your MAS skill set?
6. **Case Study**
   - Question: In Laura's career trajectory, how did open-source contributions and meetups catalyze her advancement?
7. **Short Coding Prompt**
   - Question: Write pseudocode for a function `generatePortfolioSummary(projects)` that formats MAS projects into a neat text summary for display on your personal site.

Answer Key (Suggested):

1. **Release Notes**: They highlight new features or fixes, guiding devs to adapt or adopt improvements and avoid known issues. E.g., subscribe to an **RSS feed**, or watch GitHub releases.
2. **MOOC/Research**: Coursera's "Multi-agent Systems" specialization or AAAI/ACM papers on cooperative RL.
3. **Forums**: Others provide immediate troubleshooting help or fresh viewpoints, helping devs solve issues faster and expand knowledge.
4. **Portfolio**: 1) Real-world impact metrics (e.g., "30% less idle time"), 2) Clear, well-documented code that others can run or replicate.
5. **Game Theory/Distributed**: Offers deeper insight into agent strategies, negotiations, or consensus—foundation for robust multi-agent interactions.

6. **Laura's Path**: Contributing to open-source gave her practical experience and visibility, while meetups created networking opportunities that led to job offers.
7. **Pseudocode**:

```python
def generatePortfolioSummary(projects):
    summary = ""
    for proj in projects:
        summary += f"Project Name: {proj.name}\n"
        summary += f"Domain: {proj.domain}\n"
        summary += f"Key Achievements:
{proj.achievements}\n"
        summary += f"Repo Link: {proj.repo_url}\n\n"
    return summary
```

Continuous learning and **skill development** are cornerstones of success in the evolving world of multi-agent systems. Keeping track of **DeepSeek R1** updates, immersing yourself in advanced MAS resources, and engaging with vibrant **communities** accelerate mastery and foster professional growth. Curating a strong **portfolio** of MAS projects demonstrates real competence, enabling you to capitalize on industry opportunities. Whether you pursue further education, specialized research, or advanced roles in diverse industries, a commitment to ongoing learning ensures your MAS expertise remains relevant, impactful, and future-ready.

Chapter 27: Continuous Learning and Skill Development

As **multi-agent systems (MAS)** and frameworks like **DeepSeek R1** continue to evolve, developers and researchers must **continuously learn** to stay informed about the latest methodologies, best practices, and industry trends. From tracking official DeepSeek R1 releases to immersing oneself in advanced educational resources, consistent skill development is pivotal for success. Additionally, engagement with the broader MAS community—both online and in person—offers invaluable opportunities for collaboration, feedback, and mentorship. Building a robust **portfolio** of MAS projects can demonstrate practical expertise, fueling career growth or advanced study pathways. This chapter covers strategies to **stay updated**, details **advanced learning resources**, discusses **community engagement**, explains how to **build and leverage a MAS portfolio**, outlines **future learning** avenues, and presents a **case study** illustrating career progression through MAS expertise.

---

1. Staying Updated with DeepSeek R1

1.1. Following Official Updates and Releases

DeepSeek R1 regularly introduces new features, performance enhancements, and security updates:

1. **Official Documentation and Release Notes**
   - Monitor the official DeepSeek R1 website or repository for version announcements and changelogs.
   - Pay attention to breaking changes or deprecations when upgrading.
2. **RSS Feeds and Newsletter**
   - If available, subscribe to an **RSS feed** or newsletter that announces release details, patch notes, or roadmaps.
3. **Version Compatibility**
   - Use major/minor version references (e.g., 2.x, 3.x) to track significant API evolutions or improvements.
   - Maintain test environments to validate that your MAS solution works properly before moving to production.

Tips:

- **Pin** or lock agent dependencies (e.g., certain plugin versions) if your system demands stability.
- Plan time to **test** each new release in a staging environment, ensuring no unforeseen compatibility issues.

1.2. Participating in DeepSeek R1 Community Forums

Community forums offer interactive support:

1. **Q&A and Support**
   - Post questions about advanced agent behaviors, debugging, or feature usage.
   - Search existing threads to see if your query has been previously answered.
2. **Sharing Best Practices**
   - Users with similar challenges discuss configuration tips, performance tweaks, or code patterns.
   - Encourage knowledge exchange by posting your own solutions.
3. **Contributing Ideas**
   - Submit feature requests or vote on community-driven proposals. The development team often values these inputs.

Example Forum Interaction:

```
text

Title: "Optimal load balancing strategy in DeepSeek R1"
Body:
- Summarize your MAS scenario (heavy job distribution among
10 worker agents).
- Ask for recommended config or scheduling policy to minimize
queue times.
- Mention steps you've tried, performance stats, and
environment details.
```

2. Advanced Learning Resources

2.1. Recommended Books and Research Papers

Books:

- **"An Introduction to MultiAgent Systems"** by Michael Wooldridge
  - Covers fundamental MAS principles: communication, cooperation, negotiation, game-theoretic underpinnings.
- **"Multiagent Systems: Algorithmic, Game-Theoretic, and Logical Foundations"** by Shoham and Leyton-Brown
  - Explores theoretical frameworks with emphasis on algorithmic and logical approaches.
- **DeepSeek R1 Whitepapers** (if available)
  - Offer in-depth insights on design decisions, architecture, or advanced usage.

Research Papers:

- **ACM, IEEE, AAAI**
  - Search for cutting-edge MAS topics: distributed reinforcement learning, agent-based simulations, negotiation protocols.
- **ArXiv**
  - Preprints on MAS or multi-agent RL. Keep an eye on citation counts or endorsements to gauge reliability.

2.2. Online Courses and Tutorials

1. **MOOCs (Coursera, edX, Udacity)**
   - Look for courses in **Reinforcement Learning**, **AI for Robotics**, or specialized MAS modules.
   - Many come with hands-on assignments, ensuring practical skill-building.
2. **Official DeepSeek R1 Tutorials**
   - If provided, stepwise lessons on agent deployment, integration with other libraries, or advanced debugging.
   - May include sample code or sandbox projects for direct experimentation.
3. **Conference Workshops**
   - AAMAS (Autonomous Agents and Multiagent Systems), NeurIPS, or domain-specific conferences often run half-day or full-day MAS tutorials.

Table: Potential Learning Paths

Resource Type	Example Platform/Source	Key Benefit
Academic Textbooks	Wooldridge's "Introduction to MAS," Shoham's "Multiagent Systems"	Deep theoretical grounding
Research Papers	ACM Digital Library, IEEE Xplore	Latest algorithmic or theoretical insights
MOOCs/Online Courses	Coursera, edX (e.g., "Reinforcement Learning")	Interactive learning with assignments
Official Framework Tutorials	DeepSeek R1 docs, plugin developer guides	Framework-specific tips and best practices

3. Engaging with the MAS Community

3.1. Attending Conferences and Workshops

Conferences provide face-to-face networking and specialized knowledge:

1. **AAMAS** (International Conference on Autonomous Agents and Multiagent Systems)
   o Premier MAS-focused event: posters, demos, tutorials from industry and academia.
2. **Domain-Driven Events**
   o If your MAS is used in finance, consider FinTech summits. For robotics, ICRA or IROS are suitable.
3. **Workshops**
   o Often smaller, theme-specific gatherings. Offer in-depth discussions on emerging sub-topics like multi-agent RL or agent-based simulation in social sciences.

3.2. Contributing to Open-source MAS Projects

Open-source communities bolster skill and reputation:

1. **Finding a Project**
   o Evaluate active repositories: check recent commits, open issues, clarity of CONTRIBUTING.md.
2. **Substantive Contributions**

- o Add new agent features or documentation, improve performance, fix concurrency issues, or provide localizations.
3. **Ongoing Collaboration**
   - o Long-term involvement can yield code maintainer roles or mentorship opportunities.

Tips:

- Discuss your proposed changes in an issue thread before coding large features, ensuring alignment with maintainers' roadmap.
- Respect coding styles, test guidelines, and follow the established PR process.

4. Building a Portfolio of MAS Projects

4.1. Showcasing Your Work

A **MAS portfolio** highlights real-world achievements:

1. **GitHub/GitLab Repositories**
   - o Include README overviews, architecture diagrams, sample usage commands, and test coverage badges.
   - o Provide link to recorded demos or screenshots for quick previews.
2. **Demo Videos**
   - o Briefly illustrate agents collaborating (e.g., in a simulation environment or a physical robotic setup).
   - o Keep them short (2–5 minutes), focusing on core functionalities.
3. **Technical Blogs / Websites**
   - o Summarize system design rationales, performance benchmarks, interesting agent interactions.
   - o Add code snippets or config files to help others replicate.

4.2. Leveraging Projects for Career Advancement

Professionals can leverage MAS projects for:

1. **Resume Enhancements**

- Emphasize results: e.g., "Reduced warehouse picking time by 20% with a scheduling MAS."
2. **Interviews**
   - Walk interviewers through the architecture, challenges, and how you overcame them.
3. **Freelance Consulting**
   - Potential clients see evidence of your MAS domain skill—particularly relevant for specialized industries like autonomous drones or multi-agent e-commerce solutions.

Table: Tips to Enhance MAS Project Visibility

Tip	Implementation Detail
Clear Project Branding	Give each project a memorable name or short tagline
Concise Technical Write-ups	One-page PDF or blog post summarizing architecture, metrics
Regular Updates/Changelogs	Indicate active maintenance, fosters user confidence
Cross-Linking	Share on LinkedIn, dev forums, personal websites

5. Future Learning Pathways

5.1. Exploring Related Fields: Reinforcement Learning, Distributed Systems, etc.

Broadening your skill set amplifies MAS strengths:

1. **Reinforcement Learning (RL)**
   - Agents in dynamic environments. Multi-agent RL covers cooperation vs. competition among multiple learners.
2. **Distributed Systems**
   - Knowledge of concurrency, replication, fault tolerance, enabling robust MAS with high availability.
3. **Game Theory**
   - Negotiation or resource allocation strategies among self-interested agents.

4. **Cloud/DevOps**
   - MAS at scale on container platforms or microservices architecture.

5.2. Pursuing Advanced Degrees or Certifications

1. **Masters or PhD**
   - In AI, robotics, or computational economics. Offers deeper theoretical foundation, chance to push MAS research.
2. **Professional Certifications**
   - Some organizations or platforms provide specialized AI certifications acknowledging MAS or advanced RL expertise.
3. **Ongoing Education**
   - Even short courses or part-time diplomas can accelerate your advanced skill acquisition.

Tips:

- Evaluate your career goals. An academic route suits those wanting to pioneer new theories or teach. Industry roles may emphasize targeted skills from short specialized courses.

6. Case Study: Career Growth through Multi-agent Systems Expertise

6.1. Scenario

Ravi, an engineer with a background in web development, started tinkering with **DeepSeek R1** for a small e-commerce automation project. Fascinated, he delved deeper into multi-agent scheduling, negotiation algorithms, and advanced RL-based optimization.

6.2. Action Steps

1. **Continuous Learning**
   - Ravi completed an online advanced RL course, devoting weekends to reading MAS research papers.
2. **Open-source Contributions**

- He contributed to a popular MAS library, adding a robust "task bidding" plugin.
- Gained recognition and mentorship from core maintainers.
3. **Portfolio Building**
   - Showcased a dynamic inventory system: warehouse robots collaborating to minimize picking delay.
   - Prepared short demos and wrote blog posts detailing architecture and performance gains.

6.3. Outcome

- **Promotions and New Opportunities**: Ravi's employer recognized his skill expansion, leading to a senior AI engineer role focusing on MAS-based solutions.
- **Community Influence**: He joined conferences, speaking about his open-source experiences, shaping best practices for scheduling agents.
- **Long-term Vision**: Plans to eventually create a startup offering specialized MAS logistics solutions, leveraging the strong network of contacts from open-source work.

7. End-of-Chapter Projects

Project 27: Developing Your MAS Portfolio

Objective: Assemble **multiple** MAS demonstration projects that illustrate your evolving expertise, from concept to advanced design, documented and presentable for future opportunities.

Outline

1. **Select 2–3 MAS Themes**
   - e.g., a small scheduling MAS, a multi-agent reinforcement learning environment, and a collaborative robotics scenario.
2. **Implement and Document**
   - Provide code repos with READMEs, instructions, and test coverage.
   - Add short "Insights" documents explaining architecture or performance metrics.

3. **Create Demo Videos**
   - o If feasible, record short screencasts or actual hardware demos.
   - o Upload to a hosting platform, embed in your readme or personal site.
4. **Showcase**
   - o Gather all projects in a single "portfolio" page.
   - o Soliciting feedback from mentors or the MAS community to refine your approach and highlight user interest.

---

8. Quizzes and Self-Assessments

Quiz 27: Continuous Learning Strategies

1. **Staying Updated**
   - o **Question**: Mention two ways to keep track of **DeepSeek R1** updates and ensure your MAS remains compatible.
2. **Advanced Resources**
   - o **Question**: Name a recommended **textbook** or **research source** for deepening multi-agent theory or practical techniques.
3. **Community Engagement**
   - o **Question**: Provide one reason why contributing to **open-source** MAS projects benefits professional growth.
4. **Portfolio Building**
   - o **Question**: Which elements of a **MAS project** demonstration help potential employers quickly grasp your accomplishments?
5. **Future Pathways**
   - o **Question**: How can knowledge in **distributed systems** or **Reinforcement Learning** enhance your MAS skill set?
6. **Case Study**
   - o **Question**: In Ravi's journey, name two factors that propelled him to a senior AI engineer role.
7. **Short Coding Prompt**
   - o **Question**: Write a pseudocode function `summarizeLearningPath(skills, resources)` that returns a text outline suggesting next steps for skill improvement.

Answer Key (Suggested):

1. **Tracking DeepSeek R1**:
   -
     1. Follow official release notes, 2) Participate in user forums or Slack for real-time updates.
2. **Recommended Reading**:
   - "An Introduction to MultiAgent Systems" by Wooldridge or any major AI conference proceedings (AAMAS).
3. **Open-source**:
   - Gains hands-on experience, public code presence, feedback from peers, and improved credibility in job markets.
4. **Project Demonstration**:
   - Clear architecture diagrams, performance metrics (before/after improvement), short video/demo links, and final outcomes or results.
5. **Distributed Systems / RL**:
   - **Distributed Systems** knowledge ensures robust agent messaging, scaling. **RL** fosters advanced adaptive behaviors.
6. **Ravi's Factors**:
   - Contributing code to an established project (visibility, skill demonstration) and building a high-value portfolio of MAS solutions (clearly documented).
7. **Pseudocode**:

```python
def summarizeLearningPath(skills, resources):
    outline = "Recommended Learning Path:\n"
    for skill in skills:
        outline += f"- {skill}:\n"
        if skill in resources:
            for resource in resources[skill]:
                outline += f"   * {resource}\n"
        else:
            outline += f"   * No specific resource
listed\n"
    return outline
```

Continuous learning is the cornerstone of sustained mastery in **multi-agent systems**. By staying abreast of **DeepSeek R1** updates, leveraging advanced learning materials, and actively engaging in MAS communities, you can refine your skills, forge valuable connections, and discover new opportunities. Crafting a polished **portfolio** demonstrates your accomplishments, while investigating **adjacent fields** or further education cements deeper expertise. As illustrated in the **career growth** case study, dedication to learning and community collaboration can propel you to advanced roles and catalyze meaningful contributions in the world of MAS.

Chapter 28: Marketing and Promotion of MAS Projects

After developing a robust **multi-agent system (MAS)** and ensuring its reliability, it's time to **showcase** it to the world. Effective **marketing** and **promotion** help attract users, contributors, and stakeholders who can benefit from and support your project's growth. This chapter explores **pre-launch campaigns**, **leveraging professional networks**, **building an online presence**, **communication strategies**, and **measuring marketing success**. We also highlight a **case study** on promoting an open-source MAS project and provide **projects** and a **quiz** for practical application.

---

1. Pre-launch Campaigns

1.1. Utilizing Social Media

Social media platforms—**LinkedIn**, **Twitter**, **Reddit**, **Facebook**—can generate early interest and feedback:

1. **Teaser Posts**
   - Share quick project highlights ("Our MAS will reduce warehouse picking time by 30%!").
   - Include visual teasers or short demos to spark curiosity.
2. **Scheduled Updates**
   - Regularly post progress snippets, screenshots, or success stories.
   - Encourage "likes," "shares," or comments to expand reach.
3. **Targeted Platforms**
   - For technical MAS, prefer professional networks like LinkedIn or specialized subreddits (r/MachineLearning, r/robotics).
   - If appealing to a broader audience (e.g., IoT smart homes), consider general consumer tech outlets.

Tips:

- Use relevant **hashtags** (#MultiAgentSystems, #DeepSeekR1, #AI) to reach like-minded audiences.
- Maintain consistent posting frequency to remain visible without spamming followers.

1.2. Hosting Webinars and Workshops

Interactive events drive deeper engagement:

1. **Online Webinars**
   - Present MAS's background, core features, and live demos.
   - Conduct Q&A at the end, gathering user feedback or clarifications.
2. **Workshops**
   - Organize half/full-day sessions. Provide hands-on tutorials for participants to explore your MAS.
   - Collaborate with academic or industry meetups (e.g., local AI clubs, developer groups).
3. **Cross-promotion**
   - Partner with known MAS or AI communities to co-host the event, leveraging each other's membership base.

1.3. Creating Pre-release Content

Build anticipation and readiness:

1. **Teaser Videos**
   - Show partial functionalities or success results in a short clip.
   - Combine narration, animations, or real footage of the MAS in action.
2. **Beta Access**
   - Offer a limited group early access, gather test results or quotes for marketing.
   - Encourages strong initial testimonials.
3. **Blog Series**
   - Write a multi-part blog detailing system design, challenges, and unique features. Readers appreciate transparency into development.

Table: Pre-launch Campaign Elements

Element	Purpose	Example
Social Media Teasers	Spark interest, gather early signups	Short post: "Revolutionizing warehouse tasks—30% faster!"
Webinar/Workshop	Deeper project introduction and hands-on guidance	1-hour Zoom session with live Q&A
Beta Access	Gather user feedback before full release	"Join our private Slack to test new MAS features!"

2. Leveraging Networks

2.1. Collaborating with Industry Influencers

Influencers in AI, robotics, or your target sector can amplify reach:

1. **Identify Key Figures**
   - Not just social media stars—think domain experts, respected developers, or professors.
2. **Pitch Collaboration**
   - Offer them early demos, exclusive insights, or co-creation opportunities (like a specialized module or integration).
3. **Joint Content**
   - Appear on their podcasts or have them guest blog about your MAS.
   - Combine audiences for a broader promotional boost.

2.2. Engaging with Professional Communities

Professional associations and bodies:

1. **AI or Industry Associations**
   - e.g., IEEE, ACM, local robotics clubs.
   - Present your MAS at small conferences or special interest group meetups.
2. **In-Person Networking**
   - Organize or attend hackathons, developer days, or roundtable discussions relevant to multi-agent solutions.

- Collect business cards or add new LinkedIn contacts, building potential partnership leads.

3. **Collaboration on Use Cases**
   - If your MAS addresses a domain (healthcare, finance), approach relevant companies or academic labs for pilot programs or research synergy.

Tips:

- Offer mutual benefit: a partner might test your MAS in real contexts while you refine it with field data.
- Document any pilot results for marketing case studies.

3. Building an Online Presence

3.1. Creating a Professional Website or Blog

Central hub to share all relevant details:

1. **Homepage**
   - Summarize your MAS, highlight main features and benefits, link to demos or GitHub repos.
   - Aim for clarity: short paragraphs, bullet points, and visuals.
2. **Documentation**
   - Offer quickstart guides, in-depth tutorials, and architecture diagrams.
   - Possibly integrate with auto-generated doc systems (e.g., Sphinx, Docusaurus).
3. **Testimonials & Case Studies**
   - Real user quotes or success metrics from early adopters.
   - Encourages trust and adoption.

3.2. Maintaining Active Social Media Profiles

Social channels let you:

1. **Regularly Publish Updates**
   - Share new features, success stories, or performance milestones.

2. **Cross-Promotion**
   o Link from your site to Twitter or LinkedIn for project announcements.
   o Add "share on social" widgets in your project pages.
3. **Community Engagement**
   o Answer user queries publicly, showcase quick solutions, or highlight interesting user-led modifications.

Code Example (Markdown snippet for your blog):

```markdown
# Welcome to My MAS Project

**Project Name**: Adaptive Scheduling MAS
**Description**: A multi-agent system that dynamically
schedules production tasks in real-time, reducing idle time
by 25%.

## Features
- Agent-based communication with minimal overhead
- Auto-scaling capability
- Real-time optimization feedback

[View GitHub
Repo](https://github.com/YourUser/AdaptiveSchedulingMAS)
```

- **Explanation**:
  o A simple overview for a blog or site README, pointing visitors to essential info quickly.

---

4. Effective Communication Strategies

4.1. Crafting Compelling Project Descriptions

Concise yet **impactful** descriptions are key:

1. **Highlight Unique Value**
   o Summarize how your MAS outperforms or innovates (e.g., 20% faster scheduling vs. prior solutions).
2. **Use Real Metrics**

o Concrete numbers (throughput, accuracy, cost savings) build credibility.
3. **Narrative Style**
   o Share the "why" behind your MAS: problem it solves, who benefits, and an anecdote or user story if relevant.

4.2. Showcasing Success Stories and Case Studies

Proof of impact:

1. **Before/After Comparisons**
   o Show how a client or pilot environment improved post-deployment.
   o Graphs or tables illustrating performance boosts or user satisfaction leaps.
2. **User Testimonials**
   o Quotes from project stakeholders: "Using this MAS cut our response times in half."
3. **Technical Breakdown**
   o For an engineering audience, detail how architecture or algorithmic changes led to the positive outcome.

Table: Example Communication Elements

Element	Usage	Example
Clear Value Proposition	Instantly convey major benefit	"Reduce picking cost by 20% using collaborative robots."
Metric-based Evidence	Quantify improvements	"3-month pilot increased assembly throughput by 30%."
User/Client Testimonials	Real experiences, fosters trust	"Warehouse manager: 'We handle peak loads effortlessly now.'"

5. Measuring Marketing Success

5.1. Key Metrics and KPIs

Track marketing **performance**:

1. **Website Traffic**

o Unique visitors, page views, bounce rates. Check if marketing campaigns drive relevant visits.

2. **Conversion Rates**
   o e.g., number of watchers/stars on GitHub, sign-ups for demos, or requests for pilot trials.
3. **Engagement Levels**
   o Forum or social media interaction (likes, shares, comments).
   o Newsletter open rates, webinar attendance.

5.2. Adjusting Strategies Based on Feedback

1. **User Surveys**
   o Ask new adopters or event attendees about how they heard of your MAS, what resonated or confused them.
2. **A/B Testing**
   o Test different landing page designs or ad copy to see which yields better user response.
3. **Iterative Improvement**
   o If certain content gets minimal traction, pivot or refine it. Focus on the mediums or messages that yield highest ROI.

Code Example (Pseudocode):

```python
def track_metrics(analytics_data):
    # parse relevant marketing metrics
    visitors = analytics_data["visitors"]
    signups = analytics_data["signups"]
    conversion_rate = signups / visitors if visitors else 0
    print(f"Visitors: {visitors}, Sign-ups: {signups}, Conversion rate: {conversion_rate:.2%}")
```

- **Explanation**:
   o A simple function for summarizing basic marketing metrics. Real usage might tie into Google Analytics or custom dashboards.

6. Case Study: Successfully Promoting an Open-source MAS Project

6.1. Scenario

A small group of developers creates an **open-source** MAS for **urban traffic management**. Initially, it struggles to gain traction despite robust features.

6.2. Campaign Strategies

1. **Pre-launch Sneak Peeks**
   - They posted short demonstration videos showing real-time simulations at small scale. Social media teased major improvements over legacy models.
2. **Targeted Webinars**
   - Organized free 1-hour sessions where urban planners and academic researchers joined to see live demos and Q&A.
3. **Influencer Collaboration**
   - Team partnered with a well-known AI researcher who tweeted about the project, adding credibility and user influx.

6.3. Results

- **Sharp Increase** in GitHub Stars: from 50 to 300 in two weeks following the influencer's endorsement.
- **Active Community**: More bug reports, new feature suggestions, and external plugin contributions.
- **Pilot Projects**: Two mid-sized cities tested the system in simulation for traffic light optimization, leading to real-world trials.

Table: Marketing Gains

Metric	Before Campaign	After Campaign	Improvement
GitHub Stars	50	300+	+500% increase
Forum Activity	Infrequent	10+ new threads/wk	Community discussions flourish
City Pilot Interest	0	2 city pilots	Gaining real municipal engagement

7. End-of-Chapter Projects

Project 28: Designing a Marketing Plan for Your MAS Project

Objective: Develop and execute a well-rounded **marketing strategy** for an MAS you've created or are actively contributing to.

Outline

1. **Identify Target Audience**
   - e.g., industrial robotics managers, academic researchers, or open-source hobbyists.
2. **Create Core Collateral**
   - A concise pitch deck or webpage with a compelling project summary, key benefits, and a short demo video.
3. **Plan a Pre-launch**
   - Teaser posts, short blog series, possibly an early-access or invite-only community event.
4. **Leverage Networks**
   - Reach out to influencers, relevant conferences, or domain-specific user groups.
5. **Measure and Adapt**
   - Track metrics: site traffic, sign-up rates, contributor growth.
   - Adjust messaging or mediums as you learn what resonates best.

---

8. Quizzes and Self-Assessments

Quiz 28: Marketing and Promotion Techniques

1. **Pre-launch**
   - **Question**: Why is hosting a **webinar** or workshop prior to official release effective for building early interest?
2. **Leveraging Networks**
   - **Question**: Name one benefit of **collaborating** with an industry influencer or domain expert for your MAS.
3. **Online Presence**
   - **Question**: Provide two essential elements you'd include in a professional **MAS project** website.
4. **Communication Strategies**

- ○ **Question**: Mention one way to make **project descriptions** stand out, capturing potential adopters' attention.
5. **Measuring Success**
   - ○ **Question**: Identify a **KPI** (key performance indicator) that indicates strong user engagement with your MAS.
6. **Case Study**
   - ○ **Question**: In the open-source traffic management example, what triggered a jump in GitHub stars and new user interest?
7. **Short Coding Prompt**
   - ○ **Question**: Write pseudocode for `publishAnnouncement(title, body, social_channels)` that posts an MAS announcement to multiple networks (e.g., Twitter, LinkedIn, a forum).

Answer Key (Suggested):

1. **Webinar**: Demonstrates features, fosters direct user Q&A, and gathers immediate feedback, building **hype** and trust.
2. **Influencer Collaboration**: Gains **wider reach**, as their followers or domain contacts engage, boosting credibility.
3. **Website Essentials**:
   - ○
     1. Clear overview of MAS benefits,
   - ○
     2. Step-by-step guides or demos for easy adoption.

4. **Compelling Descriptions**: Emphasize **real metrics** or success stories, plus short, clear language.
5. **KPI**: e.g., **conversion rate** from site visitors to download or pilot trial signups.
6. **GitHub Star Surge**: An AI influencer's **endorsement** led to a large audience discovering the project.
7. **Pseudocode**:

```python
def publishAnnouncement(title, body, social_channels):
    for channel in social_channels:
        if channel == "twitter":
            post_twitter(title, body)
        elif channel == "linkedin":
            post_linkedin(title, body)
        elif channel == "forum":
```

```
    post_forum(title, body)
print("Announcement posted to all channels!")
```

Effective **marketing** and **promotion** are as vital to a **multi-agent system** project's success as robust architecture or advanced features. Through careful **pre-launch** planning, utilizing **professional networks**, crafting **clear online presences**, and implementing data-driven **communication strategies**, your MAS gains visibility and adoption. Monitoring metrics guides iterative improvements, ensuring your project resonates with the target audience. As shown by the open-source case study, well-executed campaigns can transform a small project into a thriving community with real-world deployments.

Appendices

The following **appendices** provide detailed references, instructions, sample resources, and expert insights essential for mastering **DeepSeek R1** and multi-agent systems (MAS). They serve as a comprehensive supplement to the main chapters, guiding you through in-depth technical details, setup instructions, terminology, and additional learning opportunities.

Appendix A: DeepSeek R1 API Reference

This appendix offers an **in-depth** overview of the **DeepSeek R1** core APIs. It is designed for quick lookups and deeper exploration of advanced features.

A.1. Agent Lifecycle and Management

1. **Agent Initialization**
   o **Constructor** parameters, agent ID configuration, optional environment settings.
   o Example usage snippet:

   ```python
   from deepseek_r1_sdk import AgentBase

   class MyAgent(AgentBase):
       def on_start(self):
           print(f"{self.agent_id} started!")

   agent = MyAgent(agent_id="Agent01")
   agent.run()
   ```

2. **Lifecycle Hooks**
   o **on_start()**: Called once the agent is ready.
   o **on_message()**: Handles inbound messages.
   o **on_shutdown()**: Cleanup logic prior to agent termination.

A.2. Communication APIs

1. **Messaging Methods**

- o **send_message(self, message)**: Send a dictionary-like message (sender, receiver, content_type, payload).
- o **broadcast_message(self, payload)**: Publish updates to multiple agents or a topic.

2. **Message Format**
   - o Typically JSON-based for clarity, but supports binary or custom formats if configured.
   - o Example:

```python
message = {
  "sender": "Agent01",
  "receiver": "Agent02",
  "content_type": "TASK_ASSIGNMENT",
  "payload": {"task_id": "T123", "priority":
"high"}
}
agent.send_message(message)
```

A.3. Task Scheduling and Coordination

1. **TaskManager**
   - o Subsystem for distributing tasks among capable agents.
   - o Methods: `submit_task(task)`, `check_task_status(task_id)`.
2. **Coordinator or Manager APIs**
   - o **AgentManager** handles agent registration, discovery, and lifecycle events.
   - o Example usage in a small snippet:

```python
manager = AgentManager()
agent1 = WorkerAgent(agent_id="Worker1")
manager.register_agent(agent1)
manager.run()
```

A.4. Extended Features and Plugins

1. **Conflict Resolution**
   - o Optional conflict resolution module, e.g., negotiation or arbitration plugins.
2. **Reasoning and Decision-making**

- o Integrations with external AI or rule engines; reference the sub-library for configuring advanced reasoning.
3. **Customization**
   - o Hooks to override default behavior, add custom logging, or implement specialized agent roles.

Note: For each feature, cross-reference the official docs or source code for deeper parameter details and code examples.

Appendix B: Installation Guides for Different Platforms

A streamlined approach to **installing** and configuring **DeepSeek R1** across major operating systems and environments.

B.1. Windows

1. **Prerequisites**
   - o Python 3.9+ (if using Python-based agents).
   - o Optional: Docker Desktop if containerizing.
2. **Installation Steps**

   bash

   ```
   pip install deepseek_r1_sdk
   ```

   - o Confirm PATH environment variables.
   - o For advanced usage, configure a dedicated environment or use conda.
3. **Common Issues**
   - o **Missing Build Tools**: If building from source, install MSVC Build Tools or the Windows SDK.
   - o **Firewall Prompts**: Windows Defender firewall may block inter-agent communication. Create exceptions for agent ports.

B.2. macOS

1. **Homebrew**

- o Install dependencies (Python, Docker, etc.) using `brew install python docker`.

2. **Cloning Repo**

```bash
git clone https://github.com/YourUser/deepseek_r1.git
cd deepseek_r1
python setup.py install
```

3. **Virtual Environments**
   - o Recommended to isolate project dependencies.
   - o `python3 -m venv env && source env/bin/activate`.

B.3. Linux (Ubuntu Example)

1. **Package Requirements**
   - o `sudo apt-get update`, then `sudo apt-get install python3 python3-pip build-essential`.
2. **DeepSeek R1 SDK**
   - o `pip install deepseek_r1_sdk` or build from source.
3. **Systemd Service Setup**
   - o You may run agent processes as a systemd service for easy start/stop on boot.

Tips:

- Always verify library versions with `pip list`.
- Use containerization (Docker, Kubernetes) for consistent cross-platform behavior if desired.

Appendix C: Glossary of Terms

A concise **reference** defining key MAS and DeepSeek R1 terminology.

Term	Definition
Agent	An autonomous entity capable of perceiving, reasoning, and acting within an environment

Term	Definition
Agent Manager	A module handling agent registration, lifecycle management, and message routing
Conflict Resolution	Mechanisms ensuring agents avoid deadlocks, resource clashes, or priority inversions
MAS (Multi-agent System)	A system in which multiple autonomous agents collaborate or compete to achieve goals
DeepSeek R1	The MAS framework described in this book, providing APIs for agent design, scheduling, etc.
Task Manager	A subsystem distributing tasks among suitable agents
Hot Swap	Replacing or adding agents at runtime without stopping the entire system
Publish/Subscribe	A communication pattern where senders publish events to channels and interested agents subscribe to them

Use this glossary as a **quick reference** for key concepts throughout the book.

Appendix D: Additional Resources and Further Reading

Recommended **supplementary materials** to deepen your MAS expertise:

1. **Academic Journals and Proceedings**
   - **Autonomous Agents and Multi-Agent Systems** (Springer).
   - **AAMAS Conference Proceedings** for cutting-edge research.
2. **Online Tutorials & Blogs**
   - MAS-focused channels on Medium, specialized YouTube series on agent-based modeling.
3. **Podcasts**
   - AI-themed shows often feature guests discussing multi-agent breakthroughs (Lex Fridman podcast, The TWIML AI Podcast).
4. **Professional Groups**

o   IEEE Computer Society's chapters, AAAI special interest groups on Agents.

Table: Example Additional Resources

Resource	Link / Info	Why It's Useful
AAMAS Conference	http://www.aamas-conference.org/	Latest academic and industry MAS research
MAS-Focused YouTube Channels	e.g., "MultiAgent AI - Tutorials"	Visual demonstrations, step-by-step explanations
AI Blogs (Medium, personal)	"Agent-based Simulation" curated topics	Practical insights, field updates

Appendix E: Sample Code Repositories and Projects

An assortment of **practical** MAS references you can clone, study, or extend:

1. **Basic Multi-Agent Coordination**
   o   https://github.com/ExampleOrg/coordination-mas
   o   Demonstrates simple messaging and task distribution among agents.
2. **DeepSeek R1 Plugin Collection**
   o   https://github.com/DeepSeekR1Community/plugins
   o   Community-contributed plugins for specialized tasks (e.g., negotiation-based scheduling).
3. **Reinforcement Learning Agents**
   o   https://github.com/ExampleUser/multiagent-rl
   o   Example code bridging RL libraries with MAS environments.

Tips:

- Always read each repo's README or wiki for setup instructions.
- Contribute bug fixes or improvements if you find issues or see potential enhancements.

Appendix F: Video Tutorials and Webinars

A curated list of **video-based** learning materials:

1. **DeepSeek R1 Official Tutorials**
   - Short YouTube or Vimeo playlists demonstrating agent creation, messaging, conflict resolution approaches.
   - Also includes Q&A segments with project maintainers.
2. **Conference Presentations**
   - Videos from AAMAS or other AI events, providing slides plus commentary on advanced MAS topics.
3. **Workshops and Webinars**
   - Recordings from official or community-run MAS training sessions. Access them via your project's website or community pages.

Example:

```
text

Title: "Introduction to DeepSeek R1" (45 mins)
Link: https://youtu.be/IntroDeepSeekR1
Highlights:
- Basic agent setup, messaging demos, agent manager usage
- Q&A on best deployment practices
```

- *Explanation*: Showcases a typical reference to help new watchers quickly locate relevant video training.

Appendix G: Interview Transcripts with Industry Experts

Conversations with **leading MAS practitioners** illuminate advanced insights, real-world challenges, and potential future trends. These transcripts can guide your solutions and spark new ideas.

1. **Dr. Alicia Gomez** – Senior Researcher in Agent-based Simulation
   - Topics: Urban traffic management, large-scale agent modeling, bridging academic and industry solutions.

2. **Marton Li** – Architect at a FinTech MAS platform
   o Emphasizes real-time data ingestion, multi-agent risk calculations, and compliance obligations.
3. **Elena Rossi** – Robotics Engineer implementing swarm-based inspection agents
   o Discusses cross-industry robotics synergy, agent-based mission planning, and swarm integration with IoT.

Suggested Reading Approach:

- Skim each transcript's highlights for direct quotes or best practices.
- Dive deeper into the sections relevant to your domain.
- Reflect on how each expert overcame domain-specific or technical hurdles to apply lessons to your MAS.

These **appendices** serve as a comprehensive resource, providing **API references**, **installation** guidelines, an easy-to-navigate **glossary**, and curated **further reading**. Sample projects, code repositories, video tutorials, and real-world expert insights deliver practical, readily actionable knowledge. By leveraging these appendices—along with the main content of the book—you'll have at your fingertips everything necessary to confidently build, maintain, and continuously improve **multi-agent systems** with **DeepSeek R1** and beyond.

Index

Below is a **comprehensive, alphabetically ordered index** of the key topics, terms, and references covered throughout this book on **DeepSeek R1** and **multi-agent systems (MAS)**. Each entry highlights **where** in the book the concept is primarily discussed, including **chapters**, **sections**, and (when applicable) relevant **appendices** or notable **code examples**. This index helps you **quickly locate** the detailed explanations and implementations discussed in the preceding chapters and appendices.

A

Accessibility

- **Definition**: Ensuring that MAS user interfaces and agent interactions accommodate users with disabilities or varied technical backgrounds.
- **Key References**:
    - Chapter 17 / Section 4 (Sustainable and Responsible AI Practices)
    - Chapter 27 / Section 4 (Building a Portfolio of MAS Projects, inclusivity in demos)

Accountability

- **Definition**: Assigning responsibility for decisions or outcomes in multi-agent contexts where multiple entities may be involved.
- **Key References**:
    - Chapter 17 / Section 1 (Ethical Challenges in MAS)
    - Chapter 25 / Section 1 and 2 (Ensuring agent actions remain transparent and traceable)

Adaptive Agents

- **Definition**: Agents capable of **learning** or modifying behaviors in real-time based on environmental changes or user feedback.
- **Key References**:
    - Chapter 21 / Section 1 (Dynamic Environment Handling)
    - Chapter 4 / Section 4 (Implementing Agent Behaviors)

Agent Lifecycle

- **Definition**: The creation, initialization, run-time operation, and shutdown phases of an MAS agent.
- **Key References**:
  - Appendix A (DeepSeek R1 API Reference)
  - Chapter 4 / Section 1 (Agent Architecture)

Agent Manager

- **Definition**: A subsystem or module overseeing **agent registration**, **lifecycle**, and sometimes **messaging** or **task distribution**.
- **Key References**:
  - Chapter 2 / Section 2 (DeepSeek R1 Architecture)
  - Appendix A / A.1 (DeepSeek R1 API for agent management)

Agent Roles

- **Definition**: Specialized tasks or functions assigned to an agent (e.g., scheduling, monitoring, or data processing).
- **Key References**:
  - Chapter 4 / Section 2 (Defining Agent Roles and Responsibilities)
  - Chapter 7 / Section 1 (Task Allocation strategies)

AI Ethics

- **Definition**: The moral and responsible use of AI technology, focusing on fairness, privacy, and accountability.
- **Key References**:
  - Chapter 17 (Ethical Considerations and Responsible AI in MAS)
  - Chapter 25 (Ethical Considerations and Responsible AI in MAS)

Architecture (MAS)

- **Definition**: The structural design guiding how agents, communication, and environment interactions are organized.
- **Key References**:
  - Chapter 4 / Section 1 (Agent Architecture)
  - Chapter 2 / Section 2 (DeepSeek R1 Architecture)

Automated Maintenance

- **Definition**: Scripts or mechanisms that handle routine system upkeep (log rotation, agent restarts, backups) without manual intervention.
- **Key References**:
  - Chapter 20 / Section 4 (Automated Maintenance Tasks)

B

Bias and Fairness

- **Definition**: The tendency of an MAS or AI model to produce systematically skewed decisions that disadvantage particular groups or contexts.
- **Key References**:
  - Chapter 17 / Section 1 (Ethical Challenges)
  - Chapter 25 / Section 1 (Ethical Challenges in MAS)

Big Data

- **Definition**: Large, complex data sets requiring specialized technologies to handle analytics and real-time insights.
- **Key References**:
  - Chapter 15 / Section 5 (Big Data and Analytics)

Black Box Models

- **Definition**: AI or agent decision processes that are opaque to inspection, making them harder to interpret or explain.
- **Key References**:
  - Chapter 17 / Section 2 (Designing Ethical Agents, ensuring transparency)
  - Chapter 25 / Section 2 (Incorporating Ethical Decision-Making)

Blockchain

- **Definition**: A distributed ledger technology that can be used for secure, tamper-proof logs or agent transactions.

- **Key References**:
  - o Chapter 16 / Section 5 (Intrusion Detection and logs) – though not specifically blockchain, related to tamper-proof record-keeping discussion

Broadcasting Messages

- **Definition**: Sending a single message to multiple agents or an entire topic.
- **Key References**:
  - o Chapter 2 / Section 2.1 (Messaging Systems in DeepSeek R1, direct vs. broadcast)
  - o Appendix A / A.2 (Communication APIs)

C

Case Studies

- **Definition**: Real-world or hypothetical scenarios illustrating MAS solutions and best practices.
- **Key References**:
  - o Each chapter ends with a relevant case study (e.g., Chapter 6 for financial trading, Chapter 10 for autonomous vehicle fleets).

CI/CD

- **Definition**: Continuous Integration and Continuous Deployment pipelines ensuring code changes are tested and deployed automatically.
- **Key References**:
  - o Chapter 19 / Section 3 (Continuous Integration and Continuous Deployment)
  - o Chapter 22 / Section 4 (Automated Testing with DeepSeek R1)

Cloud Deployment

- **Definition**: Hosting agents or entire MAS on cloud infrastructure (AWS, Azure, GCP) for scalability and reduced maintenance overhead.
- **Key References**:
  - Chapter 19 / Section 1 (Deployment Strategies)
  - Chapter 19 / Section 2 (Containerization, using Docker/Kubernetes)

Collaboration

- **Definition**: Agents (and possibly humans) working together, sharing tasks and resources to achieve goals.
- **Key References**:
  - Chapter 4 / Section 2 (Defining Agent Roles and Responsibilities)
  - Chapter 2 / Section 3 (Core Features: Multi-agent Coordination)

Community Forums

- **Definition**: Online or offline spaces where developers, users, and enthusiasts discuss MAS topics, share solutions, and collaborate.
- **Key References**:
  - Chapter 24 / Section 3 (Engaging with the MAS and DeepSeek R1 Communities)
  - Chapter 27 / Section 1.2 (Participating in DeepSeek R1 Community Forums)

Conflict Resolution

- **Definition**: Methods to handle resource contention, deadlocks, or agent priority inversions.
- **Key References**:
  - Chapter 8 (Conflict Resolution and Robustness in MAS)

Containerization

- **Definition**: Packaging an application (including MAS agents) and dependencies into lightweight containers (Docker) for consistent deployment.
- **Key References**:
  - Chapter 19 / Section 2 (Containerization and Virtualization)

Continuous Learning

- **Definition**: The process of consistently updating or retraining agent logic based on new data or user feedback.
- **Key References**:
    - Chapter 21 / Section 1 (Real-time Learning and Adaptation)
    - Chapter 27 (Continuous Learning and Skill Development)

D

Data Privacy

- **Definition**: Safeguarding user or organizational data processed by agents, respecting relevant laws like GDPR.
- **Key References**:
    - Chapter 16 / Section 4 (Data Privacy in MAS)
    - Chapter 23 / Section 2 (Data Protection and Privacy Laws)

DeepSeek R1

- **Definition**: A multi-agent system framework supporting agent orchestration, messaging, scheduling, conflict resolution, and more.
- **Key References**:
    - Chapter 2 / Section 1 (What is DeepSeek R1?)
    - Appendix A (DeepSeek R1 API Reference)

Distributed Systems

- **Definition**: Systems in which components located on networked computers communicate and coordinate by passing messages to achieve a common goal.
- **Key References**:
    - Chapter 15 / Section 2 (Reinforcement Learning in MAS, distributed aspects)
    - Chapter 5 (Communication and Coordination Among Agents)

Docker

- **Definition**: A platform enabling container-based application deployment, common for MAS with microservices or agent-based architectures.
- **Key References**:
  - Chapter 19 / Section 2 (Using Docker and Kubernetes with DeepSeek R1)

E

Edge Computing

- **Definition**: Processing agent logic at or near data sources (like IoT devices), reducing latency and bandwidth usage.
- **Key References**:
  - Chapter 26 / Section 1.2 (Edge Computing and MAS)

Encryption

- **Definition**: Securing data in transit or at rest to prevent unauthorized access.
- **Key References**:
  - Chapter 16 / Section 2 (Implementing Secure Communication)
  - Chapter 23 / Section 2 (Data Protection and Privacy Laws)

Ethical Agent

- **Definition**: An agent designed with explicit moral or legal constraints to ensure fair, safe, and respectful decisions.
- **Key References**:
  - Chapter 17 / Section 2 (Designing Ethical Agents)
  - Chapter 25 / Section 2 (Incorporating Ethical Decision-Making Frameworks)

Explainable AI (XAI)

- **Definition**: AI approaches that provide human-understandable reasons for decisions, fostering trust and accountability.
- **Key References**:

F

Fault Tolerance

- **Definition**: The capacity of an MAS to continue operating even if some agents or nodes fail.
- **Key References**:

Feedback Loops

- **Definition**: Mechanisms by which agent or user feedback continuously refines agent behavior or system performance.
- **Key References**:

Financial Trading MAS

- **Definition**: Systems employing multi-agent solutions for real-time trade execution, risk checks, or market analysis.
- **Key References**:

Forum Participation

- **Definition**: Engaging with user communities, Q&A, and discussion boards for knowledge exchange and support.

- **Key References**:
    - Chapter 24 / Section 3.1 (Engaging with the MAS Community)
    - Chapter 27 / Section 1.2 (Participating in DeepSeek R1 Community Forums)

G

GDPR

- **Definition**: EU regulation for data privacy, ensuring user consent, data minimization, and user's right to erasure or portability.
- **Key References**:
    - Chapter 16 / Section 4 (Data Privacy)
    - Chapter 23 / Section 2 (Data Protection and Privacy Laws)

Git / GitHub

- **Definition**: Version control and hosting platforms crucial for open-source MAS collaboration.
- **Key References**:
    - Chapter 24 / Section 4 (Collaborative Development Strategies)
    - Chapter 27 / Section 3.2 (Contributing to Open-source MAS Projects)

Glossary

- **Definition**: A compiled reference of key terms used throughout the book for quick lookup.
- **Key References**:
    - Appendix C (Glossary of Terms)

H

Healthcare MAS

- **Definition**: Systems applying multi-agent paradigms to manage patient data, scheduling, or diagnosis support in healthcare.
- **Key References**:
  - Chapter 22 / Section 6 (Case Study on Healthcare)
  - Chapter 23 / Section 3.1 (Industry-Specific Regulations: Healthcare)

Hot Swapping Agents

- **Definition**: Replacing or adding agent instances on the fly without shutting down the entire MAS.
- **Key References**:
  - Chapter 21 / Section 2 (Hot Swapping Agents)

I

Installation

- **Definition**: Steps to set up DeepSeek R1 and dependencies on various operating systems.
- **Key References**:
  - Appendix B (Installation Guides for Different Platforms)
  - Chapter 3 / Section 2 (Installation Guide)

Integration Testing

- **Definition**: Verifying that multiple agents interact correctly, handling real or mock data flows.
- **Key References**:
  - Chapter 22 / Section 2 (Testing Methodologies for MAS)

IoT (Internet of Things)

- **Definition**: A broad network of smart devices with sensors and actuators. MAS can orchestrate or coordinate these devices.
- **Key References**:
  - Chapter 15 / Section 3 (MAS in IoT)
  - Chapter 26 / Section 3 (MAS in Internet of Things)

K

Key Performance Indicators (KPIs)

- **Definition**: Metrics that track and quantify MAS effectiveness (throughput, latency, error rates, etc.).
- **Key References**:
  - Chapter 20 / Section 2 (Performance Metrics and KPIs)

Knowledge Graphs

- **Definition**: Graph-based structures storing and linking information, enhancing agent reasoning.
- **Key References**:
  - Chapter 15 / Section 3 (Knowledge Graphs and Semantic Web Technologies)

L

Licensing

- **Definition**: Legal frameworks defining how others can use, modify, or redistribute MAS or related software.
- **Key References**:
  - Chapter 23 / Section 4 (Intellectual Property Considerations)
  - Chapter 24 / Section 5.1 (Open-sourcing Your Projects)

Load Balancing

- **Definition**: Distributing workloads or tasks among multiple agents or servers to optimize performance.
- **Key References**:
  - Chapter 5 / Section 1, 2 (Communication and Coordination, especially resource distribution)
  - Chapter 21 / Section 5 (Automated Scaling and Resource Management)

M

Marketing MAS Projects

- **Definition**: Strategies to promote multi-agent solutions, attract contributors, and secure user adoption.
- **Key References**:
  - Chapter 28 (Marketing and Promotion of MAS Projects)

MAS

- **Definition**: Multi-agent systems, where multiple autonomous entities coordinate or compete within an environment.
- **Key References**:
  - Chapters 1, 4, entire book.

Microservices Architecture

- **Definition**: A design approach splitting large systems into small, independent services that can correspond to specialized agents.
- **Key References**:
  - Chapter 19 / Section 2 (Containerization and Virtualization)

Monitoring

- **Definition**: Continuous observation and metric collection for system or agent performance, used to detect anomalies.
- **Key References**:
  - Chapter 20 / Section 1 (Real-time Monitoring Tools)

N

Negotiation Protocols

- **Definition**: Formal methods enabling agents to propose, counter-propose, or bid for resources or tasks.
- **Key References**:

- Chapter 5 / Section 2 (Coordination Mechanisms, Contract Net Protocol)
- Chapter 8 / Section 2.1 (Negotiation-Based Conflict Resolution)

Network Failures

- **Definition**: Communication breakdowns in distributed MAS, leading to partial or total agent isolation.
- **Key References**:
  - Chapter 3 / Section 1.1 (Potential connectivity issues)
  - Chapter 20 / Section 3 (Troubleshooting Common Issues)

O

On-Premises vs. Cloud

- **Definition**: Distinctions between hosting MAS on local data centers or using third-party cloud services.
- **Key References**:
  - Chapter 19 / Section 1 (Deployment Strategies)

Open-source Collaboration

- **Definition**: Community-driven approach enabling public contributions to MAS frameworks or projects.
- **Key References**:
  - Chapter 24 (Community Engagement and Open-source Collaboration)
  - Chapter 27 / Section 3.2 (Contributing to Open-source MAS Projects)

P

Performance Tuning

- **Definition**: Optimizing agent algorithms, messaging, or resource usage to maximize MAS throughput or reduce latency.
- **Key References**:
  - Chapter 14 (Scalability and Performance Optimization in MAS)

Privacy

- **Definition**: Ensuring user or organizational data is protected from unauthorized access and handled per regulations.
- **Key References**:
  - Chapter 16 / Section 4 (Data Privacy in MAS)
  - Chapter 23 / Section 2 (Data Protection and Privacy Laws)

Project Portfolio

- **Definition**: A curated set of MAS projects demonstrating one's expertise and accomplishments.
- **Key References**:
  - Chapter 27 / Section 4 (Building a Portfolio of MAS Projects)

Q

Quantum Computing

- **Definition**: A paradigm that uses quantum bits (qubits) to achieve potential computational speedups, relevant for some MAS optimization tasks.
- **Key References**:
  - Chapter 26 / Section 1.1 (Integration of Quantum Computing)

Quizzes and Self-Assessments

- **Definition**: End-of-chapter sets of questions verifying comprehension and reinforcing learning.
- **Key References**:
  - Found at the end of each chapter, e.g., Chapter 2 / Section 7, Chapter 28 / Section 8, etc.

R

Reactive Agents

- **Definition**: Agents that respond immediately to environmental changes without extensive internal state or planning.
- **Key References**:
  - Chapter 4 / Section 4.1 (Reactive Behaviors)
  - Chapter 6 / Section 2.1 (Agent Architectures in advanced reasoning)

Redundancy

- **Definition**: Duplicating critical agent roles or nodes so if one fails, another continues service seamlessly.
- **Key References**:
  - Chapter 8 / Section 4.1 (Fault tolerance)
  - Chapter 19 / Section 1.2 (Hybrid models with failover)

Rolling Updates

- **Definition**: Methodically replacing old agent versions with new ones without halting the entire MAS.
- **Key References**:
  - Chapter 19 / Section 5 (Maintenance and Updates)

S

Scalability

- **Definition**: The ability of an MAS to handle growing loads, additional agents, or expanded data volumes.
- **Key References**:
  - Chapter 14 (Scalability and Performance Optimization in MAS)
  - Chapter 21 / Section 5 (Automated Scaling and Resource Management)

Security

- **Definition**: Measures to safeguard agent communications and data (encryption, authentication, intrusion detection).
- **Key References**:
    - Chapter 16 (Security and Privacy in MAS)
    - Chapter 19 / Section 1.2 (Ensuring safe deployment across networks)

Simulation-based Validation

- **Definition**: Testing agent logic within a controlled, artificial environment before real-world deployment.
- **Key References**:
    - Chapter 22 / Section 3.1 (Validation Techniques)

Smart Manufacturing

- **Definition**: Using MAS and collaborative robots (cobots) to optimize production lines, inventory management, and quality control.
- **Key References**:
    - Chapter 11 (Smart Manufacturing with Collaborative Robots)

T

Task Allocation

- **Definition**: MAS approach to distributing jobs among specialized or generalist agents based on capabilities, availability, or priority.
- **Key References**:
    - Chapter 7 (Task Allocation and Load Balancing)

Testing Methodologies

- **Definition**: Frameworks for validating correctness, performance, and stability in MAS—unit, integration, system tests.
- **Key References**:
    - Chapter 22 (Testing and Validation in MAS)

Transparency

- **Definition**: Ensuring MAS decisions or processes are interpretable to human operators and stakeholders.
- **Key References**:
    - Chapter 17 / Section 2 (Designing Ethical Agents)
    - Chapter 25 / Section 2.2 (Ensuring Transparency in Agent Actions)

U

Unit Testing

- **Definition**: Verifying individual agent methods or logic in isolation.
- **Key References**:
    - Chapter 22 / Section 2.1 (Testing Methodologies for MAS)

User Interface (UI)

- **Definition**: The visual or interactive layer through which human operators interact with MAS.
- **Key References**:
    - Chapter 18 / Section 2 (Designing User-Friendly Interfaces)

V

Version Control

- **Definition**: Systems (Git, Mercurial) used to track changes to agent code, enabling collaborative development.
- **Key References**:
    - Chapter 24 / Section 4.1 (Version Control and Collaborative Tools)

W

Workshops and Webinars

- **Definition**: Interactive sessions or online events offering in-depth MAS tutorials, Q&A, or collaborative problem-solving.
- **Key References**:
    - Chapter 28 / Section 1.2 (Hosting Webinars and Workshops)
    - Chapter 27 / Section 3.1 (Attending Conferences and Workshops)

Zero Downtime Deployment

- **Definition**: Rolling out new MAS versions or agent updates without interrupting service availability.
- **Key References**:
    - Chapter 19 / Section 5 (Maintenance and Updates, rolling updates)

This **Index** is designed to help you quickly **locate** critical topics—ranging from agent lifecycle management to advanced ethical considerations—by referencing the relevant **chapters** and **appendices**. Each entry provides a **brief description** and direct **pointer** to where the content is explained **in-depth** within the book. Use this as a **handy cross-reference** whenever you need to revisit a specific concept, methodology, or example.

www.ingramcontent.com/pod-product-compliance
Lightning Source LLC
LaVergne TN
LVHW080111070326
832902LV00015B/2530